Real-Resumes For Sports Industry Jobs

Anne McKinney, Editor

PREP PUBLISHING

FAYETTEVILLE, NC

PREP Publishing
1110 ½ Hay Street
Fayetteville, NC 28305
(910) 483-6611

Copyright © 2004 by Anne McKinney

Library of Congress Cataloging-in-Publication Data

Real-resumes for sports industry jobs / Anne McKinney, editor.
       p. cm. -- (Real-resumes series)
  ISBN 1-885288-41-7
  1. Resumes (Employment) 2. Sports--Vocational guidance. I. McKinney, Anne, 1948- II. Series.

  HF5383.R39623 2004
  650.14'2--dc22   2004044285

Printed in the United States of America

PREP Publishing

Business and Career Series:

RESUMES AND COVER LETTERS THAT HAVE WORKED, Revised Edition

RESUMES AND COVER LETTERS THAT HAVE WORKED FOR MILITARY PROFESSIONALS

GOVERNMENT JOB APPLICATIONS AND FEDERAL RESUMES

COVER LETTERS THAT BLOW DOORS OPEN

LETTERS FOR SPECIAL SITUATIONS

RESUMES AND COVER LETTERS FOR MANAGERS

REAL-RESUMES FOR COMPUTER JOBS

REAL-RESUMES FOR MEDICAL JOBS

REAL-RESUMES FOR FINANCIAL JOBS

REAL-RESUMES FOR TEACHERS

REAL-RESUMES FOR STUDENTS

REAL-RESUMES FOR CAREER CHANGERS

REAL-RESUMES FOR SALES

REAL ESSAYS FOR COLLEGE & GRADUATE SCHOOL

REAL-RESUMES FOR AVIATION & TRAVEL JOBS

REAL-RESUMES FOR POLICE, LAW ENFORCEMENT & SECURITY JOBS

REAL-RESUMES FOR SOCIAL WORK & COUNSELING JOBS

REAL-RESUMES FOR CONSTRUCTION JOBS

REAL-RESUMES FOR MANUFACTURING JOBS

REAL-RESUMES FOR RESTAURANT, FOOD SERVICE & HOTEL JOBS

REAL-RESUMES FOR MEDIA, NEWSPAPER, BROADCASTING & PUBLIC AFFAIRS JOBS

REAL-RESUMES FOR RETAILING, MODELING, FASHION & BEAUTY JOBS

REAL-RESUMES FOR HUMAN RESOURCES & PERSONNEL JOBS

REAL-RESUMES FOR NURSING JOBS

REAL-RESUMES FOR AUTO INDUSTRY JOBS

REAL RESUMIX & OTHER RESUMES FOR FEDERAL GOVERNMENT JOBS

REAL KSAS--KNOWLEDGE, SKILLS & ABILITIES--FOR GOVERNMENT JOBS

REAL BUSINESS PLANS & MARKETING TOOLS

REAL-RESUMES FOR ADMINISTRATIVE SUPPORT, OFFICE & SECRETARIAL JOBS

REAL-RESUMES FOR FIREFIGHTING JOBS

REAL-RESUMES FOR JOBS IN NONPROFIT ORGANIZATIONS

REAL-RESUMES FOR SPORTS INDUSTRY JOBS

REAL-RESUMES FOR LEGAL & PARALEGAL JOBS

Judeo-Christian Ethics Series:

SECOND TIME AROUND

BACK IN TIME

WHAT THE BIBLE SAYS ABOUT...Words that can lead to success and happiness

A GENTLE BREEZE FROM GOSSAMER WINGS

BIBLE STORIES FROM THE OLD TESTAMENT

Contents

Real-Resumes For Sports Industry Jobs

Anne McKinney, Editor

A WORD FROM THE EDITOR:
ABOUT THE REAL-RESUMES SERIES

Welcome to the Real-Resumes Series. The Real-Resumes Series is a series of books which have been developed based on the experiences of real job hunters and which target specialized fields or types of resumes. As the editor of the series, I have carefully selected resumes and cover letters (with names and other key data disguised, of course) which have been used successfully in real job hunts. That's what we mean by "Real-Resumes." What you see in this book are *real* resumes and cover letters which helped real people get ahead in their careers.

The Real-Resumes Series is based on the work of the country's oldest resume-preparation company known as PREP Resumes. If you would like a free information packet describing the company's resume preparation services, call 910-483-6611 or write to PREP at 1110½ Hay Street, Fayetteville, NC 28305. If you have a job hunting experience you would like to share with our staff at the Real-Resumes Series, please contact us at preppub@aol.com or visit our website at http://www.prep-pub.com.

We hope the superior samples will help you manage your current job campaign and your career so that you will find work aligned to your career interests.

The resumes and cover letters in this book are designed to be of most value to people already in a job hunt or contemplating a career change. If we could give you one word of advice about your career, here's what we would say: Manage your career and don't stumble from job to job in an incoherent pattern. Try to find work that interests you, and then identify prosperous industries which need work performed of the type you want to do. Learn early in your working life that a great resume and cover letter can blow doors open for you and help you maximize your salary.

As the editor of this book, I would like to give you some tips on how to make the best use of the information you will find here. Because you are considering a career change, you already understand the concept of managing your career for maximum enjoyment and self-fulfillment. The purpose of this book is to provide expert tools and advice so that you *can* manage your career. Inside these pages you will find resumes and cover letters that will help you find not just a job but the type of work you want to do.

Overview of the Book
Every resume and cover letter in this book actually worked. And most of the resumes and cover letters have common features: most are one-page, most are in the chronological format, and most resumes are accompanied by a companion cover letter. In this section you will find helpful advice about job hunting. Step One begins with a discussion of why employers prefer the one-page, chronological resume. In Step Two you are introduced to the direct approach and to the proper format for a cover letter. In Step Three you learn the 14 main reasons why job hunters are not offered the jobs they want, and you learn the six key areas employers focus on when they interview you. Step Four gives nuts-and-bolts advice on how to handle the interview, send a follow-up letter after an interview, and negotiate your salary.

The cover letter plays such a critical role in a career change. You will learn from the experts how to format your cover letters and you will see suggested language to use in particular career-change situations. It has been said that "A picture is worth a thousand words" and, for that reason, you will see numerous examples of effective cover letters used by real individuals to change fields, functions, and industries.

The most important part of the book is the Real-Resumes section. Some of the individuals whose resumes and cover letters you see spent a lengthy career in an industry they loved. Then there are resumes and cover letters of people who wanted a change but who probably wanted to remain in their industry. Many of you will be especially interested by the resumes and cover letters of individuals who knew they definitely wanted a career change but had no idea what they wanted to do next. Other resumes and cover letters show individuals who knew they wanted to change fields and had a pretty good idea of what they wanted to do next.

Whatever your field, and whatever your circumstances, you'll find resumes and cover letters that will "show you the ropes" in terms of successfully changing jobs and switching careers.

Before you proceed further, think about why you picked up this book.
- Are you dissatisfied with the type of work you are now doing?
- Would you like to change careers, change companies, or change industries?
- Are you satisfied with your industry but not with your niche or function within it?
- Do you want to transfer your skills to a new product or service?
- Even if you have excelled in your field, have you "had enough"? Would you like the stimulation of a new challenge?
- Are you aware of the importance of a great cover letter but unsure of how to write one?
- Are you preparing to launch a second career after retirement?
- Have you been downsized, or do you anticipate becoming a victim of downsizing?
- Do you need expert advice on how to plan and implement a job campaign that will open the maximum number of doors?
- Do you want to make sure you handle an interview to your maximum advantage?

Introduction:
The Art of
Changing
Jobs...
and Finding
New Careers

- Would you like to master the techniques of negotiating salary and benefits?
- Do you want to learn the secrets and shortcuts of professional resume writers?

Using the Direct Approach

As you consider the possibility of a job hunt or career change, you need to be aware that most people end up having at least three distinctly different careers in their working lifetimes, and often those careers are different from each other. Yet people usually stumble through each job campaign, unsure of what they should be doing. Whether you find yourself voluntarily or unexpectedly in a job hunt, the direct approach is the job hunting strategy most likely to yield a full-time permanent job. The direct approach is an active, take-the-initiative style of job hunting in which you choose your next employer rather than relying on responding to ads, using employment agencies, or depending on other methods of finding jobs. You will learn how to use the direct approach in this book, and you will see that an effective cover letter is a critical ingredient in using the direct approach.

The "direct approach" is the style of job hunting most likely to yield the maximum number of job interviews.

Lack of Industry Experience Not a Major Barrier to Entering New Field

"Lack of experience" is often the last reason people are not offered jobs, according to the companies who do the hiring. If you are changing careers, you will be glad to learn that experienced professionals often are selling "potential" rather than experience in a job hunt. Companies look for personal qualities that they know tend to be present in their most effective professionals, such as communication skills, initiative, persistence, organizational and time management skills, and creativity. Frequently companies are trying to discover "personality type," "talent," "ability," "aptitude," and "potential" rather than seeking actual hands-on experience, so your resume should be designed to aggressively present your accomplishments. Attitude, enthusiasm, personality, and a track record of achievements in any type of work are the primary "indicators of success" which employers are seeking, and you will see numerous examples in this book of resumes written in an all-purpose fashion so that the professional can approach various industries and companies.

Using references in a skillful fashion in your job hunt will inspire confidence in prospective employers and help you "close the sale" after interviews.

The Art of Using References in a Job Hunt

You probably already know that you need to provide references during a job hunt, but you may not be sure of how and when to use references for maximum advantage. You can use references very creatively during a job hunt to call attention to your strengths and make yourself "stand out." Your references will rarely get you a job, no matter how impressive the names, but the way you use references can boost the employer's confidence in you and lead to a job offer in the least time.

You should ask from three to five people, including people who have supervised you, if you can use them as a reference during your job hunt. You may not be able to ask your current boss since your job hunt is probably confidential.

A common question in resume preparation is: "Do I need to put my references on my resume?" No, you don't. Even if you create a references page at the same time you prepare your resume, you don't need to mail, e-mail, or fax your references page with the resume and cover letter. Usually the potential employer is not interested in references until he meets you, so the earliest you need to have references ready is at the first interview. Obviously there are exceptions to this standard rule of thumb; sometimes an ad will ask you to send references with your first response. Wait until the employer requests references before providing them.

An excellent attention-getting technique is to take to the first interview not just a page of references (giving names, addresses, and telephone numbers) but an actual letter of reference written by someone who knows you well and who preferably has supervised or employed you. A professional way to close the first interview is to thank the interviewer, shake his or her hand, and then say you'd like to give him or her a copy of a letter of reference from a previous employer. Hopefully you already made a good impression during the interview, but you'll "close the sale" in a dynamic fashion if you leave a letter praising you and your accomplishments. For that reason, it's a good idea to ask supervisors during your final weeks in a job if they will provide you with a written letter of recommendation which you can use in future job hunts. Most employers will oblige, and you will have a letter that has a useful "shelf life" of many years. Such a letter often gives the prospective employer enough confidence in his opinion of you that he may forego checking out other references and decide to offer you the job on the spot or in the next few days.

Whom should you ask to serve as references? References should be people who have known or supervised you in a professional, academic, or work situation. References with big titles, like school superintendent or congressman, are fine, but remind busy people when you get to the interview stage that they may be contacted soon. Make sure the busy official recognizes your name and has instant positive recall of you! If you're asked to provide references on a formal company application, you can simply transcribe names from your references list. In summary, follow this rule in using references: If you've got them, flaunt them! If you've obtained well-written letters of reference, make sure you find a polite way to push those references under the nose of the interviewer so he or she can hear someone other than you describing your strengths. Your references probably won't ever get you a job, but glowing letters of reference can give you credibility and visibility that can make you stand out among candidates with similar credentials and potential!

The approach taken by this book is to (1) help you master the proven best techniques of conducting a job hunt and (2) show you how to stand out in a job hunt through your resume, cover letter, interviewing skills, as well as the way in which you present your references and follow up on interviews. Now, the best way to "get in the mood" for writing your own resume and cover letter is to select samples from the Table of Contents that interest you and then read them. A great resume is a "photograph," usually on one page, of an individual. If you wish to seek professional advice in preparing your resume, you may contact one of the professional writers at Professional Resume & Employment Publishing (PREP) for a brief free consultation by calling 1-910-483-6611.

Part One: Some Advice About Your Job Hunt

What if you don't know what you want to do?

Your job hunt will be more comfortable if you can figure out what type of work you want to do. But you are not alone if you have no idea what you want to do next! You may have knowledge and skills in certain areas but want to get into another type of work. What *The Wall Street Journal* has discovered in its research on careers is that most of us end up having at least three distinctly different careers in our working lives; it seems that, even if we really like a particular kind of activity, twenty years of doing it is enough for most of us and we want to move on to something else!

That's why we strongly believe that you need to spend some time figuring out *what interests you* rather than taking an inventory of the skills you have. You may have skills that you simply don't want to use, but if you can build your career on the things that interest you, you will be more likely to be happy and satisfied in your job. Realize, too, that interests can change over time; the activities that interest you now may not be the ones that interested you years ago. For example, some professionals may decide that they've had enough of retail sales and want a job selling another product or service, even though they have earned a reputation for being an excellent retail manager. We strongly believe that interests rather than skills should be the determining factor in deciding what types of jobs you want to apply for and what directions you explore in your job hunt. Obviously one cannot be a lawyer without a law degree or a secretary without secretarial skills; but a professional can embark on a next career as a financial consultant, property manager, plant manager, production supervisor, retail manager, or other occupation if he/she has a strong interest in that type of work and can provide a resume that clearly demonstrates past excellent performance in *any* field and *potential* to excel in another field. As you will see later in this book, "lack of exact experience" is the last reason why people are turned down for the jobs they apply for.

How can you have a resume prepared if you don't know what you want to do?

You may be wondering how you can have a resume prepared if you don't know what you want to do next. The approach to resume writing which PREP, the country's oldest resume-preparation company, has used successfully for many years is to develop an "all-purpose" resume that translates your skills, experience, and accomplishments into language employers can understand. What most people need in a job hunt is a versatile resume that will allow them to apply for numerous types of jobs. For example, you may want to apply for a job in pharmaceutical sales but you may also want to have a resume that will be versatile enough for you to apply for jobs in the construction, financial services, or automotive industries.

Based on more than 20 years of serving job hunters, we at PREP have found that your best approach to job hunting is **an all-purpose resume** and **specific cover letters tailored to specific fields** rather than using the approach of trying to create different resumes for every job. If you are remaining in your field, you may not even need more than one "all-purpose" cover letter, although the cover letter rather than the resume is the place to communicate your interest in a narrow or specific field. An all-purpose resume and cover letter that translate your experience and accomplishments into plain English are the tools that will maximize the number of doors which open for you while permitting you to "fish" in the widest range of job areas.

Figure out what interests you and you will hold the key to a successful job hunt and working career. (And be prepared for your interests to change over time!)

"Lack of exact experience" is the last reason people are turned down for the jobs for which they apply.

Your resume will provide the script for your job interview.
When you get down to it, your resume has a simple job to do: Its purpose is to blow as many doors open as possible and to make as many people as possible want to meet you. So a well-written resume that really "sells" you is a key that will create opportunities for you in a job hunt.

This statistic explains why: The typical newspaper advertisement for a job opening receives more than 245 replies. And normally only 10 or 12 will be invited to an interview.

But here's another purpose of the resume: it provides the "script" the employer uses when he interviews you. If your resume has been written in such a way that your strengths and achievements are revealed, that's what you'll end up talking about at the job interview. Since the resume will govern what you get asked about at your interviews, you can't overestimate the importance of making sure your resume makes you look and sound as good as you are.

So what is a "good" resume?
Very literally, your resume should motivate the person reading it to dial the phone number or e-mail the screen name you have put on the resume. When you are relocating, you should put a local phone number on your resume if your physical address is several states away; employers are more likely to dial a local telephone number than a long-distance number when they're looking for potential employees.

If you have a resume already, look at it objectively. Is it a limp, colorless "laundry list" of your job titles and duties? Or does it "paint a picture" of your skills, abilities, and accomplishments in a way that would make someone want to meet you? Can people understand what you're saying? If you are attempting to change fields or industries, can potential employers see that your skills and knowledge are transferable to other environments? For example, have you described accomplishments which reveal your problem-solving abilities or communication skills?

How long should your resume be?
One page, maybe two. Usually only people in the academic community have a resume (which they usually call a *curriculum vitae*) longer than one or two pages. Remember that your resume is almost always accompanied by a cover letter, and a potential employer does not want to read more than two or three pages about a total stranger in order to decide if he wants to meet that person! Besides, don't forget that the more you tell someone about yourself, the more opportunity you are providing for the employer to screen you out at the "first-cut" stage. A resume should be concise and exciting and designed to make the reader want to meet you in person!

Should resumes be functional or chronological?
Employers almost always prefer a chronological resume; in other words, an employer will find a resume easier to read if it is immediately apparent what your current or most recent job is, what you did before that, and so forth, in reverse chronological order. A resume that goes back in detail for the last ten years of employment will generally satisfy the employer's curiosity about your background. Employment more than ten years old can be shown even more briefly in an "Other Experience" section at the end of your "Experience" section. Remember that your intention is not to tell everything you've done but to "hit the high points" and especially impress the employer with what you learned, contributed, or accomplished in each job you describe.

Your resume is the "script" for your job interviews. Make sure you put on your resume what you want to talk about or be asked about at the job interview.

The one-page resume in chronological format is the format preferred by most employers.

Once you get your resume, what do you do with it?

You will be using your resume to answer ads, as a tool to use in talking with friends and relatives about your job search, and, most importantly, in using the "direct approach" described in this book.

When you mail your resume, always send a "cover letter."

A "cover letter," sometimes called a "resume letter" or "letter of interest," is a letter that accompanies and introduces your resume. Your cover letter is a way of personalizing the resume by sending it to the specific person you think you might want to work for at each company. Your cover letter should contain a few highlights from your resume—just enough to make someone want to meet you. Cover letters should always be typed or word processed on a computer—never handwritten.

Never mail or fax your resume without a cover letter.

1. Learn the art of answering ads.

There is an "art," part of which can be learned, in using your "bestselling" resume to reply to advertisements.

Sometimes an exciting job lurks behind a boring ad that someone dictated in a hurry, so reply to any ad that interests you. Don't worry that you aren't "25 years old with an MBA" like the ad asks for. Employers will always make compromises in their requirements if they think you're the "best fit" overall.

What about ads that ask for "salary requirements?"

What if the ad you're answering asks for "salary requirements?" The first rule is to avoid committing yourself in writing at that point to a specific salary. You don't want to "lock yourself in."

There are two ways to handle the ad that asks for "salary requirements."

First, you can ignore that part of the ad and accompany your resume with a cover letter that focuses on "selling" you, your abilities, and even some of your philosophy about work or your field. You may include a sentence in your cover letter like this: "I can provide excellent personal and professional references at your request, and I would be delighted to share the private details of my salary history with you in person."

What if the ad asks for your "salary requirements?"

Second, if you feel you must give some kind of number, just state a range in your cover letter that includes your medical, dental, other benefits, and expected bonuses. You might state, for example, "My current compensation, including benefits and bonuses, is in the range of $30,000-$40,000."

Analyze the ad and "tailor" yourself to it.

When you're replying to ads, a finely tailored cover letter is an important tool in getting your resume noticed and read. On the next page is a cover letter which has been "tailored to fit" a specific ad. Notice the "art" used by PREP writers of analyzing the ad's main requirements and then writing the letter so that the person's background, work habits, and interests seem "tailor-made" to the company's needs. Use this cover letter as a model when you prepare your own reply to ads.

Date

Exact Name of Person
Exact Title
Exact Name of Company
Address
City, State, Zip

Dear Exact Name of Person (or Dear Sir or Madam if answering a blind ad):

With the enclosed resume, I would like to make you aware of my interest in exploring current or future opportunities as Director of Tennis with your club.

A previous employer recruited me for my current position as Director of Tennis at a prestigious club. Although I am held in the highest regard and am excelling in a position which could be mine for life, I am selectively exploring other opportunities. The main reason I am "looking" is that I feel I have done nearly everything that can be done at the club where I work. I have brought the tennis program up to an extraordinarily high level, but simply maintaining an excellent program does not appeal to me as a job forever. I suppose I yearn to go on to "bigger and better things," and I am interested in applying my extensive background to benefit a larger organization in a larger market.

Because of my in-depth experience, I have much to offer. Textbook learning is a valuable thing but, through working in the tennis field for 15 years, I have learned how to teach every shot in tennis using multiple approaches. It is no exaggeration to say that I can teach the serve 30 different ways. I have also become "a pro" at working in the unique environment of a membership organization, and I have learned how to work congenially with all personality types. With a reputation as a resourceful manager, I offer highly refined skills in managing every aspect of a dynamic tennis program.

I hold the highest certifications given to tennis professionals. I am certified by the Professional Tennis Registry as a Tennis Professional, the highest of three ratings, and have held that certification since 1990. I am also a USPTR National Testers in Utah.

After beginning my tennis career as a Tennis Pro, I have worked for only two clubs since 1993. At both clubs I dramatically increased tennis participation, boosted the number of USTA league teams, started multiple programs for juniors and adults, conducted USPTR coaches' workshops for persons seeking certifications or upgrades, became an influential tennis spokesperson in the community, managed successful tournaments, managed budgets in excess of $100,000, and supervised other tennis pros. My reputation in the tennis community is outstanding, and I can provide exemplary references from my current club at the appropriate time.

If you feel that your current or future needs might require a top-level tennis professional and manager such as myself, I hope you will contact me.

Yours sincerely,

Moses Lock

Employers are trying to identify the individual who wants the job they are filling. Don't be afraid to express your enthusiasm in the cover letter!

2. Talk to friends and relatives.

Don't be shy about telling your friends and relatives the kind of job you're looking for. Looking for the job you want involves using your network of contacts, so tell people what you're looking for. They may be able to make introductions and help set up interviews.

About 25% of all interviews are set up through "who you know," so don't ignore this approach.

3. Finally, and most importantly, use the "direct approach."

The "direct approach" is a strategy in which you choose your next employer.

More than 50% of all job interviews are set up by the "direct approach." That means you actually mail, e-mail, or fax a resume and a cover letter to a company you think might be interesting to work for.

To whom do you write?

In general, you should write directly to the *exact name* of the person who would be hiring you: say, the vice-president of marketing or data processing. If you're in doubt about to whom to address the letter, address it to the president by name and he or she will make sure it gets forwarded to the right person within the company who has hiring authority in your area.

How do you find the names of potential employers?

You're not alone if you feel that the biggest problem in your job search is finding the right names at the companies you want to contact. But you can usually figure out the names of companies you want to approach by deciding first if your job hunt is primarily geography-driven or industry-driven.

In a **geography-driven job hunt,** you could select a list of, say, 50 companies you want to contact **by location** from the lists that the U.S. Chambers of Commerce publish yearly of their "major area employers." There are hundreds of local Chambers of Commerce across America, and most of them will have an 800 number which you can find through 1-800-555-1212. If you and your family think Atlanta, Dallas, Ft. Lauderdale, and Virginia Beach might be nice places to live, for example, you could contact the Chamber of Commerce in those cities and ask how you can obtain a copy of their list of major employers. Your nearest library will have the book which lists the addresses of all chambers.

In an **industry-driven job hunt,** and if you are willing to relocate, you will be identifying the companies which you find most attractive in the industry in which you want to work. When you select a list of companies to contact **by industry,** you can find the right person to write and the address of firms by industrial category in *Standard and Poor's, Moody's,* and other excellent books in public libraries. Many Web sites also provide contact information.

Many people feel it's a good investment to actually call the company to either find out or double-check the name of the person to whom they want to send a resume and cover letter. It's important to do as much as you feasibly can to assure that the letter gets to the right person in the company.

On-line research will be the best way for many people to locate organizations to which they wish to send their resume. It is outside the scope of this book to teach Internet research skills, but librarians are often useful in this area.

What's the correct way to follow up on a resume you send?

There is a polite way to be aggressively interested in a company during your job hunt. It is ideal to end the cover letter accompanying your resume by saying, "I hope you'll welcome my call next week when I try to arrange a brief meeting at your convenience to discuss your current and future needs and how I might serve them." Keep it low key, and just ask for a "brief meeting," not an interview. Employers want people who show a determined interest in working with them, so don't be shy about following up on the resume and cover letter you've mailed.

STEP THREE: Preparing for Interviews

But a resume and cover letter by themselves can't get you the job you want. You need to "prep" yourself before the interview. Step Three in your job campaign is "Preparing for Interviews." First, let's look at interviewing from the hiring organization's point of view.

What are the biggest "turnoffs" for potential employers?

One of the ways to help yourself perform well at an interview is to look at the main reasons why organizations *don't* hire the people they interview, according to those who do the interviewing.

Notice that "lack of appropriate background" (or lack of experience) is the *last* reason for not being offered the job.

The 14 Most Common Reasons Job Hunters Are Not Offered Jobs (according to the companies who do the interviewing and hiring):

1. Low level of accomplishment
2. Poor attitude, lack of self-confidence
3. Lack of goals/objectives
4. Lack of enthusiasm
5. Lack of interest in the company's business
6. Inability to sell or express yourself
7. Unrealistic salary demands
8. Poor appearance
9. Lack of maturity, no leadership potential
10. Lack of extracurricular activities
11. Lack of preparation for the interview, no knowledge about company
12. Objecting to travel
13. Excessive interest in security and benefits
14. Inappropriate background

Department of Labor studies have proven that smart, "prepared" job hunters can increase their beginning salary while getting a job in *half* the time it normally takes. (4½ months is the average national length of a job search.) Here, from PREP, are some questions that can prepare you to find a job faster.

Are you in the "right" frame of mind?

It seems unfair that we have to look for a job just when we're lowest in morale. Don't worry *too* much if you're nervous before interviews. You're supposed to be a little nervous, especially if the job means a lot to you. But the best way to kill unnecessary

It pays to be aware of the 14 most common pitfalls for job hunters.

fears about job hunting is through 1) making sure you have a great resume and 2) preparing yourself for the interview. Here are three main areas you need to think about before each interview.

Do you know what the company does?

Don't walk into an interview giving the impression that, "If this is Tuesday, this must be General Motors."

Research the company
before you go to
interviews.

Find out before the interview what the company's main product or service is. Where is the company heading? Is it in a "growth" or declining industry? (Answers to these questions may influence whether or not you want to work there!)

Information about what the company does is in annual reports, in newspaper and magazine articles, and on the Internet. If you're not yet skilled at Internet research, just visit your nearest library and ask the reference librarian to guide you to printed materials on the company.

Do you know what you want to do for the company?

Before the interview, try to decide how you see yourself fitting into the company. Remember, "lack of exact background" the company wants is usually the last reason people are not offered jobs.

Understand before you go to each interview that the burden will be on you to "sell" the interviewer on why you're the best person for the job and the company.

How will you answer the critical interview questions?

Anticipate the questions
you will
be asked at the interview,
and prepare your
responses in advance.

Put yourself in the interviewer's position and think about the questions you're most likely to be asked. Here are some of the most commonly asked interview questions:

Q: "What are your greatest strengths?"

A: Don't say you've never thought about it! Go into an interview knowing the three main impressions you want to leave about yourself, such as "I'm hard-working, loyal, and an imaginative cost-cutter."

Q: "What are your greatest weaknesses?"

A: Don't confess that you're lazy or have trouble meeting deadlines! Confessing that you tend to be a "workaholic" or "tend to be a perfectionist and sometimes get frustrated when others don't share my high standards" will make your prospective employer see a "weakness" that he likes. Name a weakness that your interviewer will perceive as a strength.

Q: "What are your long-range goals?"

A: If you're interviewing with Microsoft, don't say you want to work for IBM in five years! Say your long-range goal is to be *with* the company, contributing to its goals and success.

Q: "What motivates you to do your best work?"

A: Don't get dollar signs in your eyes here! "A challenge" is not a bad answer, but it's a little cliched. Saying something like "troubleshooting" or "solving a tough problem" is more interesting and specific. Give an example if you can.

Q: *"What do you know about this organization?"*

A: Don't say you never heard of it until they asked you to the interview! Name an interesting, positive thing you learned about the company recently from your research. Remember, company executives can sometimes feel rather "maternal" about the company they serve. Don't get onto a negative area of the company if you can think of positive facts you can bring up. Of course, if you learned in your research that the company's sales seem to be taking a nose-dive, or that the company president is being prosecuted for taking bribes, you might politely ask your interviewer to tell you something that could help you better understand what you've been reading. Those are the kinds of company facts that can help you determine whether or not you want to work there.

Go to an interview prepared to tell the company why it should hire you.

Q: *"Why should I hire you?"*

A: "I'm unemployed and available" is the wrong answer here! Get back to your strengths and say that you believe the organization could benefit by a loyal, hard-working cost-cutter like yourself.

In conclusion, you should decide in advance, before you go to the interview, how you will answer each of these commonly asked questions. Have some practice interviews with a friend to role-play and build your confidence.

STEP FOUR: Handling the Interview and Negotiating Salary

Now you're ready for Step Four: actually handling the interview successfully and effectively. Remember, the purpose of an interview is to get a job offer.

A smile at an interview makes the employer perceive of you as intelligent!

Eight "do's" for the interview

According to leading U.S. companies, there are eight key areas in interviewing success. You can fail at an interview if you mishandle just one area.

1. **Do wear appropriate clothes.**
You can never go wrong by wearing a suit to an interview.

2. **Do be well groomed.**
Don't overlook the obvious things like having clean hair, clothes, and fingernails for the interview.

3. **Do give a firm handshake.**
You'll have to shake hands twice in most interviews: first, before you sit down, and second, when you leave the interview. Limp handshakes turn most people off.

4. **Do smile and show a sense of humor.**
Interviewers are looking for people who would be nice to work with, so don't be so somber that you don't smile. In fact, research shows that people who smile at interviews are perceived as more intelligent. So, smile!

5. **Do be enthusiastic.**
Employers say they are "turned off" by lifeless, unenthusiastic job hunters who show no special interest in that company. The best way to show some enthusiasm for the employer's operation is to find out about the business beforehand.

6. Do show you are flexible and adaptable.

An employer is looking for someone who can contribute to his organization in a flexible, adaptable way. No matter what skills and training you have, employers know every new employee must go through initiation and training on the company's turf. Certainly show pride in your past accomplishments in a specific, factual way ("I saved my last employer $50.00 a week by a new cost-cutting measure I developed"). But don't come across as though there's nothing about the job you couldn't easily handle.

7. Do ask intelligent questions about the employer's business.

An employer is hiring someone because of certain business needs. Show interest in those needs. Asking questions to get a better idea of the employer's needs will help you "stand out" from other candidates interviewing for the job.

8. Do "take charge" when the interviewer "falls down" on the job.

Go into every interview knowing the three or four points about yourself you want the interviewer to remember. And be prepared to take an active part in leading the discussion if the interviewer's "canned approach" does not permit you to display your "strong suit." You can't always depend on the interviewer's asking you the "right" questions so you can stress your strengths and accomplishments.

Employers are seeking people with good attitudes whom they can train and coach to do things their way.

An important "don't": Don't ask questions about salary or benefits at the first interview. Employers don't take warmly to people who look at their organization as just a place to satisfy salary and benefit needs. Don't risk making a negative impression by appearing greedy or self-serving. The place to discuss salary and benefits is normally at the second interview, and the employer will bring it up. Then you can ask questions without appearing excessively interested in what the organization can do for you.

Now...negotiating your salary

Even if an ad requests that you communicate your "salary requirement" or "salary history," you should avoid providing those numbers in your initial cover letter. You can usually say something like this: "I would be delighted to discuss the private details of my salary history with you in person."

Once you're at the interview, you must avoid even appearing *interested* in salary before you are offered the job. Make sure you've "sold" yourself before talking salary. First show you're the "best fit" for the employer and then you'll be in a stronger position from which to negotiate salary. **Never** bring up the subject of salary yourself. Employers say there's no way you can avoid looking greedy if you bring up the issue of salary and benefits before the company has identified you as its "best fit."

Don't appear excessively interested in salary and benefits at the interview.

Interviewers sometimes throw out a salary figure at the first interview to see if you'll accept it. You may not want to commit yourself if you think you will be able to negotiate a better deal later on. Get back to finding out more about the job. This lets the interviewer know you're interested primarily in the job and not the salary.

When the organization brings up salary, it may say something like this: "Well, Mary, we think you'd make a good candidate for this job. What kind of salary are we talking about?" You may not want to name a number here, either. Give the ball back to the interviewer. Act as though you hadn't given the subject of salary much thought and respond something like this: "Ah, Mr. Jones, I wonder if you'd be kind enough to tell me what salary you had in mind when you advertised the job?" Or ... "What is the range you have in mind?"

Don't worry, if the interviewer names a figure that you think is too low, you can say so without turning down the job or locking yourself into a rigid position. The point here is to negotiate for yourself as well as you can. You might reply to a number named by the interviewer that you think is low by saying something like this: "Well, Mr. Lee, the job interests me very much, and I think I'd certainly enjoy working with you. But, frankly, I was thinking of something a little higher than that." That leaves the ball in your interviewer's court again, and you haven't turned down the job either, in case it turns out that the interviewer can't increase the offer and you still want the job.

Last, send a follow-up letter.

Mail, e-mail, or fax a letter right after the interview telling your interviewer you enjoyed the meeting and are certain (if you are) that you are the "best fit" for the job. The people interviewing you will probably have an attitude described as either "professionally loyal" to their companies, or "maternal and proprietary" if the interviewer also owns the company. In either case, they are looking for people who want to work for *that* company in particular. The follow-up letter you send might be just the deciding factor in your favor if the employer is trying to choose between you and someone else. You will see an example of a follow-up letter on page 16.

A cover letter is an essential part of a job hunt or career change.

Many people are aware of the importance of having a great resume, but most people in a job hunt don't realize just how important a cover letter can be. The purpose of the cover letter, sometimes called a **"letter of interest,"** is to introduce your resume to prospective employers. The cover letter is often the critical ingredient in a job hunt because the cover letter allows you to say a lot of things that just don't "fit" on the resume. For example, you can emphasize your commitment to a new field and stress your related talents. The cover letter also gives you a chance to stress outstanding character and personal values. On the next two pages you will see examples of very effective cover letters.

Special help for those in career change

We want to emphasize again that, especially in a career change, the cover letter is very important and can help you "build a bridge" to a new career. A creative and appealing cover letter can begin the process of encouraging the potential employer to imagine you in an industry other than the one in which you have worked.

As a special help to those in career change, there are resumes and cover letters included in this book which show valuable techniques and tips you should use when changing fields or industries. The resumes and cover letters of career changers are identified in the table of contents as "Career Change" and you will see the "Career Change" label on cover letters in Part Two where the individuals are changing careers.

Salary negotiation can be tricky.

A follow-up letter can help the employer choose between you and another qualified candidate.

A cover letter is an essential part of a career change.

Please do not attempt to implement a career change without a cover letter. A cover letter is the first impression of you, and you can influence the way an employer views you by the language and style of your letter.

Date

**Addressing the Cover
Letter:** Get the exact
name of the person to
whom you are writing. This
makes your approach
personal.

Exact Name of Person
Exact Title
Exact Name of Company
Address
City, State, Zip

Dear Exact Name of Person (or Dear Sir or Madam if answering a blind ad):

I would like to take this opportunity to introduce you to a recent college graduate who offers a reputation for exceptional leadership skills as well as a special talent for motivating others to set and achieve high goals.

Second Paragraph: You
have a chance to talk
about whatever you feel is
your most distinguishing
feature.

As you will see from my enclosed resume, I am recognized as a personable and articulate young professional who excels in bringing out the best in others through my own determination to be the best at what ever I attempt. I received my B.S. in Recreational Management from Marywood University, Scranton, PA, which I attended on an athletic scholarship. During spring semester 2004, I had the opportunity to work as the pitching coach for the college baseball team. This internship allowed me to further refine my abilities as a mentor, instructor, and role model as I played a major role in transforming an average pitching staff into one of the top ten college pitching staffs in the country.

Third Paragraph: You
bring up your next most
distinguishing qualities and
try to
sell yourself.

You will also notice that I was an award-winning athlete both at the college level and earlier in high school and was consistently named to All-Conference, All-State, and All-Region teams as well as being honored with the Best Pitcher Award two years in college.

Fourth Paragraph: Here
you have another
opportunity to reveal
qualities or achievements
which will impress your
future employer.

Through sports, I have learned how to compete, how to win, and how to persist. I believe any job in recreational management, in the teaching/coaching field, or in any other type of job I might hold would require the same highly disciplined and highly motivated attitude which has led me to be successful in sports.

Final Paragraph: He asks
the employer to contact
him. Make sure your
reader knows what the
"next step" is.

If you can use a hard charger with unlimited personal initiative and a drive to become part of a winning team with a championship company, I hope you will contact me to suggest a time when we might meet to discuss your needs.

Sincerely,

Dean McNeill

**Alternate Final
Paragraph:** It's more
aggressive (but not too
aggressive) to let the
employer know that you
will be calling him or her.
Don't be afraid to be
persistent. Employers are
looking for people who
know what they want to
do.

Date

Exact Name of Person
Title or Position
Name of Company
Address (no., street)
Address (city, state, zip)

Dear Exact Name of Person: (or Dear Sir or Madam if answering a blind ad.)

    I would appreciate an opportunity to talk with you soon about how I could contribute to your organization through my background as a successful coach and athletic director who offers experience as a head coach and six as an athletic director.

    As you will see from my resume, the bulk of my experience is in coaching football and I am now at Bismarck Senior High School in Bismarck, ND, a 3A school which has averaged 10 wins a year for the past two seasons in a conference recognized as the toughest and most competitive in the state. In fact, in my two years here, I have guided the team to an impressive current streak of scoring in double figures for the past 21 games, a fact recently publicized by the *High School Football News*. Earlier I led the football team at Fargo High School, the state's smallest 3A school which had not been to a playoff since 1971, to four consecutive playoff seasons.

    A versatile professional, I have also excelled in coaching track, basketball, wrestling, and golf. I am confident that I can build any sports program into a successful one while guiding young people to prosper academically and grow in character through athletics. My track record will show that I am not only a talented coach and administrator, but also an enthusiastic, intelligent, and motivated professional who handles pressure well. I am extremely effective in molding groups of young people into productive, winning teams. For example, when I became the youngest 3A Head Coach in North Dakota at Evergreen High School in Fargo, in 1994, I quickly produced a team with the most conference wins in the school's history.

    I can provide a school system with a winning coach who is also an excellent teacher, administrator, and communicator. I will cheerfully relocate, and I can provide outstanding personal and professional references from all previous employers.

    I hope you will call or write me soon to suggest a time convenient for us to meet and discuss your current and future needs and how I might serve them. Thank you in advance for your time.

Sincerely yours.

Jesse Underhill

This accomplished professional is responding to an advertisement in a professional trade magazine. He analyzed the job vacancy opening very closely and he has made sure that he has tailored his letter of interest to the areas mentioned in the vacancy announcement. A "letter of interest" is also referred to simply as a cover letter.

Date

Exact Name of Person
Title or Position
Name of Company
Address (number and street)
Address (city, state, and zip)

Follow-up Letter

A great follow-up letter
can motivate the
employer
to make the job offer,
and the salary offer may
be influenced by the
style and tone of your
follow-up
letter, too!

Dear Exact Name:

I am writing to express my appreciation for the time you spent with me on 9 December, and I want to let you know that I am sincerely interested in the position of Marketing Director for the Carolina Panthers which we discussed.

I feel confident that I could skillfully interact with your 60-person staff, and I would cheerfully relocate to Charlotte.

As you described to me what you are looking for in the person who fills this position, I had a sense of "déjà vu" because my current employer was in a similar position when I went to work for his organization. The managing partner needed someone to come in and be his "right arm" and take on an increasing amount of his management responsibilities so that he could be freed up to do other things. I have played a key role in the growth and profitability of his team, and his firm has come to depend on my sound advice as much as well as my proven ability to "cut through" huge volumes of work efficiently and accurately. Since this is one of the busiest times of the year in the industry, I feel that I could not leave during that time. I could certainly make myself available by mid-January.

It would be a pleasure to work for your well-known and prestigious law firm, and I am confident that I could contribute significantly not only through my background as a player but also through my strong qualities of loyalty, reliability, and trustworthiness. I am confident that I could quickly learn your style and procedures, and I would welcome being trained to do things your way.

Yours sincerely,

Jacob Evangelisto

In this section, you will find resumes and cover letters of folks who want to work in jobs related to the sports industry. Why should there be a book dedicated to people seeking jobs in the sports industry? Based on more than 20 years of experience in working with job hunters, this editor is convinced that resumes and cover letters which "speak the lingo" of the field you wish to enter will communicate more effectively than language which is not industry-specific. This book is designed to help people (1) who are seeking to prepare their own resumes and (2) who wish to use as models "real" resumes of individuals who have successfully launched careers in the sports industry or advanced in the field. You will see a wide range of experience levels reflected in the resumes in this book. Some of the resumes and cover letters were used by individuals seeking to enter the field; others were used successfully by senior professionals to advance in the field.

Newcomers to an industry sometimes have advantages over more experienced professionals. In a job hunt, junior professionals can have an advantage over their more experienced counterparts. Prospective employers often view the less experienced workers as "more trainable" and "more coachable" than their seniors. This means that the mature professional who has already excelled in a first career can, with credibility, "change careers" and transfer skills to other industries.

Newcomers to the field may have disadvantages compared to their seniors. Almost by definition, the inexperienced professional—the young person who has recently entered the job market, or the individual who has recently received certifications respected by the industry—is less tested and less experienced than senior managers, so the resume and cover letter of the inexperienced professional may often have to "sell" his or her potential to do something he or she has never done before. Lack of experience in the field she wants to enter can be a stumbling block to the junior manager, but remember that many employers believe that someone who has excelled in anything— academics, for example—can excel in many other fields.

Some advice to inexperienced professionals...
If senior professionals could give junior professionals a piece of advice about careers, here's what they would say: Manage your career and don't stumble from job to job in an incoherent pattern. Try to find work that interests you, and then identify prosperous industries which need work performed of the type you want to do. Learn early in your working life that a great resume and cover letter can blow doors open for you and help you maximize your salary.

Special help for career changers...
For those changing careers—either out of sports or into sports—you will find useful the resumes and cover letters marked "Career Change" on the following pages. Consult the Table of Contents for page numbers showing career changers.

Date

Exact Name of Person
Title or Position
Name of Company
Address (no., street)
Address (city, state, zip)

Dear Exact Name of Person: (or Dear Sir or Madam if answering a blind ad):

ACCOUNT EXECUTIVE WITH BACKGROUND AS AN NFL DRAFT PICK.

When an individual excels as an athlete, that accomplishment stays with him or her for a lifetime and is respected by people in all walks of life. In this cover letter and resume, this jobhunter highlights the fact that he was an NFL draft pick.

With the enclosed resume, I would like to make you aware of my interest in exploring employment opportunities with your organization. I am seeking an organization that can use a versatile professional with experience in personnel recruiting and administration along with proven skills in sales, marketing, and business/operations management.

As you will see from my resume, I obtained a B.A. in Sociology from Merrimack College and studied Computer Technology. Currently employed as an Account Executive, I am excelling in a job which is essentially a sales position in the human services field. My major duties are handling administrative matters related to Workman's Compensation, payroll corrections, employee wage increases, and employee terminations/disciplinary actions. I also perform pre-employment drug screening, background and reference checks, and tests for skills and dexterity.

You will notice from my resume that I was an NFL draft pick for the Houston Falcons and played as a professional football player for four years. My extensive sports experience shaped my personality in significant ways and instilled in me a determination to win and succeed despite obstacles and setbacks. I bring the attitude of "a winner, no matter what" to your organization.

I hope you will call or write me soon to suggest a time convenient for us to meet to discuss your current and future needs. Thank you in advance for you time.

Sincerely yours,

Bruce Thomas

BRUCE THOMAS

1110½ Hay Street, Fayetteville, NC 28305   •   preppub@aol.com   •   (910) 483-6611

OBJECTIVE   To benefit an organization that can use a versatile professional with a strong background of knowledge and experience in human resources and personnel recruiting/administration along with proven skills in sales, marketing, and business/operations management.

EDUCATION   **B.A. degree in Sociology,** Merrimack College, North Andover, MA, 1992.
Studied **Computer Technology,** Suffolk University, Boston, MA.
- Was elected Student Body President, Pinebrook Senior High School.

SPORTS
HONORS
- NFL Draft Pick, Houston Falcons, 1992.
- Pre-Season All-Conference Selection, 1991.
- All-Conference, All-City-County Player of the Year, Andrews Player of the Year, Team MVP, High School All-American, Team Captain,.
- Named Best Field Athlete in *Track;* Best Defensive Player in *Basketball;* and Best Offensive Player in *Football,* was Co-Captain and Co-MVP Football and Basketball.

EXPERIENCE   **ACCOUNT EXECUTIVE.** Celtic Employment Staffing/Employment, Inc., Andover, MA (2002-present). Work with human resources executives and personnel managers throughout Massachusetts in order to meet their needs for temporary and permanent employees.
- For one major account, play a key role in revising the employee handbook; for another major account, assist in the formulation of a testing/screening module.
- Handle administrative matters related to Workman's Compensation, payroll corrections, employee wage increases, and employee terminations/disciplinary actions.
- Perform pre-employment drug screening, background and reference checks, and tests for various types of skills and dexterity.
- Was recruited for this position in Andover after excelling in a supervisory role in Lawrence with one of the largest temporary personnel placement firms in MA; supervised 350 temporary employees (90% of Hispanic origin) in a corrugated and packaging facility.

TERRITORY MANAGER. John Deere, Andover, MA (1997-02). Began with John Deere as a Sales Representative I, was rapidly promoted to Sales Representative II, and then was selected as Territory Manager.
- Serviced wholesale and retail accounts, both chains and independents, in our designated territory.
- Developed a weekly strategy and trained merchandisers on implementation methods after making key management decisions including targeting areas for greatest production yields. In 1998, was named to a Direct Sales President's Club, a sales honor reserved for top sales producers.
- In a national corporate competition entitled "Deere Race," led my team to win thousands of dollars in prizes as we finished in first, second, and third place nationally three years in a row based on sales volume as well as numerous technical measures related to inventory control, shelf space increases, and customer service.
- Trained/managed employees promoting John Deere products on displays and through sampling at retail, special events, trade shows, and store sales.

PRO FOOTBALL PLAYER. Houston Falcons, Houston, TX (1992-96). Was a running back for four years.

PERSONAL   Can provide exceptional professional references.

Date

Exact Name of Person
Title or Position
Name of Company
Address (no., street)
Address (city, state, zip)

ADMINISTRATIVE AIDE, ATHLETIC OFFICE

Dear Exact Name of Person: (or Dear Sir or Madam if answering a blind ad.)

I would appreciate an opportunity to talk with you soon about how I could contribute to your organization through my proven ability to "get things done" as well as through my management aptitude, communication skills, and versatile public relations ability.

You will see from my resume that I have excelled in jobs which have helped me refine my ability to serve the public in a gracious manner. I completely financed my college education while simultaneously pursuing a rigorous business management curriculum and excelling as a member of the varsity tennis team and varsity track team. I hope this will demonstrate to you that I am a hard worker with a proven ability to set high goals and then organize my time in the most efficient manner for achieving those goals.

In my most recent job in the Athletic Office of the NCAA college which I attended, I displayed my ability to handle numerous simultaneous activities including sales, billing and finance, scheduling, statistical analysis, media relations, office administration, and data entry. In a previous job, I was chosen to supervise other employees in the absence of the owner because of my excellent problem-solving and decision-making skills.

You would find me to be an enthusiastic young professional who prides myself on adding value to any organization of which I am a part. I can provide outstanding personal and professional references at your request.

I hope you will call or write me soon to suggest a time convenient for us to meet to discuss your current and future needs and how I might serve them. Thank you in advance for your time.

Sincerely yours,

Wanda Martin

WANDA MARTIN

1110½ Hay Street, Fayetteville, NC 28305 • preppub@aol.com • (910) 483-6611

OBJECTIVE
To contribute to an organization that can use a highly motivated self-starter with excellent customer service and public relations skills, along with a proven ability to solve problems and discover efficient new operational methods.

EDUCATION
Bachelor of Science degree in Management, University of Houston, Houston, TX, 2004.
Associate of Science degree, Arizona State University, Tempe, AZ, 2002.

EXPERIENCE
ADMINISTRATIVE AIDE. Blue Cloud Athletic Office, Houston, TX (2003-present). Excelled in this part-time job while personally financing all my college educational expenses.
- **Sales**: Coordinated the sale of season tickets for this NCAA athletic office.
- **Scheduling**: Established and administered the schedule for the use of athletic facilities.
- **Statistics**: Analyzed data and prepared statistical reports which analyzed factors pertaining to athletes and facilities.
- **Mass mailings**: Prepared bulk mailings.
- **Billing & finance**: Handled accounts receivable and coordinated the billing of season ticket holders.
- **Computer operation**: Performed data entry and routinely used a computer for word processing and spreadsheet preparation.
- **Media relations**: Learned to deal effectively with television, radio, and print media through frequent telephone conversations and through information I prepared for media press kits.
- **Office administration**: Operated a wide variety of office machines and contributed to the efficient administration of this bustling office.

WAITRESS. Wood Country Gold Club, Houston, TX (2003). In a summer job between my junior and senior year of college, worked at an elegant country club serving food at private parties and at special banquets.
- Was commended for my management skills after transforming a variety of tasks into an organized system for getting the job done.
- Learned how to deal with demanding customers and keep them very satisfied.

SUPERVISOR/CLERK. Quick Stop, Tempe, AZ (2002). In a summer job, excelled at cashiering, inventory control, and employee supervision in the absence of the owner. In my first management job, learned how to supervise other people while doing my own job.

SALES ASSOCIATE. Payless Shoes, Phoenix, AZ (2000-01). Conducted sales, cashiering, inventory control, data entry, and display design and setup; was responsible for opening and closing the store.

SALES ASSOCIATE. Sears, Phoenix, AZ (1999-2000). While learning the basics of retail management, was responsible for conducting sales, operating the cash register, performing inventory, and scheduling employees.

PERSONAL
Am able to get along with people from all different backgrounds. Adapt new environments quickly and easily. Excellent references.

Date

Exact Name of Person
Title or Position
Name of Company
Address (no., street)
Address (city, state, zip)

**AEROBICS
INSTRUCTOR**

This recent graduate is
relocating with her
husband. This generic
cover letter can be used
to approach school
systems or private
companies seeking a
sports industry
professional.

Dear Exact Name of Person: (or Dear Sir or Madam if answering a blind ad):

With the enclosed resume, I would like to make you aware of my interest in exploring employment opportunities with your organization.

As you will see from my resume, I recently graduated from college with a B.S. in Exercise & Sports Science and Elementary Physical Education. Although I am currently excelling in my position as an Aerobics Instructor and Personal Trainer, my husband and I are in the process of relocating to California, where we both grew up and where our extended families live. I can provide outstanding references from my current employer at the appropriate time.

Although I am a recent graduate, I have had considerable experience in working with the public since graduating from San Diego High School. I completely financed my college education while excelling in demanding professional positions. I also excelled in two lengthy internships with an elementary school and a parks & recreation department in the process of earning my college degree. Through my considerable work experience, I have become very comfortable in dealing with the public, and I am confident that will be a valuable asset as I establish my career in the sports industry.

I hope you will call or write me soon to suggest a time convenient for us to meet to discuss your current and future needs. Thank you in advance for you time.

Sincerely yours,

Kimberly Burns

KIMBERLY BURNS

1110½ Hay Street, Fayetteville, NC 28305   •   preppub@aol.com   •   (910) 483-6611

OBJECTIVE   To benefit an organization in need of an enthusiastic, young professional with excellent public relations, customer service, and office management skills who possesses a knack for planning, problem-solving, and decision-making.

EDUCATION   **Bachelor of Science degree** in Exercise & Sports Science/Elementary Physical Education, Jacksonville University, Jacksonville, FL, 2004.
Internships: As part of my degree requirements, completed two three-month internships:
- *Student Teacher.* Jackson Elementary School, Jacksonville, FL (2004). Taught first and second grade children a wide range of structured motor development exercises and activities; created and implemented all lesson plans.
- *Recreation Assistant.* Jacksonville Parks & Recreation Department, Jacksonville, FL (2003). Assisted in planning recreational activities for 12 children with Muscular Dystrophy, Down's Syndrome, and other handicaps.

Courses: Coursework included:

Physiological exercise	Physical activities
Theories of sports techniques	Motor learning
Foundations of exercise and sports	Tests and measurements
Movement in sport and fitness activities	General psychology
Rhythm and motor coordination	Nutritional health
Physical activity and recreation for handicapped children	Sports and fitness
Theory of sports techniques	Industrial psychology

EXPERIENCE   **AEROBICS INSTRUCTOR.** Gold's Gym, Orlando, FL (2004-present). Refined my motivational and communication abilities teaching three aerobics classes a week at this popular local gym; praised by management for emphasizing safety guidelines. Act as Personal Trainer to three customers, planning workout and nutrition schedules and guidelines.

Gained valuable customer-service and time-management experience working in a variety of jobs while simultaneously attending college full-time:
ASSISTANT OFFICE MANAGER/REAL ESTATE ASSISTANT. ReMax, Jacksonville, FL (2001-03). Utilized my time-management skills while working part-time overseeing a wide range of office management and real estate functions.
- Showed properties; negotiated and typed leases; scheduled maintenance visits for homes, condos, and apartment units; handled administrative duties.
- Learned the "nuts and bolts" of property management while solving numerous "crisis" maintenance problems and other customer difficulties.

WAITRESS. Hard Rock Café, Orlando, FL (2000-2001). Excelled at providing excellent customer service at this trendy, popular restaurant.
- Earned a reputation for resolving thorny customer-service problems in a courteous, timely manner while guaranteeing customers had a pleasant dining experience.

SALES ASSOCIATE. Belk, Orlando, FL (1997-99). Performed sales, merchandising, and inventory functions while working for this upscale retailer. Designed displays and coordinated outfits for customers. Assisted in the planning and coordination of area fashion shows.

PERSONAL   Am a versatile professional who enjoys people. Can handle pressure and react logically to emergencies. Love working with children. Adapt easily to new situations and function smoothly in handling simultaneous responsibilities. Know some Japanese. Enjoy aerobics.

CAREER CHANGE

Date

Exact Name of Person
Title of Profession
Name of Company
Address (no., street)
Address (city, state, zip)

AEROBICS INSTRUCTOR

seeks position as a Cruise
Ship Recreation Director.

Dear Sir or Madam:

With the enclosed resume as a means of formally introducing myself, I would like to make you aware of my interest in the position of Recreation Director for your cruise ship. I am single and can travel as extensively as your needs require.

As you will see, I earned my Associate's degree in Nutrition and Fitness Physiology and then completed credentials related to Aerobics and CPR Certification. In my current position, I work for Muscle Gym where I teach aerobics for approximately 50 students daily. I feel a tremendous sense of accomplishment when I can boost an individual's self-esteem level by educating them on nutrition and physical fitness and devising a specialized exercise regiment suitable to their physical endurance, stamina, body weight, and overall fitness level.

In a previous job with Sam's Club, I advanced to increasing responsibilities as an Administrative Assistant while handling electronic data processing, payroll, collections, sales audits, quality inspections, inventory control, and membership enrollment.

With a reputation as a doer and achiever, I have worked since I was 16 years old. I am a dedicated, enthusiastic, and committed individual. I enjoy challenges and repeatedly have applied my creative problem-solving abilities in developing new programs and transforming problem systems into efficient, productive operations.

You would find me in person to be a congenial individual who would represent your cruise line with poise and professionalism. I hope you will contact me soon to suggest a time when we could meet to discuss your needs and how I might be of service to you.

Yours sincerely,

Linda Lowery

LINDA LOWERY

1110½ Hay Street, Fayetteville, NC 28305　　•　　preppub@aol.com　　•　　(910) 483-6611

OBJECTIVE

To contribute to an organization that can use a dynamic and resourceful young professional with excellent communication and public relations skills along with a reputation for unquestioned integrity, unflagging enthusiasm, and a tireless dedication to excel.

EDUCATION

Bachelor of Arts degree in Nutrition and Fitness Physiology, Saint Xavier University, Chicago, IL, 2002.

Completed Aerobics Convention Training Seminar, 2004.

Completed ADP Payroll Training Seminar, ADP, 2003.

Completed Life & Health Insurance Seminar, MetLife, 2002.

Completed In-House Payroll Training Course (ADP), 2002.

CPR Certified, 2002. Received AFAA Primary Aerobics Certification, 2002.

EXPERIENCE

AEROBICS INSTRUCTOR. Muscle Gym, Chicago, IL (2003-present). Have earned a reputation as an enthusiastic and hard-working professional who has improved every aspect of the Aerobics program at this successful physical fitness center; manage 50 students daily.

- Through my excellent sales abilities, unique ability to motivate others, and creative, innovative teaching strategies, I have dramatically increased aerobics participation and membership.
- Create specialized physical fitness regiments for individuals depending on their physical endurance, stamina, body weight, and overall physical condition and health; motivate students to excel athletically and personally.
- Provide encouragement and support to individuals suffering from obesity; feel a sense of accomplishment and personal gratification when I can restore an individual's self-esteem and self-worth.
- Provide weight training and instruction; familiar with Nautilus and Free fitness equipment. Have polished my communication skills while educating participants on nutrition, physical fitness, and program regiments; teach Hi/Low, Step, Spinning Class Training, Slide, and abdominal floor exercises.

INSURANCE AGENT. All-State, Chicago, IL (2002-03). Provided financial consultation to families, educating them about insurance options and various packages.

- Assisted customers in completing application information; wrote insurance policies while also handling a wide range of office duties including answering phones, making bank deposits, opening and responding to mail, receiving/collecting payments, and working with national insurers.

ADMINISTRATIVE ASSISTANT. Sam's Club, Chicago, IL (1995-2002). Quickly earned rapid promotion from Caller/Cashier to Administrative Assistant handling all aspects of this wholesale distributor including electronic data processing, payroll, collections, quality inspections, inventory control, and membership applications.

- As a Caller/Cashier, was responsible for handling company funds and retail sales transactions. Approved and processed new membership applications and refunds.

PERSONAL

I am a dedicated, enthusiastic, and committed individual who adapts readily to any environment and rapidly masters new tasks. I enjoy challenges and apply my creative problem-solving abilities in developing new programs and transforming problem systems into efficient, productive operations. I enjoy hiking, cycling, jogging, and traveling.

CAREER CHANGE

Date

Exact Name of Person
Title or Position
Name of Company
Address (no., street)
Address (city, state, zip)

AQUATICS COACH   Dear Exact Name: (or Dear Sir or Madam if answering a blind ad.)

I am enclosing a resume in application for the job as Aquatic Supervisor.

As you will see from my enclosed resume, I offer extensive expertise in the aquatics, swimming, and water safety field. I offer proven expertise in every area described in your ad. I have supervised lifeguards, taught swimming to people of all ages, given lifesaving instruction, and received all appropriate certifications that the job requires.

I am in the process of taking early retirement from my job at a manufacturing facility where I have worked for more than 20 years. Even while working full-time, you will see from my resume that I have always held a part-time job in the aquatics field. It is now my desire to make aquatics my full-time career, and I offer a wealth of experience in organizing and coaching teams, teaching swimming and aquatics to people at all skill levels, and developing new aquatics programs. It would be my privilege to take a fine program to even higher levels of excellence and popularity, and I offer the proven leadership to do that.

I can provide excellent personal and professional references, and I would welcome the opportunity to show you in person that I have the aquatics expertise, instructional skills, and supervisory abilities that you are seeking.

Yours sincerely,

Mark Reed

MARK REED

1110½ Hay Street, Fayetteville, NC 28305   •   preppub@aol.com   •   (910) 483-6611

OBJECTIVE	To benefit an organization that can use a hard-working and reliable professional who offers expertise in aquatics and water safety instruction along with proven supervisory ability.
EXPERIENCE	**Am excelling in two jobs simultaneously:** **2000-present: AQUATICS COACH.** (Part-time). Philadelphia YMCA, Philadelphia, PA . In addition to my job on the third shift with Poultry's, Inc., am utilizing the years of experience I have acquired in aquatics as an Aquatics Coach. **1985-present: ASSISTANT SHIPPING FOREMAN** (Full-time). Poultry's, Inc., Philadelphia, PA. Through my supervisory skills, have helped this company decrease its inventory costs by my excellent management of shipping and receiving as well as my resourceful control of perishable food items. • Monitor inventory levels by analyzing computer printouts. • Have been commended for my efficiency in ordering products and materials. **Other part-time experience in the aquatics and recreation field:** **WATER SAFETY INSTRUCTOR**. Philadelphia Club, Philadelphia, PA (2002-04). Served as a lifeguard and instructed swim lessons to youth and adults. • From May-Aug 2003, worked for the PA Department of Parks and Recreation as a **Managing Lifeguard**; managed swimming pool activities and assigned duties to other lifeguards while acting as **Water Safety Instructor** and supervising five other lifeguards. **WATER SAFETY INSTRUCTOR**. Sports Center, Philadelphia, PA (2000-03). Trained people of all ages in water survival training while also serving as an instructor in the Aquatics Program: this program aims to develop self-esteem and therapeutic skills in cooperation with other organizations including Pennsylvania Hospital. • Served as the Junior Olympics Aquatic Coach. **ASSISTANT CENTER DIRECTOR**. Philadelphia Parks and Recreation Department, Philadelphia, PA (1990-99). Planned, organized, and implemented recreational and educational programs for area residents while conducting training and practice for both youth and adults in a wide variety of sporting events. • Supervised and taught recreation center operations to youth employees. Highlights of previous experience: • Worked as a **Lifeguard** and **Water Safety Instructor** for the PA Pitt's League Center. • Worked as **Chief Lifeguard** for the State of PA Department of Recreation. • Was a **Probation Officer** with the PA State Home for Boys in Pittsburgh, PA.
EDUCATION	Studied Physical Education and Psychology, Carnegie Mellon University, Pittsburgh, PA, 1987-1989.
TRAINING	Am certified as a **Water Safety Instructor, Lifeguard Instructor,** and **Adapted Aquatic Instructor** by Life Safety.
PERSONAL	Earned many awards because of aquatics expertise and water safety skills.

Date

Exact Name of Person
Title or Position
Name of Company
Address (no., street)
Address (city, state, zip)

**ASSISTANT COACH &
PHYSICAL EDUCATION
TEACHER**

Dear Exact Name of Person: (or Dear Sir or Madam if answering a blind ad):

With the enclosed resume, I would like to make you aware of my interest in exploring employment opportunities with your organization.

As you will see from my resume, I worked full-time while earning my B.S. degree in Education. It was my volunteer experience which actually led me to earn my degree in Education and embark upon a career which would involve me in teaching and motivating youth.

While excelling in full-time sales positions, I volunteered as a Little League Coach and discovered that I possess a talent for motivating children to set high goals and work hard to achieve them.

I felt honored that I was offered a full-time position as a Teacher and Assistant Coach based on excellent performance in my student teaching assignment. Recently I played a key role in coaching a team which had posted a losing season last year to a conference title. In the process of coaching that team, I discovered the thrill of teaching while on a field or court, and I have decided that I wish to become a part of the coaching staff at a school which can use an effective motivator. I feel privileged to be a part of the teaching and coaching profession, and I am confident that I could become a valuable part of your staff.

I hope you will call or write me soon to suggest a time convenient for us to meet to discuss your current and future needs. Thank you in advance for you time.

Sincerely yours,

Roger Young

ROGER YOUNG

1110½ Hay Street, Fayetteville, NC 28305 • preppub@aol.com • (910) 483-6611

OBJECTIVE   To contribute to an organization that can use a vivacious and enthusiastic communicator who seeks to contribute to the success of my students in life as well as in the classroom.

EDUCATION   Earned a **Bachelor's degree in Education**, The Georgetown University, Washington, DC, 2004.
- Worked in full-time sales positions while earning my college degree.
- Excelled in numerous courses which emphasized sports education. Became knowledgeable about the techniques used to teach sports to beginners.

EXPERIENCE   **ASSISTANT COACH & PHYSICAL EDUCATION TEACHER.** Constitution Senior High School, Washington, DC (2004-present). Was offered a full-time position after excelling in my student internship. Teach Physical Education and Health to high school students.
- As Assistant Coach of the varsity baseball team, played a key role in motivating a high school team which had a losing season in 2003 to win the conference title in 2004.
- Prepare lesson plans for six classes a day, and teach nearly 150 students daily.

RECREATION & WEIGHT TRAINING TEACHER. Constitution Senior High School, Washington, DC (2003). As a student teacher, taught recreation and weight training courses to high school students, including varsity athletes.
- Excelled in working with students, teachers, and parents. Because of my outstanding performance, was offered a full-time position upon college graduation.

SALES ASSOCIATE. Hecht's, Washington, DC (1998-2003). Worked full-time while earning my college degree. Provided top-quality customer service while consistently maintaining and exceeding sales per hour quotas and percentage quotas in sales of maintenance agreement contracts.

SALES ASSOCIATE. Lord & Taylor, Washington, DC (1995-97). After high school graduation, worked at this retail giant; strengthened my natural customer service skills.

Volunteer experience:
- Little League Volunteer. Coached Little League teams, and discovered that I possess a talent for motivating children to set high goals and work hard to achieve them.
- Volunteer in group home for mentally and physically challenged adults. Enjoyed working with the geriatric population.
- Volunteer in local city community outreach centers.
- Volunteer as the basketball coach for my church's high school basketball team, which won the church league championship in 2001.
- Volunteer in local city community outreach centers.

COMPUTERS   Offer strong computer skills including proficiency with Microsoft Word and PowerPoint.

PERSONAL   Am very flexible and willing to do what it takes to ensure the highest quality of service. Willing to work long hours to achieve maximum results. Have an optimistic and friendly personality. Strongly believe in providing excellent customer service to everyone.

CAREER CHANGE

Date

Exact Name of Person
Title or Position
Name of Company
Address (no., street)
Address (city, state, zip)

ASSISTANT DIRECTOR, AQUATICS CAMP.

Here you see the resume of an accomplished young teacher who feels that she has "found her niche" because of her involvement in a prestigious summer internship.

Dear Exact Name of Person: (or Dear Sir or Madam if answering a blind ad):

With the enclosed resume, I would like to make you aware of my interest in applying for the position as Director of the Eastern Aquatics Camp. It was my privilege this past summer to serve as Assistant Director of the Summer Youth Science Camp sponsored by the Eastern Aquatics Camp, and I have decided that I wish to be permanently associated with this organization.

As you will see from my resume, I am an accomplished and respected educator with an undergraduate degree in Biology. Although I have excelled in the teaching profession as a Science and Math teacher, I have decided that I wish to be involved in activities which will fully utilize my strong management abilities as well as my teaching skills and research interests.

As you are aware, I was handpicked for the position as Assistant Director of the Summer Youth Science initiative in 2004, and I thoroughly enjoyed my work and responsibilities. I am fully capable of assuming the responsibilities of Director, and I am excited about the contributions I could make in that role. I can provide outstanding references.

I hope you will call or write me soon to suggest a time convenient for us to meet to discuss your current and future needs. Thank you in advance for you time.

Sincerely yours,

Catherine Jones

CATHERINE JONES

1110½ Hay Street, Fayetteville, NC 28305 • preppub@aol.com • (910) 483-6611

OBJECTIVE

To benefit an organization seeking a hard-working professional experienced with top-notch communication, planning, and organizational, and management skills.

EDUCATION

Bachelor of Science degree in Biology, University of South Carolina, Columbia, SC, 2002; graduated with honors.
- Areas of study included histology, genetics, microbiology, animal physiology, advanced ecology, biological oceanography, animal behavior, organic chemistry, physics, and electron microscopy techniques.
- Performed one-year honors research project. Member of Psi Beta Biology Honor Society.
- Awarded a four-year scholarship for academic excellence.

EXPERIENCE

ASSISTANT DIRECTOR. Summer Youth Science Camp sponsored by the Eastern Aquatics Camp, SC Aquarium, Charleston, SC (Summer 2004).
- Was handpicked by the board of directors for this prestigious summer position.
- Organized activities and provided instruction to students at this summer camp sponsored by CSU Charleston and the SC Aquarium.

Teaching Experience

SCIENCE/MATH TEACHER. Columbus School, Columbia, SC (2002-04). Taught science and math to sixth grade students.

Assisted in paying for my college education while working in various summer jobs:
REMEDIAL AND ENRICHMENT TUTOR. Columbus School, Columbia, SC (2002). Polished organizational skills developing individualized reading and math programs for children aged four to ten years old at this innovative private school and educational development center; integrated computer software into learning programs.
- Taught remedial as well as academically gifted/enrichment classes in math, science, and reading; liaised with parents concerning student needs and goals.

ADMINISTRATIVE ASSISTANT. Columbus School, Columbia, SC (2001). Assisted in student enrollment and curriculum development in addition to providing a wide range of administrative functions; handled accounts receivable.
- Administered placement tests (Gesell and Metropolitan); analyzed results and conducted conferences with parents for placement recommendations and determinations.

Science Experience

RESEARCH PROJECT MANAGER. University of South Carolina, Columbia, SC (2001-02). Refined research techniques and utilization of advanced laboratory equipment while conducting independent research on the tissue culturing of ginkgos and cycads, including attempts at the micropropagation of ginkgos from lateral buds, stem piths, embryos, and other explants.
- Became expert at plant tissue culturing techniques and the staining and preparation of permanent slides. Maintained all documentation, including laboratory notebook; compiled and wrote a paper on the results.
- Required to defend results in an oral examination before a panel of expert professors, passing with outstanding marks.

AFFILIATIONS

S.C. Council of Teachers of Mathematics; NSTA (National Science Teachers Association)

PERSONAL

Am a dedicated, versatile biologist who enjoys challenges, problem-solving, and maximizing available resources and information. Am proficient with Microsoft Word.

Date

Exact Name of Person
Title or Position
Name of Company
Address (no., street)
Address (city, state, zip)

ASSISTANT GENERAL MANAGER, PRO BASKETBALL TEAM

Dear Exact Name of Person: (or Dear Sir or Madam if answering a blind ad.)

I am sending you a resume and three professional references in response to your advertisement for a Director of Marketing.

In my current job I have recently been promoted from Director of Marketing to Assistant General Manager of The Jersey Dunkers. We have become recognized as one of the most effective marketing operations in our league because of my management and public relations expertise and versatile management abilities. I have adeptly handled all the areas you mention in your ad—fundraising, marketing, public relations, business management, ticket sales, and event operations. In addition to initiating exciting national press coverage in respected media for The Dunkers, I have been the "voice and face" of The Dunkers on frequent public speaking engagements. I have organized and directed many different types of promotions while also selling corporate sponsorships and business packages, arranging press conferences, and coordinating events and contests to boost the image of The Dunkers.

Although I have recently been promoted to Assistant General Manager because of my marketing and public relations success in "putting the team on the map," I have felt the strong desire for some time to become a valuable part of a college athletic program. I feel my experience in "the pro's" would give me a body of knowledge that could be used as a "magnet" to attract interest and financial support.

You would find me to be a congenial and "down-to-earth" professional who has a talent for easily establishing rapport with people from all kinds of backgrounds. Since effective public relations in professional sports requires "a jack of all trades," I feel comfortable in every area of team public relations, including developing and supervising ticket sales of all types.

I hope you will write or call me soon to suggest a time when we might meet in person to discuss the objectives you have for the Director of Marketing and how I might help you achieve them. Thank you in advance for your time.

Yours sincerely,

Travis Arnold

TRAVIS ARNOLD

1110½ Hay Street, Fayetteville, NC 28305 • preppub@aol.com • (910) 483-6611

OBJECTIVE

To apply my education and my experience in the areas of marketing, public relations, and sales to an organization that can benefit from my specialized knowledge of sports marketing as well as my organizational and planning abilities.

EDUCATION

B.S. in Sports Management, Rider University, Lawrenceville, NJ, 2001.
- Specialized in Sports Information, Marketing, and Promotion.
- Partially financed my education while gaining experience in these jobs:
  Recreation Center Manager. (1998-01). Managed a $10 million complex.
  Sports Writer. (1997-99). Gained experience in college-level sports marketing and promotion while writing promotional materials and stories for the local newspaper.

EXPERIENCE

ASSISTANT GENERAL MANAGER. Jersey Pro Basketball, Inc., Jersey City, NJ (2004-present). Oversee all budgeting, marketing, public relations, advertising, and supervisory operations for the Jersey Dunkers, a professional basketball team in the American Basketball Association.
- Entrusted with the management of an investment totaling $700,000.
- Control expenses, payroll, and bookkeeping of a $450,000 operating budget.
- Develop marketing, advertising, and public relations campaigns to enhance visibility and popularity of team. Coordinate sales of season tickets, group and small business packages, and corporate sponsorships.

MARKETING DIRECTOR. The Jersey Dunkers, Jersey City, NJ (2003-04). Controlled marketing, sales, and public relations for a basketball team in its first year of operation in the new American Basketball Association.
- Sold season tickets and $132,000 in corporate sponsorships and small business packages in the franchise's first seven months of existence. Provided statistical information, handled press conferences and press releases, and arranged public appearances for team members.
- Coordinated entertainment and promotions including booking halftime acts.
- Led the sales staff by accounting for 85% of all advance ticket sales: sold $14,000 in preseason small business packages in a 45-day period. Have become recognized as one of the league's most effective marketing operations through my management style.

SPORTS MARKETING SPECIALIST. American Advertising, Lawrenceville, NJ (2002-03). Coordinated information from high school athletic directors and created the design for producing a sports calendar for local businesses.
- Generated $25,000 in sales of advertising space in a 4 1/2 month period.

PUBLIC RELATIONS DIRECTOR. The Lawrence Strykers, Lawrenceville, NJ (2001-02). Earned rapid promotion from assistant director to handle public relations duties for this professional basketball team. Trained three interns.
- Wrote press releases, organized press conferences, arranged public appearances, and maintained statistics. Made the year's largest group sale: 1,200 tickets for one game.

COMPUTER KNOWLEDGE

Use Apple Macintosh computers and software including Adobe PageMaker, Microsoft Word, C-Scan, MacPaint, and MacWrite.

PERSONAL

Am a licensed softball umpire, baseball umpire, and basketball official. Offer a willingness to work long, hard hours to ensure quality results. Excellent references.

Exact Name of Person
Title or Position
Name of Company
Address (no., street)
Address (city, state, zip)

ASSISTANT GOLF COURSE MANAGER

Dear Exact Name of Person: (or Dear Sir or Madam if answering a blind ad.)

With the enclosed resume, I would like to make you aware of my interest in becoming associated with your organization as Director of Golf Operations. I am responding to your recent advertisement in "Golfing World."

As you will see from my resume, I will soon be graduating from Hawaii Pacific University with a B.S. in Business Administration along with a minor concentration in Professional Golf Management. You are probably aware that Hawaii Pacific University is considered one of the country's top three Professional Golf Management programs. As a member of the college's golf team, I have played a key role in helping the university win the National Golf Club championship for the past two years.

While earning my college degree, I have worked part-time as Assistant Manager at one of the country's finest golf courses. I have demonstrated my ability to interact effectively with club members as well as with co-workers, and I am confident that I am ready to assume the responsibilities of Director of Golf Operations.

I hope you will welcome my call soon to arrange a brief meeting at your convenience to discuss your current and future needs and how I might serve them. Thank you in advance for your time.

Sincerely yours,

Monica Evans

Alternate last paragraph:
I hope you will call or write soon to suggest a time convenient for us to meet and discuss your current and future needs and how I might serve them. Thank you in advance for your time.

MONICA EVANS

1110½ Hay Street, Fayetteville, NC 28305 • preppub@aol.com • (910) 483-6611

OBJECTIVE To contribute through my broad base of experience in sales, education in business administration, and reputation as a hard-working and dedicated professional who offers outstanding communication, motivational, and public relations abilities.

EDUCATION Attend Hawaii Pacific University, Honolulu, HI; will receive a B.S. in **Business Administration** with a minor concentration in Professional Golf Management, spring 2005.
- Am on the college's team which has won the National Golf Club championship for the last two years consecutively.
- Attended several seminars on golf rules and teaching methods.
- Refined my time management skills while attending college and working to finance my education.
- Have a strong interest in science and have taken numerous classes including:

chemistry	physical science	biology
earth science	anatomy & physiology	kinesiology

- Will complete a "practicum" with an advertising agency during my last semester.

Previously studied Business Administration at University of Hawaii-Maui Community College, Kahului, HI and attended on a golfing scholarship.

EXPERIENCE **ASSISTANT GOLF COURSE MANAGER**. Honolulu Golf Course, Honolulu, HI (2002-present). Gained experience in all facets of golf course management from merchandising/sales/inventory of pro shop stock, setting up tee times, working in the snack bar, and answering inquiries by phone and in person.
- Use my communication skills and knowledge of the game of golf while giving lessons to students of all ages and levels of play.
- Assist in planning and conducting tournaments and leagues.
- Have polished my managerial abilities overseeing four employees.
- Applied my computer knowledge while implementing a new inventory control program.

SALES AND CUSTOMER SERVICE REPRESENTATIVE. Luau Golf Club, Honolulu, HI (2000-01). Learned to deal with people as individuals and handle their problems and concerns in a professional and appropriate manner while involved in pro shop sales.
- Used my education in business to develop an improved system of billing customers.

APPRAISER. Islands Mapping Co., Kahului, HI (1999-00). Used maps and other available documents and information to reappraise land & properties.
- Became experienced in dealing tactfully with upset, and often irate, individuals who were aware that my appraisal could influence their property taxes.

SUPERVISORY LANDSCAPER. Coral Club, Kahului, HI (1998-99). Oversaw four employees while taking care of planting, cutting, and maintaining golf course grounds including pool and tennis court areas. Became skilled in the proper methods for maintaining golf course grounds and in using heavy equipment.

Highlights of other experience: Taught swimming and water safety to people of all ages as a lifeguard at a city park for two summers.

PERSONAL An award-winning high school basketball player. Am a creative thinker with outstanding negotiation, research, and time management skills. Excellent references.

Date

Exact Name of Person
Title or Position
Name of Company
Address (no., street)
Address (city, state, zip)

ASSISTANT GOLF PRO SEEKING POSITION AS HEAD PRO

Dear Exact Name: (or Dear Sir or Madam if answering a blind ad.)

With the enclosed resume, I would like to make you aware of my interest in the position as Head Golf Pro at your club.

You will see from my resume that I was a champion junior player in high school and won the state high school golfing championship during my senior year. After high school graduation, I was recruited by the leading retailer of golfing supplies to become a salesman, and I won numerous sales contests and exceeded all sales goals. After graduating from college with a B.S. in Business Administration, I was aggressively recruited by a leading retailer to become a Store Manager. Although I excelled in sales and management, I missed being "a player" and working with other players, so I found my way back to the golf course community as an Assistant Golf Pro.

Prior to becoming an assistant pro, I managed an off-course shop where I gained a wealth of knowledge in merchandising, customer service, and club repair. We were totally computerized in maintaining inventory levels, price structure, and customer accounts. In my current position with the Beacon Club and tournament program, we post all scores and update handicaps twice a month. I also teach private lessons and work with a junior program that has increased 300 percent from last year.

If you find yourself in need of a golfing professional to join your team, I would appreciate your contacting me. I am confident that I could be an asset to your club. I hope I will have the pleasure of meeting you in person soon in order to discuss your needs and goals.

Yours sincerely,

Samuel Johnson

SAMUEL JOHNSON

1110½ Hay Street, Fayetteville, NC 28305   •   preppub@aol.com   •   (910) 483-6611

OBJECTIVE
I want to contribute to an organization that can use an outgoing individual who offers a proven ability to manage all aspects of golf course operations while effectively interfacing with club members, vendors, and others.

EDUCATION
B.S. degree in Business Administration, Hampton University, Hampton, VA, 2000.
Graduated from South Columbia High School, South Columbia, GA, 1996.
- Lettered in three sports. Won the high school state golfing championship in 1996. Was named Most Valuable Player for four years during high school.

EXPERIENCE
ASSISTANT GOLF PRO. Beacon Club, Richmond, VA (2004-present). As second assistant, ensure overall service to club members and assist with both pro-shop and outside operations. This includes merchandise displays, club repair, cart-boy management, inventory decisions, and tournament setup through the Beacon Club and its tournament program.
- Provide private lessons to golfers of all ages.
- Have played a key role in significantly expanding the junior program. Have attracted promising new juniors to the club's program, and manage a junior program that has increased 300 percent from last year.

STORE MANAGER. Go Golf, Richmond, VA (2000-04). Responsibilities included inventory control, advertising decisions, and designs, bank deposits, training, scheduling and managing salesmen and daily accounting work.
- Performed computerized swing analysis to better fit and service our customers when buying clubs.
- Provided on-the-spot club repair and taught private lessons in a hitting area.
- During this period I took the store from near bankruptcy to annual sales of $550,000 while maintaining a 32 percent margin.

LANDSCAPE TECHNICIAN. Virginia & Co., Richmond, VA (1999). Performed lawn maintenance, pruning, spraying, and soil preparation activities.
- Performed landscaping at various golf clubs in the Richmond area.

SALESMAN. Golf, Etc., Hampton, VA (1996-99). Sold golf equipment, performed club repair, and controlled inventory.

Other experience (high school).
MANAGER TRAINEE. Taco Bell, Hampton, VA (1993-96). Was entrusted with occasionally managing this store after learning the internal workings of this fast-food preparation and delivery business serving the Hampton area.

Scheduled/directed drivers.	Ordered food/supplies.
Balanced daily receipts.	Answered phones/took orders.
Made bank deposits.	Prepared/delivered food.

COMPUTERS
Proficient with software including Word and Excel.

PERSONAL
Outstanding personal and professional references upon request.

Date

Exact Name of Person
Title or Position
Name of Company
Address (no., street)
Address (city, state, zip)

ASSISTANT RECREATION CENTER DIRECTOR.

Sometimes you don't know what you want to do professionally until you try different things. This individual was employed as a recreation center director and then as a teacher, and now he has decided that he wishes to get back into the management of recreational centers.

Dear Exact Name of Person: (or Dear Sir or Madam if answering a blind ad):

With the enclosed resume, I would like to make you aware of my interest in exploring employment opportunities with your organization.

As you will see from my resume, I earned a B.S. in Health, Physical Education, and Recreation from Pacific Lutheran University in Tacoma, Washington, where I am a member of the Washington Recreation and Parks Society. I was recently recognized for my service to the mentally handicapped.

As an Assistant Center Director, I perform professional recreation work in the development and direction of a variety of recreation activities. In addition to planning and promoting a variety of activities and events for various ages and special interest groups, I assist center supervisors and recreation staff during special programs.

With outstanding personal and professional references, I offer a reputation as an effective manager of human and financial resources as well as a resourceful planner and programmer. Although I am held in high regard in my current position, I am seeking a position in which my responsibilities would be greater and more complex. I enjoy the challenges of managing multiple activities, and I offer a proven ability to manage a busy recreation center.

I hope you will call or write me soon to suggest a time convenient for us to meet to discuss your current and future needs. Thank you in advance for you time.

Sincerely yours,

David Simpson

DAVID SIMPSON

1110½ Hay Street, Fayetteville, NC 28305   •   preppub@aol.com   •   (910) 483-6611

OBJECTIVE

To contribute to an organization that can use a skilled manager of finances, projects, and programs who offers strong teaching, coaching, and motivational skills.

EDUCATION

B.S., Health, Physical Education, and Recreation, Pacific Lutheran University, Tacoma, WA, 1996.
- Played intramural volleyball and basketball; led my team to a first-place finish in the annual intramural league championship, 1996.

HONORS

Recognized for service to Mentally Handicapped, 2004.
Received a certificate for participation in Violence Intervention Workshop, 2003.
Awarded Certificate of Appreciation for volunteer work during Summer Games, 2000.

EXPERIENCE

ASSISTANT RECREATION CENTER DIRECTOR. Seattle Parks and Recreation, Seattle, WA (2004-present). Perform professional recreation work in the development and direction of a variety of recreation activities.
- Plan and promote a variety of activities and events for various ages and special interest groups.
- Assist center supervisor and recreation staff during special programs.
- Plan and execute center programs for special events.

PHYSICAL EDUCATION INSTRUCTOR. Pacific Middle School, Seattle, WA (2002-03). Instructed 6th, 7th, and 8th grade students in the areas of health and physical education. Supervised track and field, and football activities.
- Assisted with non-instructional duties including bus duty and lunchroom duty.

CENTER DIRECTOR. Tacoma Parks and Recreation, Tacoma, WA (1999-02). Organized, scheduled, and programmed for all ages while working in a recreation center.
- Planned and supervised various city-wide programs.
- Prepared and maintained program files and records.
- Issued, received, and maintained recreating equipment.
- Interacted with public to resolve conflicts.

TEACHER'S ASSISTANT. Chinook High School, Seattle, WA (1996-99). Assisted in devising and implementing Behavior Modification Programs for high school students. Supervised the high school's In-School Suspension Program.
- Offered assistance with extracurricular activities including, track and field, wrestling, and football.
- Assisted with non-instructional duties including bus duty and lunchroom duty.

VOLUNTEER EXPERIENCE

DIRECT CARE VOLUNTEER. Northwest Group Home, Tacoma, WA (1996-99). Ensured the overall grooming, nutrition, and therapy of six mentally handicapped young men. Helped clients to maintain clean/comfortable living quarters. Transported clients to area day program.

ACTIVITIES

Member of Washington Recreation and Parks Society

PERSONAL

Excellent references on request. Proven ability to handle multiple tasks and interact effectively with others. Am known for my enthusiastic and outgoing personality.

CAREER CHANGE

Date

Exact Name of Person
Title or Position
Name of Company
Address (no., street)
Address (city, state, zip)

ATHLETIC TRAINER.
This individual is working at a high school, but she is aggressively pursuing professional sports teams. The cover letter is "all purpose" and generic, and she is sending the cover letter and resume to dozens of professional sports teams throughout the U.S.

Dear Exact Name of Person: (or Dear Sir or Madam if answering a blind ad):

With the enclosed resume, I would like to make you aware of my interest in exploring employment opportunities with your organization.

As you will see from my resume, I offer experience as an Athletic Trainer along with education at the master's degree level. A graduate of the University of Illinois with a Masters of Arts in Health Education and Sports Medicine, I am working as a Teacher and Head Athletic Trainer at Northview Senior High School. Although I enjoy the challenge of educating high school students about physical fitness and athletic training, I feel that my extensive knowledge would be better suited to a professional sports team, and it has been my dream for many years to become a trainer with a professional sports team. I am confident that I could favorably impact the bottom line of a professional sports team through my ability to help athletes stay fit and ready to play.

As you will see from my resume, I have attended many sports medicine clinics and conferences, and I am frequently invited to present my professional opinions in the form of papers and speeches. I would enjoy putting my knowledge to work for your organization.

I hope you will call or write me soon to suggest a time convenient for us to meet to discuss your current and future needs. Thank you in advance for you time.

Sincerely yours,

Krystal Gooding

KRYSTAL GOODING

1110½ Hay Street, Fayetteville, NC 28305 • preppub@aol.com • (910) 483-6611

OBJECTIVE
To benefit a high school, college, or professional organization that can use an accomplished professional educated in sports medicine and certified as an athletic trainer.

EDUCATION
Masters of Arts in Health Education/Sports Medicine, University of Illinois at Chicago, Chicago, IL, 2001.
Bachelor of Arts Degree, Biology, University of Chicago, Chicago, IL, 1998.
Certifications: Illinois Teaching Certificate; National Athletic Trainer's Association Certification

SPORTS
MEDICINE
CLINICS
Attended numerous sports medicine clinics including:
Arthur Sports Medicine Clinic. Harrisburg, IL (2003-04).
The Matthews Sports Medicine Clinic. Chicago, IL (2003).
District Two Sports Medicine Conference. Springfield, IL (2002).
University of Chicago Medicine Conference. Chicago, IL (2003). Supervised and facilitated the learning of Student Athletic Trainers.
University of Illinois at Chicago Sports Medicine Conferences. Chicago, IL (1999, 2000, 2001, and 2004).

EXPERIENCE
TEACHER & HEAD ATHLETIC TRAINER. Northview Senior High School, Chicago, IL (2001-present). Teach physical education courses to high school students while overseeing the school's athletic training programs. Oversee assessment, treatment, rehabilitation, organization and administration while supervising all sports and student trainers.

INSTRUCTOR. Family Medicine Clinic, Wendler High School, Chicago, IL (2001). As a volunteer, taught rehabilitation techniques and principles to third-year student athletic trainers.

STUDENT ATHLETIC TRAINER. University of Illinois at Chicago (1999-01). As a volunteer trainer, trained under the supervision of certified athletic trainers in the following sports:

Football	Swimming	Tennis
Basketball	Volleyball	Golf
Soccer	Baseball and softball	Cross Country

• Worked as a Volunteer Athletic Trainer for the Chicago Panthers, a minor league baseball team, and the Vienna Gym for Chicago Sports Medicine.

TEACHER. Churchill Middle School, Chicago, IL (1998-99). Taught Biology to middle school students.

AUXILIARY
SKILLS
• Certified in adult, child and infant CPR.
• Certified in First Aid.
• Member of National Athletic Trainer's Association
• Member of the Safety Committee at Northview Senior High School.
• Member of the Student Involvement Committee at Northview Senior High.
• Co-advisor of Northview Senior High Key Club.
• Member of IL Science Teacher's Association.

AWARDS &
HONORS
• Invited to present a paper, Chicago District Sports Medicine Conference, 2001.
• Member, Kappa Beta Health Honor Society – University of Illinois at Chicago.

Exact Name of Person
Title or Position
Name of Company
Address (no., street)
Address (city, state, zip)

BASKETBALL COACH   Dear Exact Name of Person: (or Dear Sir or Madam if answering a blind ad.)

I would appreciate an opportunity to talk with you soon about the Basketball Head Coach vacancy in your organization.

As you will see from my resume, I offer "hands-on" experience in coaching basketball, volleyball, and track. I have been named "Coach of the Year" and have coached athletes who were named "Player of the Year." I strongly believe in the value of athletics to inspire human excellence and shape character, and I consider it an honor to be a part of the coaching profession.

With a Master's degree in physical education, I offer knowledge of the latest fitness techniques used in teaching physical education. I have a sincere interest in seeing young people become physically fit, and I enjoy motivating them to achieve this fitness.

You would find me to be an enthusiastic and dedicated professional who works well independently or as part of a team. I thrive on meeting challenging situations.

I hope you will call or write me soon to suggest a time convenient for us to meet and discuss your current and future needs and how I might serve them. Thank you in advance for your time.

Sincerely yours,

Michael Stein

MICHAEL STEIN

1110½ Hay Street, Fayetteville, NC 28305 • preppub@aol.com • (910) 483-6611

OBJECTIVE	To benefit a school that can use a talented educator and coach who is dedicated to encouraging athletes to excel physically and mentally and who is skilled in producing winning teams.
CERTIFICATION	Hold a Maine Physical Education Certificate, grades K-12.
COACHING EXPERIENCE	**In these simultaneous coaching roles, excelled in a "track record" of achievements in a variety of sports, Bridgeton High School, Augusta, ME.**

2001-present: HEAD COACH, WOMEN'S TRACK. Led a team which had won only three dual meets in three years to achieve this record:
- 2003-04: 8-10 in quad meets and finished fourth in Northeast Conference.
- 2002-03: 5-1 in dual meets and finished third in Northeast Conference.
- 2001-02: 4-2 in dual meets and finished fifth in Northeast Conference.

2000-present: HEAD COACH, WOMEN'S VOLLEYBALL. Took charge of a team with only two returning players and, in three years, won the first conference championship in the school's history; held a 19-3 record and reached the state quarter finals.
- Made playoffs for second consecutive year with a 13-4 record, 2003.
- Was named Northeast "Coach of the Year," 2002.
- Coached the "Player of the Year," two first-team selections, and three second-team selections named to the All-Conference Team.

1997-present: HEAD COACH, JUNIOR VARSITY BASKETBALL. Began an after school study hall program which virtually eliminated academic failure among athletes.
- 2003-04, overall 9-9; finished 9-5 in conference for third place.
- Served four years as assistant head coach; in 2002-03, finished my first season as head coach with a 10-10 record.
- Led the team to finish first in its conference.

1997-present: ASSISTANT COACH, VARSITY BASKETBALL. As a volunteer assistant and assistant coach, played a key role in helping head coach Bill Oats motivate young athletes.

Other experience: ASSISTANT COACH, MEN'S TRACK. (1997-00). Coached the school's first 1600 meter champion while coaching distance runners.

EDUCATION	**M.Ed. degree in Physical Education,** University of Maine at Augusta, ME, 1999.

- Taught students and coached two sports while earning my degree.

B.S. degree in Physical Education (graduated cum laude), University of Maine at Augusta, ME, 1997.
- Earned the highest GPA in the Health, Physical Education, and Recreation and Education programs; elected to honor society.

Athletic Achievements
- Was an active athlete: lettered in tennis, was elected vice-president of the Physical Education Majors Club, and was assistant intramural director.

A.A. degree in General Education, University of Southern Maine, Gorham, ME, 1994.
- Managed a women's basketball team which participated in a national championship!
- Lettered in tennis; was intramural team captain and intramural basketball MVP.

PERSONAL	A native of Augusta, am dedicated to the advancement of local athletes. Believe in "going the extra mile" by being available to my players on and off the field. Thrive on helping devoted athletes improve their performance. Excellent references.

Date

Exact Name of Person
Title or Position
Name of Company
Address (no., street)
Address (city, state, zip)

CART & DRIVING RANGE ATTENDANT SEEKING FIRST PROFESSIONAL POSITION AFTER COLLEGE

Dear Exact Name of Person: (or Dear Sir or Madam if answering a blind ad):

With the enclosed resume, I would like to make you aware of my interest in exploring employment opportunities with your organization.

As you will see from my resume, I attended summer workshops sponsored by "Golf Forever" magazine and was honored as the "Most Valuable Player." I am currently pursuing my B.S. degree in Business Administration with a concentration in Professional Golf Management at the University of Arkansas. I am a member of the golf team which has won the Collegiate Athletic Association championships for the past two consecutive years!

During the summers when not attending school, I worked full-time to pay for college. My most recent employment was as a Cart & Driving Range attendant for a popular elite private country club which has a total of 750 members. I handled cart cleaning and scheduling in addition to bag drop and driving range operations. I also assisted during tournament preparations including marking the course and scoring during tournaments.

In previous summers, I worked as a Club Operations Assistant of a 400-member public golf club where I applied my instructional abilities while conducting highly successful clinics for women and youth members. I became skilled in applying what was taught in college to practical situations by seeing rules and handicapping in action.

I hope you will call or write me soon to suggest a time convenient for us to meet to discuss your current and future needs. Thank you in advance for you time.

Sincerely yours,

Chad Atkins

CHAD ATKINS

1110½ Hay Street, Fayetteville, NC 28305 • preppub@aol.com • (910) 483-6611

OBJECTIVE

To benefit an organization that can use a knowledgeable and well-educated young professional who can contribute through creativity, hard work, and enthusiasm as well as through practical experience in golf course management and tournament play.

EDUCATION

Attend University of Arkansas at Little Rock, Little Rock, AR: will receive a B.S. degree in Business Administration with a concentration in **Professional Golf Management,** spring 2005.
- Am a member of the golf team which has won the Collegiate Athletic Association championship for the past two years.
- Excelled in specialized course work in these subjects:

pro shop management	agronomy	rules of golf
tournament operations	club repair	effective instruction
cost accounting	managerial finance	management
principles of accounting	micro/macro economics	marketing
human resource management	Swing techniques	computer applications

- Gained valuable practical experience in summer internships.

TRAINING

Attended 2000 and 2001 summer workshops sponsored by "Golf Forever" magazine.
- Was honored as "Most Outstanding Player for 2001."

EXPERIENCE

CART & DRIVING RANGE ATTENDANT. Little Rock Country Club, Magnolia, AR (summer 2004). Working for the head golf pro, Jason Freeman, provided services to the playing membership of 270 and the 750 total members of an elite private club.
- Handled cart cleaning and scheduling in addition to bag drop and driving range operations.
- Assisted during tournament preparations including marking the course and then helped with scoring during tournaments.
- Was selected to serve on the rules committee.

CLUB OPERATIONS ASSISTANT. Santa Vista Golf Club, Magnolia, AR (summers 2001-03). Assisted the director of golf club operations, Noel Parker, in all aspects of running a 400-member public golf course.
- Applied my instructional abilities while conducting highly successful clinics for women and youth members.
- Learned to take charge of promotional activities while organizing and operating leagues and club-sponsored tournaments.
- Was involved in the day-to-day practical operational areas including cart cleanliness and storage, club repair, range maintenance and resupply, and as a starter.
- Became skilled in applying what was taught in college to practical situations by seeing rules and handicapping in action.

VOLUNTEER SERVICE

Refined my knowledge by helping in preparations for and the conduct of tournaments:
- Back-to-Camp Tournament at Little Rock Country Club, Little Rock, AR
- the first Smiley Jones Invitational at Classic Golf and Country Club, Atlanta, GA

PERSONAL

Offer a reputation as a warm and friendly young professional, highly skilled in handling and welcoming customers. Am very creative with experience in sales, display, and advertising.

Date

Exact Name of Person
Title or Position
Name of Company
Address (no., street)
Address (city, state, zip)

CROSS COUNTRY and TRACK & FIELD COACH.

This talented athlete who became a teacher is seeking to swap his position at a prominent private academy for a coaching and teaching job at a college.

Dear Exact Name of Person: (or Dear Sir or Madam if answering a blind ad.)

I was surprised to find that the cross country and track and field position at Mary Washington College was vacant, having spoken to Anthony Baker about helping with the track team just prior to his departure for the National Track and Field Championships. At that time, I was in the midst of "bartering" with the headmaster at Harper Academy to release me from my softball coaching duties so that I might pursue my goals of coaching track and cross country while teaching at the college level.

A successful program such as the one which Anthony Baker has helped build will surely have no shortage of qualified applicants wanting to fill the position. However, I am confident that my blend of academic knowledge, motivational and leadership skills, and the experience of a seasoned professional is unique. My background in the sport is extensive, having competed at University of North Carolina at Chapel Hill under the internationally known track and cross-country coach, Bill Smith, in addition to two other Olympic coaches and numerous national team coaches. I have studied the sport and have had success in coaching the sport at the high school level. There are perhaps a handful of universities in this country that can offer the kind of experience that track athletes at UNC Chapel Hill are exposed to. Unlike long jump skills, middle distance workouts, meet procedures, and other purely technical aspects of the sport, the understanding of a highly competitive program cannot be learned from a book, it must be experienced. I offer that experience.

A successful college such as Mary Washington depends not only upon its athletic reputation, but also upon its academic reputation, and I feel that my experience in the classroom would support your reputation for teaching excellence. I was an Associate Instructor at Chapel Hill while finishing my Master's degree and have since taught physical education and science at the junior and senior high school level. The bulk of my experience has always been in the sciences, in particular the physical sciences, and anatomy and physiology. I have always felt this is a positive step towards a collegiate physical education position because it is both relevant and provides the unique organizational and teaching skills of the typical classroom.

I am excited about the prospect of working with Mary Washington College. I enjoy teaching and coaching; it has never been just a job to me. During my teaching experience, I have had just a single sports season off. I would appreciate the opportunity to meet and talk with you soon about Mary Washington College's coaching and teaching needs and how I might serve them.

Sincerely,

Rochelle Lee

ROCHELLE LEE

1110½ Hay Street, Fayetteville, NC 28305   •   preppub@aol.com   •   (910) 483-6611

OBJECTIVE   To contribute my outstanding skills and experience as a track and field and cross-country coach, as well as my background in teaching, to an organization that can use an energetic professional who excels at motivating people to reach their full potential.

EDUCATION   **M.S.**, Physical Education, 2001, University of North Carolina at Chapel Hill (UNC). Worked as an Associate Instructor as a graduate student.
B.S., Physical Education, (with distinction) 1998, UNC.

EXPERIENCE   **TEACHER, COACH, & ASSISTANT ATHLETIC DIRECTOR.** Harper Academy, Richmond, VA (2003-present). Teach science classes grades 7-12 with particular emphasis on physical sciences; increased hands-on lab work by over 100%. Organize an experiential learning experience where students used hands-on science to understand physical laws of motion using "roller coaster physics."
- Initiate, develop, and teach anatomy and physiology curriculum using exercise science to create interest among students. Develop new goals, objectives, and curriculum guide to enhance the physical education department, grades 8-9.
- Increased physical education budget through sports merchandise and uniform sales.
- Organized a fitness project where students trained for and ran a 5K road race.

TEACHER & COACH. E.G. Lyman High School, Chapel Hill, NC (2000-02). As a science teacher, wrote all five class objectives, goals, and curriculum guides. In two years as track and field coach, turned a last-place county and conference meet team into a top contender, finishing second and fifth respectively in first year and first and fourth in the second year.
- Implemented weight training program for track team and created meet result handouts to assist students in assessing progress towards goals. Served on the NC State Department of Education committee to rewrite physical education proficiencies.

RELEVANT EXPERIENCE & ACCOMPLISHMENTS
- Competed on UNC Chapel Hill cross-country and indoor and outdoor track and field teams, captain of cross-country team during senior year, Scholastic Athlete of the Year in junior and senior year.
- Attended Coaching of Track and Field class under head coaches Bill Smith and Tom Anderson. Particular coaching strengths in middle distance and distance events, high jump, pole vault, and shot put. Attended UNC Chapel Hill Track and Field Clinic.
- In order to foster leadership skills, interpersonal relationships, global environmental and cultural awareness, and lifetime fitness potential, independently planned, organized, and chaperoned Rocky Mountain field trips for area students. Responsible for all financial management, travel arrangements, advertising, and recruiting.
- Initiated and coached a summer travel team in softball that finished seventh nationally in both the Eastern Coast and All-American tournament and won the National Team Sportsmanship Award. Raised over $11,000 for travel and entry fees.
- Winner of UNC Chapel Hill Morris G. Oliver public speaking contest.
- Graduate emphasis on pedagogy and Sports History. Did significant, original research on the history of women's track and field in the U.S. and the role of the Amateur Athletic Union in its development.

PERSONAL   Possess outstanding written and verbal communications skills. Excellent references.

CAREER CHANGE

Date

Exact Name of Person
Title or Position
Name of Company
Address (no., street)
Address (city, state, zip)

CROSS COUNTRY COACH & HIGH SCHOOL TEACHER.

This talented teacher and coach is seeking a new challenge within the high school academic environment.

Dear Exact Name of Person: (or Dear Sir or Madam if answering a blind ad.)

With the enclosed resume, I would like to make you aware of my interest in the position as Assistant School Principal which you advertised recently.

As you will see from my resume, I have excelled as a Teacher, Coach, and Advisor with the Detroit Schools since 1990. I have gained experience with all types of student populations ranging from behaviorally and emotionally challenged youth, to Advanced Placement (AP) students. I have established a new AP course at Delta Pine High School and implemented a new Peer Mediation Program.

I have also helped students excel outside the traditional classroom environment. While serving as sponsor of the National Honor Society, I provided the leadership which enabled the school's chapter to become a national Service Award winner as well as a State Award winner. While serving as sponsor of the Delta Pine Student Council, I provided guidance which enabled the council to earn Honor Council distinction and to be named Best Workshop Host.

The students I have taught and coached, and the colleagues with whom I have worked, have honored me in numerous ways. I have been named State Cross Country Coach of the Year, Senior Class Teacher of the Year (twice), National Honor Society Advisor of the Year (twice), and have been named to "Who's Who Among America's Teachers."

At this point in my career, I feel that my strong communication skills and resourceful problem-solving abilities could be best utilized if I were serving in a position as Assistant School Principal. I would appreciate an opportunity to talk with you in person about the vacancy.

Yours sincerely,

Joe Carter

JOE CARTER

1110½ Hay Street, Fayetteville, NC 28305   •   preppub@aol.com   •   (910) 483-6611

OBJECTIVE

To contribute to the Detroit schools through my strong planning, organizational, and communication skills as well as my proven ability to inspire students to set high goals for themselves in character development, community service, and academic achievement.

PUBLICATIONS & HONORS

Authored an article published in 2004 in *Quality Magazine* on "Time Management: Handling Stress."

Named Senior Class **Teacher of the Year,** 2004 and 2002, Delta Pine High School.

Named MI National Honor Society **Advisor of the Year,** 2003 and 2002.

Included in **"Who's Who Among America's Teachers,"** 2003 and 2002.

Named State Conference Cross Country **Coach of the Year,** 1997.

MI National Honor Society Executive Director, 2001-2004.

Provided leadership which enabled Delta Pine High School's National Honor Society to be named a National Service Award Winner (only 10 schools in the nation annually win this award), 2003 and 2002. The Honor Society won the **State Service Award,** 2002.

Provided leadership which led Delta Pine Student Council to earn Honors Council distinction, 2003 and 2002. The Student Council was named **Best Workshop Host,** 2003.

EDUCATION

Bachelor of Arts (B.A.) degree in Political Science, Wayne State University, Detroit, MI, 1989. Completed numerous workshops including AP Workshops sponsored by the College Board and training in team building by the National Association of Student Councils.

Completed training in Peer Mediation sponsored by the National Peer Helping Institute.

- Learned how to start a mediation program and how to train others in mediation and program start-up techniques.

Received **Social Studies Certification,** Calvin College, Grand Rapids, MI, 1991.

EXPERIENCE

CROSS COUNTRY COACH & TEACHER. Detroit County Schools, Delta Pine High School, Detroit, MI (1996-present). Teach all social studies courses offered by Detroit schools to students at all proficiency levels, including AP courses.

- **Coaching:** Coached cross country for six years.
- **Leading and mentoring:** Served as the Student Council sponsor for three years and National Honor Society sponsor for six years.
- **New initiatives:** Establish a new AP course in American Government for the school. Implemented a Peer Mediation Program at Delta Pine. Organize and manage numerous field trips to locations in the U.S. and Canada.

TEACHER/COACH. Lake Michigan Junior High School, Detroit, MI (1992-96). Taught PEL and achieved the second highest End of Course scores in Detroit. Coached track and acted as Student Council sponsor.

TEACHER OF EXCEPTIONAL CHILDREN. Delta Pine Junior High School, Detroit, MI (1989-1992). Refined my skills in handling a variety of learning problems and motivational issues while teaching behaviorally and emotionally challenged students in a self-contained class.

AFFILIATIONS

Member, Professional Educators of Michigan. Have served as Treasurer of the Detroit Association of Educators.

PERSONAL

Known for exceptional creativity, resourceful problem-solving ability, and enthusiastic work ethic. Enjoy the challenge of shaping attitudes and inspiring youth to make good choices.

CAREER CHANGE

Date

Exact Name of Person
Title or Position
Name of Company
Address (no., street)
Address (city, state, zip)

DIRECTOR OF GOLF OPERATIONS.

This savvy golf pro seeks to transition from the daily business of teaching golf and supervising golf operations. He is interested in a sales representative position with a major golf retailer.

Dear Exact Name of Person: (or Dear Sir or Madam if answering a blind ad):

I would appreciate an opportunity to talk with you soon about how I could contribute to your organization through my strong desire to represent your product line throughout North Carolina and Virginia.

As you will see from my resume, since earning my B.A. degree in 1995, I have been promoted to increasing responsibilities at Queens Country Club. I began as an Assistant Golf Professional, was promoted to Head Golf Professional, and am currently Director of Golf Operations. Although many clubs and organizations have approached me over the years with employment opportunities, I was determined to remain at Queens Country Club until I developed its golf program to the highest possible standard. By every measure, I achieved that goal and, in the process, I have gained a reputation as an exceptionally strong communicator and motivator.

Frequently described as a "born salesman," I have become skilled in retail management while owning and managing the golf shop which grosses $165,000 annually.

As a lifetime resident of North Carolina, I am well acquainted with the region and have an extensive network of contacts who know of my fine personal and professional reputation. I believe my name would make an excellent "calling card," and I am certain I could contribute to your goals and continued success. I am an enthusiastic advocate of your products, and I would enjoy the opportunity to talk with you about the position of sales representative which is available. Of course I can provide outstanding personal and professional references.

I hope you will call or write me soon to suggest a time convenient for us to meet and discuss your current and future needs and how I might serve them. Thank you in advance for you time.

Sincerely yours,

Thomas Campbell

THOMAS CAMPBELL

1110½ Hay Street, Fayetteville, NC 28305 • preppub@aol.com • (910) 483-6611

OBJECTIVE

To contribute to an organization through my expertise as a golf professional, outstanding personal and professional reputation, exceptionally strong communication and sales skills, as well as my proven ability to manage operations, budgets, people, events, and assets.

EDUCATION

Bachelor of Arts (B.A.) degree in History, North Carolina State University, Raleigh, NC, 1995. Areas of concentration were Business Administration, Psychology, and Sociology.

EXPERIENCE

Queens Country Club, Raleigh, NC (1995-present). On numerous occasions, have been approached by other clubs and organizations, but have steadfastly remained at Queens Country Club in order to achieve the goal of elevating this golf program to the highest standard; have been promoted in this progression:

DIRECTOR OF GOLF OPERATIONS. (2004-present). At this 625-member private club, own and operate a retail shop grossing $165,000 annually and supervise its four employees while also managing all aspects of golf operations, including supervising a staff of eight performing course maintenance.
- Combined my creativity and writing skills to improve communication with members through the monthly newsletter.
- Directed installation of a state-of-the-art irrigation system tee-to-green.
- Added senior tees, which have been greatly appreciated by the members.

HEAD GOLF PROFESSIONAL. (1997-03). Planned and administered a $130,000 operational budget for golf shop operations while promoting, supervising, directing, and coordinating the overall golf program.
- Trained and supervised four employees retailing products in the golf shop.
- Created and directed the North Carolina Junior Golf League which began as a four-club league in 1997 and grew to 15 member clubs in three divisions by 2003.
- Established a Junior Golf Association. Was golf coach for Queens High School.
- Was featured in *Golf Magazine* for walking and playing a 100-hole golf marathon for Junior Golf, June 2001. Coordinated numerous tournaments and golf promotions.

ASSISTANT GOLF PROFESSIONAL. (1995-97). After graduating from college, served as apprentice under Joshua Cape, Golf Professional, while planning and conducting golf clinics and club tournaments, coordinating the junior golf program, and serving as Treasurer of the Golf Association. Organized a junior golf team to compete with area clubs.

PROFESSIONAL BACKGROUND & AFFILIATIONS

Golf National Education Committee, 2003
Carolinas Golf Section involvement:
Tournament Committee Chairman, 2003   Playing Ability Workshop Instructor, 2002
Junior Golf Committee Chairman, 2002   Special Events Committee Chairman, 2001
Golf Business School II, 1998, and Golf Business School I, 1997

PLAYING BACKGROUND

Winner of seven Pro-Ams and qualified for Western Pro Championship, 1999-2003:
- Winter Seminar Pro-Am Champion, 2003
- Annual League Pro-Am Champion, 2002
- Douglas Pro-Am Champion, 2002
- Tri-Country Club Pro-Am Champion, 2001
- Windy Valley Pro-Am Champion, 2001
- Western Pro-Junior Champion, 1999
- Spring Country Club Pro-Am Champion, 1999

Date

Exact Name of Person
Exact Title
Exact Name of Company
Address
City, State, Zip

DIRECTOR OF TENNIS   Dear Exact Name of Person (or Dear Sir or Madam if answering a blind ad):

With the enclosed resume, I would like to make you aware of my interest in exploring current or future opportunities as Director of Tennis with your club.

A previous employer recruited me for my current position as Director of Tennis at a prestigious club. Although I am held in the highest regard and am excelling in a position which could be mine for life, I am selectively exploring other opportunities. The main reason I am "looking" is that I feel I have done nearly everything that can be done at the club where I work. I have brought the tennis program up to an extraordinarily high level, but simply maintaining an excellent program does not appeal to me as a job forever. I suppose I yearn to go on to "bigger and better things," and I am interested in applying my extensive tennis background to benefit a larger organization in a larger market.

Because of my in-depth experience, I have much to offer. Textbook learning is a valuable thing but, through working in the tennis field for 15 years, I have learned how to teach every shot in tennis using multiple approaches. It is no exaggeration to say that I can teach the serve 30 different ways. I have also become "a pro" at working in the unique environment of a membership organization, and I have learned how to work congenially with all personality types. With a reputation as a resourceful manager, I offer highly refined skills in managing every aspect of a dynamic tennis program.

I hold the highest certifications given to tennis professionals. I am certified by the Professional Tennis Registry as a Tennis Professional, the highest of three ratings, and have held that certification since 1990. I am also a USPTR National Testers in Utah.

After beginning my tennis career as a Tennis Pro, I have worked for only two clubs since 1993. At both clubs I dramatically increased tennis participation, boosted the number of USTA league teams, started multiple programs for juniors and adults, conducted USPTR coaches' workshops for persons seeking certifications or upgrades, became an influential tennis spokesperson in the community, managed successful tournaments, managed budgets in excess of $100,000, and supervised other tennis pros. My reputation in the tennis community is outstanding, and I can provide exemplary references from my current club at the appropriate time.

If you feel that your current or future needs might require a top-level tennis professional and manager such as myself, I hope you will contact me.

Yours sincerely,

Moses Lock

MOSES LOCK

1110½ Hay Street, Fayetteville, NC 28305 • preppub@aol.com • (910) 483-6611

OBJECTIVE   I want to contribute to an organization that can use an experienced tennis professional who offers expert teaching and motivational skills along with the proven ability to develop, manage, and promote new programs which increase club prestige and member satisfaction.

CERTIFICATIONS   Am a **USPTR National Tester.**
Am certified by the Professional Tennis Registry of the U.S.A. as a Tennis Professional, the highest of three ratings (rated October 1990).
Achieved USTA Sport Science Level I certification with training in biomechanics, nutrition, fitness, and other areas; completed Sports Science Level II training.
Attended several Elite Coaches training programs conducted by the USTA and USPTR.
Completed the USTA Rating Verifier NTRP Course and Schools Program.

AFFILIATIONS   Member of the following organizations and associations: U. S. Professional Tennis Registry (USPTR); U.S. Professional Tennis Association (USPTA); U.S. Tennis Association (USTA).

EXPERIENCE   **DIRECTOR OF TENNIS.** Peak Country Club, Salt Lake City, UT (2003-present). Was aggressively recruited by this former employer—an 800-member club—to take over its tennis program; took charge of activities which had been neglected for years and developed a vibrant program.
   •   Manage a budget in excess of $100,000. Manage four people including three junior tennis pros. Boosted the number of USTA league teams from one to six. Inherited a juniors program with one member; the club now has more than 80 active juniors.
   •   Offer multiple programs weekly for adults. Am implementing a long-range plan for the club. Network aggressively in the community; have worked with USTA to get equipment donated to the local schools in order to encourage tennis participation. Have also worked closely with University of Utah's Tennis Management Program. Started up a local tennis pro association in the community.

HEAD TENNIS PRO. Townsend Country Club, Ogden, UT (1994-03). At this 700-member club, dramatically increased tennis participation; managed classes, tournaments, maintenance, and a full-service pro shop while supervising a staff of four and administering a $65,000 facility budget.
   •   Was awarded a Local Excellence Training (LET) Program, which trained youth.
   •   Ran successful USTA tournaments including Men's Invitational; developed the club's Adult Tennis Program; formed three USTA adult teams.
   •   Developed community programs to boost tennis popularity, including school programs.
   •   Conducted USPTR coaches' workshops for persons seeking certifications or upgrades.
   •   Recreated the juniors' program. Rebuilt the clay courts and redesigned the pro shop.

TENNIS PROFESSIONAL. Peak Country Club, Salt Lake City, UT (1993-94). Increased participation in the juniors' program to an all-time high. Trained over 80 young tennis players from the southeastern US. Managed juniors' tournaments.

TENNIS COACH. Avery Twin Tennis Academy, Salt Lake City, UT (1991-93). Taught daily classes and weekend clinics for junior, college, and pro-tour tennis players; traveled to ATP and WTA tours as a professional coach. Traveled on the National Junior Circuit; worked with top-ranking juniors.

PERSONAL   Proven ability to infuse fresh ideas and fresh approaches. Excellent references. Will relocate.

Date

Exact Name of Person
Title or Position
Name of Company
Address (number and street)
Address (city, state, and zip)

Dear Exact Name of Person: (or Dear Sir or Madam if answering a blind ad.)

**FIREARMS DEALER &
SALES
REPRESENTATIVE.**
This jobhunter is writing
to "a few good
companies" expressing
his interest in exploring
employment
opportunities.

With the enclosed resume, I would like to introduce the proven sales skills and extensive firearms industry knowledge which I could put at the disposal of your company.

As you will see, I recently sold a gun store which I transformed from an unprofitable company saddled with debt into a very profitable business with an excellent reputation.

As an experienced firearms dealer, I am very familiar with your company's products, and I have dealt personally with salesmen and sales representatives from all manufacturers and distributors. I strongly believe that my sales skills and congenial personality were the keys to my success as a dealer, and I am certain I could be a highly effective representative of your products.

I have grown up around guns since I was a child. Before my father became a Baptist minister, he owned the largest firearms business in Iowa, and I helped him with everything in the store. I have used the products of every manufacturer.

I attend gun shows frequently and have developed an extensive network of contacts and friends within the industry who know me and my fine personal reputation. I feel certain that I could make significant contributions to your bottom line through my expert product knowledge, outstanding personal reputation, and exceptional sales abilities. I am writing to you because I am familiar with your company's fine reputation, and I feel it would be a pleasure to become associated with your product line.

If you can use a dynamic and hard-working individual to complement your sales team, please contact me to suggest a time when we might meet to discuss your needs and how I could help you. I am married with no children, and I can travel as extensively as your needs require. Thank you for your consideration, and I look forward to hearing from you.

Sincerely,

Adam Cooke

ADAM COOKE

1110½ Hay Street, Fayetteville, NC 28305   •   preppub@aol.com   •   (910) 483-6611

OBJECTIVE

I would like to contribute to an organization that can use an experienced sales professional with expert knowledge of firearms products along with a network of outstanding relationships which I have developed with firearms dealers, manufacturers, and distributors who know of my fine reputation and trust me personally.

EXPERIENCE

Since 1998-present, have been associated with Sumner Firearms, Inc.:
FIREARMS DEALER & SALES REPRESENTATIVE. Sumner Firearms, Inc., Des Moines, IA (200-present). In 2000, bought this company after working for the company as a Salesman for two years.
- When I purchased the company, which was located in Ankeny, IA, it was unprofitable and in debt; I relocated the company to a better market and utilized effective sales and management techniques to transform an ailing organization into a highly profitable and respected company which I sold in 2004.
- Combined my expert knowledge of manufacturers and distributors with my marketing sense in determining the correct inventory for the store; carried more than 1,000 individual guns and accessories needed by shooters.
- As a dealer, have become very familiar with the products, product lines, and sales policies of all manufacturers and distributors.
- On a daily basis, used my common sense in solving uncommon problems.
- Strongly believe that my sales skills and congenial personality were the keys to my success in this business.

SALESMAN. Sumner Firearms, Inc., Ankeny, IA (1998-00). Began with the company as a salesman and increased my sales every month compared to the previous month.
- Became skilled in communicating with every type of gun lover, from high-grade collector to casual plinker.

Other experience:
MANAGER. Vernon's Furniture, Ankeny, IA (1996-98). Managed all aspects of a small furniture refinishing business; personally handled sales and customer service.
SALESMAN. Easy Living, Des Moines, IA (1994-96). Upon graduation from high school, became employed by a furniture refinishing business and rapidly discovered that I have exceptional sales and customer relations skills.
GUN STORE ASSISTANT. Cooke Gun Exchange, Des Moines, IA. As a young boy, grew up around guns since my father, who later became a Baptist minister, owned the largest firearms business in IA.
LAW ENFORCEMENT OFFICER (Reserve). (1996-present). As an unpaid volunteer, serve as a volunteer reserve Law Enforcement Officer helping to enforce the law and keep the peace.

MEMBERSHIPS

Member, National Rifle Association; Member, Central Baptist Church.

HOBBIES

Hunting, shooting, reloading, and collecting.

EDUCATION

Completed numerous courses in Law Enforcement, Des Moines Area Community College, Ankeny, IA.

PERSONAL

Can provide outstanding references inside and outside the firearms industry. Am married with no children; will travel extensively if needed.

Exact Name of Person
Title or Position
Name of Company
Address (no., street)
Address (city, state, zip)

FOOTBALL COACH   Dear Exact Name of Person: (or Dear Sir or Madam if answering a blind ad):

With the enclosed resume, I would like to make you aware of my interest in exploring employment opportunities with your organization. Currently an Assistant Football Coach at Nelson Senior High School, I would like to become the Head Football Coach of a program such as yours.

I have found that my background as a player allows me to quickly establish rapport with high school students. I was fortunate to have several years of experience as a football player in high school, college, and professionally. In positions as a running back, safety, and outside linebacker, I was fortunate enough to play professionally for the Carolina Panthers, the Massachusetts Harbors, the Boston Hooks, and the Dallas Cowboys. An injury caused me to leave the Carolina Panthers in 2000, but I have thoroughly enjoyed the challenge of coaching high school athletics. It is my goal to coach a high school team to a first-place state finish one year, and I consider it equally important to excel in the job of helping athletes become "the best they can be" in terms of character, academics, and leadership.

Since finishing my B.S. in Industrial Technology from Boston University, I have coached at Cape Fear High School and at Nelson Senior High School, where I played high school football. Although I am held in high regard in my current position and am even celebrated as a kind of "local hero," I am selectively exploring opportunities in the state of Vermont, where my wife is from and where we wish to grow roots. I can provide outstanding references at the appropriate time, but I would appreciate your not contacting my current employer until after we talk.

I hope you will call or write me soon to suggest a time convenient for us to meet to discuss your current and future needs. Thank you in advance for you time.

Sincerely yours,

John Williams

JOHN WILLIAMS

1110½ Hay Street, Fayetteville, NC 28305　　•　　preppub@aol.com　　•　　(910) 483-6611

OBJECTIVE　　To contribute to an organization that can use an experienced football player whose technical skills have been tested in professional and college environments and whose communication and coaching abilities have been refined in high school teaching and coaching roles.

**COACHING
EXPERIENCE**

2003-present　　**DEFENSE LINE COACH.** Nelson Senior High School
2001-2002　　**DEFENSE LINE/SECONDARY COACH.** Cape Fear High School
2000　　**RUNNING BACK AND OFFENSIVE COACH.** Nelson Sr. High

EDUCATION　*2000*　　**B.S.,** Industrial Technology, Boston University, Boston, MA.
Completed degree after leaving the Carolina Panthers. Lettered for four years at Boston University where I performed with distinction as Running Back and Outside Linebacker.
Was **Special Teams Captain** in 1996.
Completed nearly four years of college prior to becoming a part of the Dallas Cowboys team in 1997. After I left the Carolina Panthers in 2000, I returned to college full-time for one semester to finish my degree.

1993　　Graduated from Nelson Senior High School, Boston, MA.
Played in state championship football game in my senior year.

PROFESSIONAL PLAYING CAREER

2000　　Carolina Panthers

1999　　Massachusetts Harbors

1998　　Boston Hooks (Safety)

1997　　Dallas Cowboys (Safety)

HIGH SCHOOL PLAYING CAREER

- A native of Boston, MA, grew up playing football and basketball in Little League.
- Played football, basketball, and ran track at Bunker Hill Jr. High.
- Played football, basketball, and ran track throughout high school. Was a popular student athlete and was named "Most Likely to Succeed" in my senior year.

PERSONAL　　Outstanding personal and professional references on request.

Date

Exact Name of Person
Title or Position
Name of Company
Address (no., street)
Address (city, state, zip)

GENERAL MANAGER, NASCAR WORLD AT MYRTLE BEACH

Dear Exact Name of Person: (or Dear Sir or Madam if answering a blind ad.)

I would appreciate an opportunity to talk with you soon about how I could contribute to your organization through my strong customer service orientation and proven ability to maximize profitability.

As you will see from my resume, I have been successful in positions which required strong communication, interpersonal, and analytical skills. In my current position as General Manager, I supervise a team consisting of an assistant manager, a marketing manager, two shift supervisors, and 15 employees who work at Nascar World in Myrtle Beach, SC. Through my attention to detail and strong management skills, I have boosted profitability 10% compared to last year.

Although I am excelling in my current job and can provide outstanding references at the appropriate time, I have decided to selectively explore other opportunities.

I hope you will welcome my call soon to arrange a brief meeting at your convenience to discuss your current and future needs and how I might serve them. Thank you in advance for your time.

Sincerely yours,

Jessica Stewart

Alternate last paragraph:
I hope you will call or write me soon to suggest a time convenient for us to meet and discuss your current and future needs and how I might serve them. Thank you in advance for your time.

JESSICA STEWART

1110½ Hay Street, Fayetteville, NC 28305   •   preppub@aol.com   •   (910) 483-6611

OBJECTIVE

To benefit an organization that can use a hard working professional with the ability to successfully plan, initiate, and implement new projects, tasks, and ideas.

EXPERIENCE

Am excelling in a track record of outstanding performance with Nascar World, Myrtle Beach, SC:
GENERAL MANAGER. (2004-present). At this enormously popular Nascar World in Myrtle Beach, SC, was promoted to supervise a team consisting of an assistant manager, a marketing manager, two shift supervisors, and 15 employees involved in customer service and maintenance activities.

SENIOR ASSISTANT MANAGER. (2003-04). Managed, scheduled, and supervised up to 50 employees and handled daily cash receipts averaging $25,000 while providing excellent customer service and bookkeeping support related to payroll, sales and use tax computation, and accounts payable/receivable.
- Played a key role in the annual budgeting process.
- Was relied upon for marketing expertise and coordinated fund raising activities for groups and organizations.
- Directed maintenance and facility upkeep.

Other experience:
FINANCIAL ADVISOR. The Raymond James Company, Lawrence, KS (1999-2002). Advised families on savings, college education, and community benefits matters; analyzed financial statements, created financial programs to fit individual families, and processed paperwork.
- Became skilled in prospecting for new clients.
- Earned the respected Series 6 and Series 7 licenses.

ADMINISTRATIVE AIDE. Lincoln Yearbook Publishing, Lawrence, KS (1998). In this part-time job while earning my college degree, maintained a 7,000-word per hour typing rate while transforming rough yearbook pages received from schools into finished products. Acquired skills as a quality assurance specialist.

MILITARY EXPERIENCE

Built an excellent record during service with the U.S. Army (1990-96).
Provided advice on benefits and other financial matters while assuring that financial paper work was complete as a **Financial Advisor.** Served as a liaison with local financial institutions and maintained accurate balances and disbursements as a **Finance Specialist.** Was handpicked to troubleshoot and correct finance problems as a **Payroll Monitor.** Served as a **Finance Clerk,** using computers to process requests for payment.

EDUCATION

Bachelor of Arts degree in Management, University of Kansas, Lawrence, KS, 1998.

TRAINING

Excelled at courses in computer software and systems such as Excel and Word.
Completed college-level training in accounting, finance, and computer operations through extensive U.S. Army training courses, 1990-96.

PERSONAL

Outstanding personal and professional references on request.

Exact Name of Person
Title or Position
Name of Company
Address (no., street)
Address (city, state, zip)

**GOLF CLUB
GENERAL MANAGER
&
HEAD PRO**

Dear Exact Name of Person: (or Dear Sir or Madam if answering a blind ad):

    With the enclosed resume, I would like to make you aware of my interest in exploring employment opportunities with your organization. I am an All-American award winner for the highest scores in the Golf Professional Training Program in Arizona, and I am seeking a full-time teaching position.

    With a Bachelor of Science from the Arizona State University, I offer a proven ability to handle all aspects of being a Head Pro, from running tournaments to managing the Pro Shop and business functions. After brief experiences as an Assistant Golf Pro and First Assistant, I was recruited for my current position as General Manager and Head Pro at a prestigious country club.

    If you can use a skilled golf professional to join your team, I hope you will call or write me soon to suggest a time convenient for us to meet to discuss your current and future needs. Thank you in advance for you time.

Sincerely yours,

Duncan Pitts

DUNCAN PITTS

1110½ Hay Street, Fayetteville, NC 28305 • preppub@aol.com • (910) 483-6611

OBJECTIVE An All-American award winner for highest scores in Golf Professional Training Program in Arizona seeks a full-time teaching position. Experienced Head Professional with excellent management, supervisory, communication, interpersonal, and problem-solving skills.

EDUCATION Bachelor of Science degree, Arizona State University, Tempe, AZ, 1999.

TEACHING
- Adult Continuing Education Instructor
- Have given over 200 lessons
- Developed more than 20 clinics for beginners to advanced players
- Provided one-on-one lessons on subjects varying from basics of swing to specific problems
- Teaching Assistant at University of Phoenix
- Teaching Assistant at Arizona State University

EXPERIENCE **GENERAL MANAGER & HEAD PROFESSIONAL.** Mesa Golf Club, Tempe, AZ (2002-present). Am involved in these functional areas:

Business Management:
- Manager in charge of staffing, hiring, and terminations
- Payroll control
- Obtained financing, set budgets, and generated profits

Golf Shop Management:
- Golf Pro Shop opening and closing procedures
- Inventory management, pricing, special promotions, sales, ordering and receiving of new merchandise, and monthly inventories
- Scheduling and personnel management of shop staff

Outside Staff Management:
- Supervise maintenance of 150 golf carts
- Oversee bag storage for 200+ members and guests
- Manage staff of two mechanics, eight rangers, and four beverage cart operators

Membership Development:
- Worked on all phases of increasing and maintaining membership
- Promotional activities, public relations, and marketing
- New summer memberships and other innovative programs and clinics

Tournament Operations:
- Organized over 150 outside and member tournaments
- Acted as rules official
- Contacted sponsors
- Prepared and marked golf course
- Officiated scoring and prize presentations

Other experience:
FIRST ASSISTANT. Grand Canyon Country Club, Phoenix, AZ, 2001-02.
ASSISTANT GOLF PROFESSIONAL. Apache Creek Country Club, Phoenix, AZ, 2000.

AWARDS
- All-American Award–Highest scores in Arizona for G.P.T.P.
- Award of Merit in Community-Based Programs
- Included in U.S. National Football Yearbook for high school students
- Received the Eagle Scout Award–the highest ranking award given in Scouting

Date

Exact Name of Person
Title or Position
Name of Company
Address (no., street)
Address (city, state, zip)

**GOLF COURSE
SUPERINTENDENT**

Dear Exact Name: (or Dear Sir or Madam if answering a blind ad.)

With the enclosed resume, I would like to make you aware, confidentially at this point, of my interest in discussing the position as Golf Course Superintendent.

As a Golf Course Superintendent since 1988, I have made significant contributions to every course with which I have been associated. While serving simultaneously as Golf Course Superintendent for the Charity Golf Course and the High Park Country Club from 1988-89, I supervised major projects at two clubs which are overseeded for winter play.

At Charity, I supervised the enlargement of the greens along with their conversion from Bermuda greens to Bentgrass, and I provided oversight when the irrigation system around the greens was changed. Also at Charity, I provided the project management required when the soil mixture was changed to a more favorable Bentgrass environment based on the advice of Dr. John Smith of Tennessee State University. For both High Park and Charity, I managed separate budgets and separate crews.

With hobbies that include both freshwater and deep-sea fishing, I also am an avid golfer. With a current 1 handicap and index of 1.4, I enjoy competitive golf and have qualified and competed in numerous Amateurs, Mid-Amateurs, and local tournaments. I am a former individual winner of the Coast College Conference Championship.

As a great fan of the Morehead area, I am familiar with the reputation as well as the technical composition of your outstanding course. I believe the work being performed at Morehead City Country Club is similar to the work I performed at Charity.

You would find me in person to be a congenial individual who prides myself on my versatile technical knowledge as well as my management skills. I can provide excellent references at the appropriate time, but I would appreciate your holding my interest in your club in confidence at this point.

I hope you will give me a call to suggest a time when we might meet to discuss your needs and how I might help you. Thank you in advance for your time.

Sincerely,

Francis Steven

FRANCIS STEVEN

1110½ Hay Street, Fayetteville, NC 28305 • preppub@aol.com • (910) 483-6611

OBJECTIVE

To offer my services as a Golf Course Superintendent.

EDUCATION

Earned **Associate's degree in Applied Science in Recreational Grounds Management,** Tennessee State University, Nashville, TN, 1983.
Completed courses in Computer Engineering, State Technical Institute of Memphis, Memphis, TN.
Graduated from Melon High School, Memphis, TN, 1980.

EXPERIENCE

GOLF COURSE SUPERINTENDENT. Great Country Club, Memphis, TN (1999-present). For this semiprivate club, serve as Golf Course Superintendent in charge of a crew while also handling the purchasing and maintenance of equipment.
- Great Country Club has Bentgrass greens with Tifdwarf, 419 tees, and fairways.

GOLF COURSE SUPERINTENDENT. Charity Golf Course, Memphis, TN and High Park Country Club, Nashville, TN (1988-99). Was simultaneously the Superintendent of both courses: Charity had Tifgreen 328 greens and Tifdwarf 419 fairways; High Park Country Club has Pencross Bentgrass greens and common Bermuda grass tees and fairways.
- Provided technical leadership when Charity greens were changed from Bermuda grass to Bentgrass; I supervised all construction, which was performed inhouse.
- At Charity, supervised the successful enlargement of the greens and provided oversight when the irrigation system around the greens was changed to meet greens needs.
- Again at Charity, provided leadership when the soil mixture was changed to a more favorable Bentgrass environment based on the advice of Dr. John Smith of Tennessee State University. Upon his recommendation, greens were stripped of all sod, fumigated, and then seeded, with the entire process lasting from mid-September to mid-December.
- At Charity, gained expert knowledge of a resort course which is overseeded for winter play.
- At High Park Country Club, also a private club overseeded for winter play, supervised all grounds maintenance.
- For both the High Park and Charity courses, managed separate budgets and separate crews while actually saving the courses from the expense of a grounds mechanic, since I functioned in this role.

GOLF COURSE SUPERINTENDENT. Clove Golf Club, Nashville, TN (1987-88). Served as Golf Course Superintendent and handled duties which included hiring crew members, preparing budgets, and managing upkeep of all equipment for a course which has Tifgreen 328 Bermuda grass from tee to green.

ASSISTANT SUPERINTENDENT. Great Country Club, Memphis, TN (1984-87). As Assistant to a crew of eight people, was in charge of spraying pesticides, assisting in projects, and managing the crew.
- Great has Penncross Bentgrass greens and Tifdwarf 419 tees and fairways.

ASSISTANT SUPERINTENDENT. Superior Golf Club, Memphis, TN (1983-84). Worked as an Assistant while course was being grown in; also assisted in construction projects, tees, fairways, and other course features.

PERSONAL

Excellent references on request. Current 1 handicap and index of 1.4.

Date

Exact Name of Person
Exact Title
Exact Name of Company
Address
City, State, Zip

**GOLF COURSE
SUPERINTENDENT**

Dear Exact Name of Person (or Dear Sir or Madam if answering a blind ad):

I would appreciate an opportunity to talk with you soon about how I could contribute to your organization through my experience as a golf course superintendent with a reputation as a creative and innovative manager of resources.

As you will see from my enclosed resume, I offer a strong history as a golf course superintendent with more than 15 years of experience at several successful and heavily played courses in the West Virginia area. I was highly effective in taking on the challenge of renovating and refurbishing courses which were in need of improvements. For two 150-acre courses located in residential developments and one private club, I brought about significant changes which transformed struggling facilities. While rebuilding these facilities, I applied abilities in areas which included hiring and training personnel, coordinating the renovation of capital equipment, planning for long-range success, and completing design projects for sprinkler layout, drainage, and reconstruction of greens, tees, and fairways. I also oversaw the design and installation of water reservoirs for irrigation, including a 110-acre reservoir at Marshall Golf Course.

My organizational and time management skills have been displayed more recently while attending college full-time, excelling academically, and simultaneously creating a successful residential landscape design business. Building on my earlier A.A. degree in Agronomy and Turf Production and golf course experience, I earned a B.S. in Agribusiness and Environmental Resources in 2001.

I am in the process of relocating permanently to the Tempe area to be near family members. If you can use an experienced golf course superintendent with a broad base of experience and well-developed abilities, I hope you will contact me to suggest a time when we might meet to discuss your needs. I can assure you in advance that I could rapidly become an asset to your organization.

Sincerely,

Benjamin Allen

BENJAMIN ALLEN

1110½ Hay Street, Fayetteville, NC 28305   •   preppub@aol.com   •   (910) 483-6611

OBJECTIVE

To contribute through a versatile history of accomplishments in positions where initiative and innovative thinking along with knowledge of budgeting, capital improvements, planning, and management can combine to produce quality results and a healthy bottom line.

EDUCATION

B.S., Agribusiness and Environmental Resources with a minor in Geography, Wichita State University, Wichita, KS, 2001.
- Received a prestigious award from the School of Agribusiness and Environmental Resources in recognition of my leadership and scholastic excellence.
- Was awarded a University Legislative Internship for my scholastic achievements.
- Excelled in specialized course work which included world agriculture development, crop management and production, sales and merchandising, marketing, and finance.

A.A., Agronomy and Turf Production, West Virginia University, Morgantown, WV, 1985.
- Completed studies with a strong emphasis in the following subjects:

soil science	plant disease	turfgrass disease
pesticide application	soil reconstruction	project management
construction management (greens, tees, and fairways)		land reform

Completed a one-year internship with Kansas Farms in Topeka, KS, focusing on crop management and production of alfalfa, wheat, and cotton. Gained expertise in areas related to flood irrigation, insect control, chemical calculation, and laser leveling for flood control.

EXPERIENCE

FOUNDER & PRESIDENT. Allen Blueprints, Wichita, KS (2001-present). While excelling academically as a full-time college student, coordinated the complete start-up and operation of a successful home landscaping and design business including hiring and training a staff.
- Supervise and control all aspects of landscape and sprinkler design and installation.
- Procure all capital assets as well as developing and maintaining a satisfied client base.
- I have sold the business and am in the process of relocating to Tempe.

CLASS "A" GOLF SUPERINTENDENT. Virginia Golf Course, Morgantown, WV (1995-01). Transformed and refurbished this 150-acre golf course and residential property into one of the state's top golf facilities.
- Coordinated project management in turf, shrub, and tree production.
- Managed turf development through fertilizer, herbicide, pesticide, and fungicide applications including completing chemical calculations.

HEAD GOLF COURSE SUPERINTENDENT. Marshall Golf Course, Huntington, WV (1990-94). Was credited with successfully refurbishing a 150-acre golf course and 1,300-acre residential development and turning it into a well-managed and highly played facility.
- Coordinated project design techniques in sprinkler layout, drainage, and reconstruction of greens, tees, and fairways; developed a 110-acre water reservoir for irrigation.
- Hired and trained staff members; coordinated and renovated all capital equipment.

HEAD GOLF COURSE SUPERINTENDENT. Carter Country Club, Huntington, WV (1985-89). Brought about the successful renovation of a 150-acre private club through landscape design and the installation of trees and shrubbery.
- Coordinated project design for sprinkler layout, drainage, and the reconstruction of greens, tees, and fairways; designed and installed a 4-acre water reservoir.

PERSONAL

Offer knowledge in turf, and chemical, and biological management for all seasons/climates.

CAREER CHANGE

Date

Exact Name of Person
Title or Position
Address (no., street)
Address (city, state, zip)

GOLF PROFESSIONAL

Dear Exact Name of Person: (or Dear Sir or Madam if answering a blind ad.)

I am the strong asset that you are seeking to add to your staff. I will be able to provide leadership, management, and guidance in many areas.

I have a very strong desire to become a PGA Golf Professional. My military and civilian experience/career has helped me refine my customer service skills while working with officers, NCOs, and civilian personnel.

As you will see from my resume, I managed the golf course at Charleston AFB, SC, and was the Assistant Manager at the Davis-Monthan AFB, AZ golf course. I have taught golf, repaired golf clubs, and have worked at golf courses for over 20 years. I worked in the NCO clubs at Davis-Monthan, AZ, as well as at Kadena AB in Japan.

I have gained numerous ideas over the years which I believe constitute a "laundry list" of the best practices to follow in improving any golf course. I hope you will not find me impertinent if I share some of the insights I have learned through the years, and I freely admit that these probably will sound like "common sense" to you:

1. Better course conditions—improve maintenance.
2. Improve customer service
3. Provide quality golf instruction
4. Perform quality golf club repair
5. Create ladies and juniors programs
6. Create senior and retirees program
7. Organize team leagues to play with other courses
8. Boost sales in the pro shop
9. Increase sales through the usage of the snack bar
10. Improve relations with the community

I possess skills and knowledge which could be valuable to you, and I know I could make serious bottom-line contributions and help improve both courses. Please give me the opportunity to meet with you to discuss what I can do.

Sincerely,

Carl Kelly

CARL KELLY

1110½ Hay Street, Fayetteville, NC 28305   •   preppub@aol.com   •   (910) 483-6611

OBJECTIVE

To become a PGA Golf Professional and to contribute to a golf course using experience and knowledge gained while in the U.S. Air Force and while working part time at military golf courses and NCO clubs.

SUMMARY OF EXPERIENCE

Gained valuable experience as a military and civilian professional and also as an employee at various worldwide locations from 1980-present. Have worked in a variety of areas including: U.S. Air Force, Golf Course and Golf Pro Shop operations, NCO Club operations, supervising, managing, administrating, instructing, scheduling, planning, budgeting, security, law enforcement, developing and analyzing programs, and operational planning and procedures for worldwide missions and training.

GOLF EXPERIENCE

Have worked in service-oriented areas: Golf, both on and off the course, teaching golf, and repairing golf clubs with 20 years of experience; food service, and experience working in NCO club with a total of 35 years of experience.

Course Management

- Managed the golf course at Charleston AFB, SC; managed the Pro Shop, snack bar, and ground maintenance operations.
- Set up and ran local tournaments including the base championship and ran the American championship tournament scheduling over 2,000 players over a nine-hole course; set up and ran and juniors and ladies program.

Pro Shop/ Snack Bar Management

- As the Assistant Manager at the golf course at Davis-Monthan AFB, AZ, for four years, managed the pro shop operations and supervised pro shop and snack bar personnel; provided group clinics for beginning golfers as well as individual lessons.
- Started and ran the largest junior program in Arizona as well as started and ran the ladies program.
- Set up and ran local golf tournaments and base championships.

Dining Management

- Worked in the NCO clubs at Davis-Monthan AFB, AZ, for six months and Kadena AB in Japan for two and a half years, gaining experience in the areas of management, security, dining room, kitchen, cashier's cage, scheduling for parties and special events, and managing a bingo program.
- While working in NCO clubs, learned how to prepare food and to budget and order food, beverages, and all bar items.

Golfing Experience

- Played on the base golf team at Japan and made the Senior Tournament Champ Team, but was unable to attend due to a NATO Evaluation for the Wing.

EDUCATION

Have completed some course credits towards an associate's degree through the Arizona Western College, Yuma, AZ and Charleston Southern University, Charleston, SC.

AIR FORCE EXPERIENCE

Served in the U.S. Air Force in various worldwide locations, 1980-present. While in the service of my country, I excelled in many jobs and areas listed below:

Management:

- Prepared budgets for squadron operating expenses.
- Scheduled and managed operational flying missions in numerous NATO countries coordinating flying missions with high-ranking military and civilian officials and embassies, i.e., photo air reconnaissance for the U.S. and NATO.
- Scheduled over 6,500 students from all over the world to learn to fly the C-130.
- Provided studies, analyzed and developed a training program to allow C-130 air crew members to graduate on time, which allowed the on-time graduation rate to increase from 25% to 95% in less than 60 days; this decreased the operating costs and saved the Air Force millions of dollars.

Date

Exact Name of Person
Title or Position
Name of Company
Address (no., street)
Address (city, state, zip)

GOLF PRO   Dear Exact Name of Person: (or Dear Sir or Madam if answering a blind ad.)

I would appreciate an opportunity to talk with you soon about how I could contribute to your organization through my experience as a golf professional who offers outstanding management skills in all aspects of golf operations.

As an Assistant Golf Pro and Head Golf Pro for approximately eight years, I have been privileged to work with such outstanding professionals as Joe Blake, John Braxton, Clyde Smith, Will Jones, and Rob Finkle. In my current position at the Rivera Country Club in Jackson, MS, I have been effective in running a golf operation with 625 members.

In 2003, I earned Class "A" membership in the Professional Golfers Association of America (PGA). I offer a well-rounded background in all aspects of golf management including maintaining handicaps, using computers to control inventory and perform bookkeeping, instructing individuals, operating clinics, and organizing tournaments. My organizational skills were effectively used to plan and conduct the Marc Fueller Golf Classic which annually draws approximately 140 talented junior golfers.

I am a highly organized team player who strives to ensure that each club member is served properly. I thoroughly enjoy the game of golf and could make valuable contributions to a program's success and profitability as Head Golf Pro.

I hope you will welcome my call soon to arrange a brief meeting at your convenience to discuss your current and future needs and how I might serve them. Thank you in advance for your time.

Sincerely yours,

Donald Landers

DONALD LANDERS

1110½ Hay Street, Fayetteville, NC 28305   •   preppub@aol.com   •   (910) 483-6611

OBJECTIVE

To offer my reputation as a well-trained golf professional who can contribute expert teaching and motivational skills along with a proven ability to develop, manage, and promote tournaments, clinics, and everyday operations of a golf program.

PROFESSIONAL AFFILIATION

Was elected to a Class "A" membership in the Professional Golfers Association of America (PGA), 2003, after completing all requirements for membership.

EXPERIENCE

Have been promoted from Assistant Golf Pro to Head Golf Pro based on my business management skills, Rivera Country Club, Jackson, MS:
HEAD GOLF PROFESSIONAL. (2004-present). Accepted the challenge of managing a golf shop and course, and have applied my skills in building the facility into an even better, more successful, and more profitable one.
- Control a $130,000 operational budget and all aspects of a thriving golf operation.
- Train and supervise three employees in a golf shop projected to gross approximately $165,000 a year; provide leadership for the retail aspects of running a golf operation in addition to guidance in customer service and sales. Work closely with the course superintendent and his staff to oversee the everyday workings of the golf course itself.
- Manage the driving range, a fleet of 52 golf cars, and bag storage areas.

ASSISTANT GOLF PROFESSIONAL. (2001-04). As assistant to Head Golf Professional Joe Blake, was in charge of a wide range of functional golf shop operations required to support a membership of 625 people and ensure operations were run to their satisfaction.
- Gained valuable experience in organizing and conducting a major junior golf tournament: the Marc Fueller Golf Classic annually draws around 140 participants.
- Applied my experience in inventory control and buying plans to provide managerial guidance for a retail shop grossing approximately $165,000 annually.
- Used my computer skills to maintain accurate and up-to-date records of golf shop and club bookkeeping activities. Provided expert instructional and communication skills while giving private golf lessons and teaching golf clinics for adults and juniors.
- Gained valuable experience in effectively managing both human and fiscal resources.
- Created a new system for keeping accurate count of the number of rounds of golf played each day: increased sign-ins from 40% to near 100% for accurate guest fee charges.

Earlier experience: ASSISTANT GOLF PROFESSIONAL:
Fenton Country Club, Lorman, MS (1998-01). Displayed a great deal of flexibility working with three different Head Golf Professionals—John Braxton, Clyde Smith, and Will Jones.
Ashman Country Club, Lorman, MS (1996-98). As an assistant to Head Golf Professional Rob Finkle, was involved in tournament management and shop operations.

TRAINING

Completed professional development programs and clinics including the following:
The Professional Scoreboard Clinic—emphasis on the proper preparation, writing skills, and design of a golf scoreboard, 8 hours, 1999.
PGA Business School II—golf business advanced skills and knowledge, 40 hours, 1998.
PGA Business School I—basic skills and knowledge of the golf business, 40 hours, 1997.

EDUCATION

Bachelor in Business Administration, Jackson State University, Jackson, MS, 1996.

PERSONAL

Am well organized and a wise manager of time. Offer strong communication skills and the ability to relate to students, management, and other staff members. Will relocate.

Date

Exact Name of Person
Title or Position
Name of Company
Address (no., street)
Address (city, state, zip)

GOLF PRO   Dear Exact Name of Person: (or Dear Sir or Madam if answering a blind ad.)

With the enclosed resume, I am formally indicating my interest in the Head Golf Professional position at Holmes Country Club.

In my current job as the Head Golf Professional at Bulk Stream Country Club in Houston. I have improved every aspect of the golf program at this esteemed country club. Although I am quite happy in my current situation and am appreciated for the significant improvements I have made in every area of the golf program, it has always been my goal to become associated one day with a club such as yours. I am aware of the high-profile clientele you serve, and I feel certain I could add value to your operation and enhance the superior climate for which you already are known.

At Bulk Stream Country Club I have resourcefully found new ways to save money every year while making sure customers are satisfied with all "the little things" that can drive members crazy if they're not perfect! By those "little things" I include things such as the variety and quality of golf shop inventory, the tournament program, golf instruction, golf cart operation and bag storage, driving range administration, as well as the operation of starters and rangers. I have taken golf instruction to a new level at Bulk Stream Country Club and, while supervising seven employees, I have continually developed the instructional abilities of my assistants.

I have completed PGA Business School I, II, and III, have served on the Oral Interview Committee, and was invited by fellow PGA Professionals to act as instructor for the Creek Valley Golf League. In my previous job at Weeks Park Country Club, I gained extensive experience in organizing and managing an extensive tournament schedule including The Southern Amateur Tournament, National League Tournament, and the U.S. Golf Association Tournament.

You would find me in person to be a congenial individual who prides myself on my ability to relate well to anyone. I believe strongly in the ability of golf to teach and refine virtues including honesty, fairness, courtesy, responsibility, determination, and discipline. I can provide outstanding personal and professional references.

I hope you will write or call me to suggest a time when we might meet in confidence to discuss your current and future needs and how I might serve them. Thank you in advance for your time.

Sincerely yours,

Keith Easton

70 Part Two: Real-Resumes for Sports Industry Jobs

KEITH EASTON

1110½ Hay Street, Fayetteville, NC 28305   •   preppub@aol.com   •   (910) 483-6611

OBJECTIVE

To benefit an organization that can use a respected golf professional who offers experience in financial management, proven skills in teaching and training, as well as an intense commitment to the highest standards of excellence in both personal and professional areas.

EXPERIENCE

HEAD GOLF PROFESSIONAL. Bulk Stream Country Club, Houston, TX (2002-present). Have earned a reputation as an enthusiastic and hard-working professional who has improved every aspect of the golf program at this prestigious country club.

- **Golf shop sales and service**: Improved customer service, accounting practices, and the quality of merchandise; boosted sales from $155,000 to $177,000 in my first year, to $223,000 in my second year, and to more than $230,000 in the third year.
- **Financial administration**: Resourcefully found new ways to decrease expenses while improving services; proposed a 2003 budget that is $21,000 less than the 2002 budget and have already reduced expenses by $6,000 in 2004.
- **Tournament program**: Hosted the 2004 Texas Region Tournament and generally increased the club's level of interest in competition.
- **Golf instruction**: Continually develop the instructional abilities of my assistants and have improved the golf game of every student I have taught.
- **Starters and rangers**: Improve course scheduling, develop new approaches to helping members find games, and ensure a reasonable pace on busy days.
- **Junior Golf Program**: Expose juniors to the great virtues golf can teach—honesty, fairness, courtesy, responsibility, determination, and discipline.
- **Golf cart operation and bag storage**: Improve maintenance, repairs, and customer satisfaction with all aspects of these operations.
- **Driving range**: Develop an attractive range membership plan.
- **Employee supervision**: Supervise seven employees; am known for my fairness.

ASSISTANT GOLF PROFESSIONAL. Weeks Park Country Club, Houston, TX (1999-02). Supervised nine bag storage and cart operation personnel while managing accounts receivable/payable, inventory control, and merchandising.

- Organized and managed an extensive tournament schedule which included The Southern Amateur Tournament, National League Tournament, and U.S. Golf Association Tournament. Taught clinics and provided private instruction to men, women, and juniors.

FIRST ASSISTANT PROFESSIONAL. Western Village Country Club, Plainview, TX (1996-99). Managed part-time cart staff and pro shop staff; planned budgets for cart staff and operation costs for the driving range; and handled accounts receivable/payable, inventory control, and merchandise selection. Organized Men's and Ladies' Clinics.

FIRST ASSISTANT PROFESSIONAL. Skyview Country Club, Houston, TX (1994-96). Began as Second Assistant Professional in 1994 and was promoted to First Assistant Professional in less than a year; learned the "nuts and bolts" of golf program management.

EDUCATION

Completed **PGA Business School I, II, and III**, Houston, TX, and Richmond, VA, 1994, 1995, and 2002.
Completed workshops focused on business planning for the golf professional, techniques for outclassing the competition, improving the appearance of the club scoreboard, food and beverage principles, wage and hour laws, and computer software.

HONORS

Invited by fellow PGA Professionals to be an instructor, Creek Valley Golf League, 1997 and 1998. Appointed member, Oral Interview Committee, 1998.

Date

Exact Name of Person
Title or Position
Name of Company
Address (no., street)
Address (city, state, zip)

GOLF PRO   Dear Exact Name of Person: (or Dear Sir or Madam if answering a blind ad.)

I would appreciate an opportunity to talk with you soon about how I could contribute to your organization through my experience as a golf professional as well as through my proven ability to manage golf shop operations, develop new programs, and create business opportunities.

As you will see from my resume, I offer experience that is somewhat unique for a head golf professional. During the time I was a golf professional at the exclusive Bayside Country Club, the Hilton Corporation bought the property and transformed it into a 375-room "destination resort." Hilton named me its Convention Manager during the transition and I managed 29 people while promoting convention and golf packages. The training and experience I gained at the Hilton Corporation in marketing, promotions, publicity, and management has been enormously useful to me and to the two clubs I worked for subsequently.

In my most recent job, I transformed a poorly performing golf shop which was retailing only $20,000 a year. As the sole proprietor, I developed that underperforming business into a thriving retail shop with a reputation for its fine selection. I hosted numerous charity events, community associations, and fundraisers. In fact, I did such a great job in increasing revenues that the golf course attracted new owners from New Mexico who are in the middle of an ambitious construction program to expand the golf course!

I have had several clubs call to invite me to talk with them about their head pro job since I left Grand Valley, but I am sincerely interested in first exploring the possibility of working for Grants Country Club. I feel that my background and my knowledge of the area may be well suited to your needs. I certainly would enjoy the opportunity to talk with you about what you're looking for and what I have to offer.

Please let me know if you have an interest in my versatile background. I know of your club's fine reputation and I believe I could become a valuable asset to you in retaining members, developing new business, increasing overall profitability, and enhancing your club's reputation through my golfing expertise. I am aware that the market in Scottsdale is quite competitive, and I am certain I could make valuable contributions to your club's ability to compete successfully in this market.

Yours sincerely,

Jared Bullock

JARED BULLOCK

1110½ Hay Street, Fayetteville, NC 28305   •   preppub@aol.com   •   (910) 483-6611

OBJECTIVE   I want to contribute to the growth and financial success of an organization that can use a respected golf professional who offers a "track record" of producing outstanding results in areas including publicity and marketing, retail sales and service operations management, public relations and programming, as well as membership development and retention.

EDUCATION   Earned a **Bachelor of Science degree,** University of Southern Colorado, Pueblo, CO, 1994. Completed extensive graduate studies in **Behavioral Science,** The University of Arizona, Tucson, AZ. Completed P.G.A. Business School I and II, San Diego, CA, and Phoenix, AZ.

EXPERIENCE   **HEAD GOLF PROFESSIONAL.** Canyon Golf Club, Tucson, AZ (2004-present). Through my golf expertise and marketing skills, played a key role in transforming a privately owned, daily fee golf course with a small membership into a profitable operation which was recently sold to a buyer from New Mexico who intends to further develop and expand the business after finishing an extensive construction program.
- In less than two years, more than doubled the number of private members.
- Took over a golf pro shop which was retailing only $20,000 yearly and, as the sole proprietor of the shop and with my own capital, developed a thriving and profitable retail business which gained a word-of-mouth reputation for quality products.
- On my own initiative, started a Co-ed Golf Association.
- Increased rounds of golf from 16,000 in 2002 to 26,000 in 2004; played a key role in the growth of total revenue from $280,000 in 2002 to $385,000 in 2004.
- Developed an area golfer database for the monthly newsletter.
- Established Golf Package Accounts with all area hotels and motels.
- Conducted five-day Summer Golf Camps. Hosted charity events and fundraisers.

HEAD GOLF PROFESSIONAL & CLUB MANAGER. Grand Valley Golf Country, Tucson, AZ (2000-03). At this private country club with a membership of 325 families, was the driving force in the revitalization of club operations with the result that the club showed a profit in 2001 after many years of losing money.
- As the sole proprietor of the golf shop and snack bar/catering departments, expanded menus and improved service and presentation; supervised seven people.
- Instituted a new golf cart maintenance and recordkeeping system; increased golf cart revenue from $61,000 to $109,000 over a three-year period. Hosted the first annual "Lee Rock Golf Tournament" in 2003 and raised $15,000 for the Woodman School System.

GOLF PROFESSIONAL & CONVENTION COORDINATOR. Hilton's Bayside Golf Resort, Scottsdale, AZ (1994-99). Began as an Assistant Golf Professional at one of the world's most exclusive private clubs which catered to upscale tastes and protected the privacy of its guests who included corporate VIPs, heads of state, and entertainment industry personalities; in 1995, was named Convention Coordinator after Bayside was purchased by the Hilton Corporation, which transformed it into a 375-room posh "destination resort."
- Supervised 29 people as Convention Coordinator; marketed Bayside to all Scottsdale hotels/casinos and to major corporations for conferences and golf packages.
- Exceeded all goals within budgets of $3.4M in 1996, $3.9M in 1997, and $4.1M in 1998.
- Was a key member of the first management staff to surpass $2 million in sales in a four-week budget period (May 1998).

PERSONAL   Enjoy training and developing others, and take pride in the fact that six of my former Golf Assistants are now Head Professionals and Directors of Golf. Excellent references.

TWO-PAGE RESUME

MARTY HOGAN

1110½ Hay Street, Fayetteville, NC 28305

preppub@aol.com   •   (910) 483-6611

CAREER OBJECTIVE

A Titleist-Hicks award winner for highest scores in G.P.T.P. in Indianapolis seeks a full-time teaching position. Past owner of successful business as a General Manager and Head Professional with excellent management, supervisory, communication, interpersonal, and problem-solving skills.

EDUCATION

Vincennes University: Doctorate Degree in Science
Vincennes, IN, 1996.

Ball State University: Bachelor of Science degree
Muncie, IN, 1994.

TEACHING

- Adult Continuing Education Instructor
- Have given over 200 lessons
- Developed more than 20 clinics for beginners to advanced players
- Provided one-on-one lessons on subjects varying from basics of swing to specific problems and areas
- Teaching Assistant at Vincennes University
- Teaching Assistant at Ball State University

BACKGROUND HIGHLIGHTS

- Class "A" Member of PGA in good standing
- Successfully passed Golf Professional Training Program of PGA of America
- Player Ability Test (PAT), Indianapolis, IN

RELATED WORK EXPERIENCE

- **Harding Golf Club (Semi-Private):** Indianapolis, IN
  General Manager/Head Professional, 2004-present
- **Evergreen Country Club (Private):** Indianapolis, IN
  First Assistant, 2003-2004
- **Fairway Country Club (Private):** Vincennes, IN
  First Assistant, 2001-2003
- **Anchor Park Country Club (Semi-Private):** Vincennes, IN
  First Assistant, 2000-2001
- **Salisbury Country Club (Resort):** Indianapolis, IN
  Assistant Golf Professional, 1997-2000

BUSINESS MANAGEMENT

- General Manager–all phases
- Past owner
- Manager in charge of staffing, hiring, and terminations
- Payroll control
- All operational phases of business–obtained financing, set budgets, and generated profits

- General Manager over entire facility
- Golf Pro Shop opening and closing procedures
- Inventory management, pricing, special promotions, sales, ordering and receiving of new merchandise, and monthly inventories
- Scheduling and personnel management of shop staff

OUTSIDE STAFF MANAGEMENT
- General Manager
- Supervised maintenance of 150 golf carts
- Handled bag storage for 200+ members and guests
- Staff included two mechanics, eight rangers, and four beverage cart operators

MEMBERSHIP DEVELOPMENT
- Worked on all phases of increasing and maintaining membership
- Promotional activities, public relations, and marketing
- New summer memberships and other innovative programs and clinics

TOURNAMENT OPERATIONS
- Organized over 150 outside and member tournaments
- Acted as rules official
- Set budgets
- Contacted sponsors
- Set up operations
- Prepared and marked golf course
- Officiated scoring and prize presentations

SKILLS
- Effectively analyze and interpret situations
- Extremely punctual and reliable
- Good problem solving and communication skills especially in demanding situations
- Exceptional interpersonal skills
- Computer skills—enter data, analyze reports, and program

ACTIVITIES
- Past Vice-President of local Rotary Club
- Past member of Planning Committee
- Past Board Member—Seawood Country Club

AWARDS
- Titleist-Hicks Award—Highest scores in Indianapolis for G.P.T.P.
- Award of Merit in Community Based Programs
- Prep High School All-American Basketball Yearbook
- Received the Boy Scout Award

Date

Exact Name of Person
Title or Position
Name of Company
Address (no., street)
Address (city, state, zip)

HEAD FOOTBALL COACH & OFFENSIVE COORDINATOR

Dear Exact Name of Person: (or Dear Sir or Madam if answering a blind ad.)

I would appreciate an opportunity to talk with you soon about how I could contribute to your organization through my background as a successful coach and athletic director who offers experience as a head coach and athletic director.

As you will see from my resume, the bulk of my experience is in coaching football and I am now at Bismarck Senior High School in Bismarck, ND, a 3A school which has averaged 10 wins a year for the past two seasons in a conference recognized as the toughest and most competitive in the state. In fact, in my two years here, I have guided the team to an impressive current streak of scoring in double figures for the past 21 games, a fact recently publicized by the *High School Football News*. Earlier I led the football team at Fargo High School, the state's smallest 3A school which had not been to a playoff since 1971, to four consecutive playoff seasons.

A versatile professional, I have also excelled in coaching track, basketball, wrestling, and golf. I am confident that I can build any sports program into a successful one while guiding young people to prosper academically and grow in character through athletics. My track record will show that I am not only a talented coach and administrator, but also an enthusiastic, intelligent, and motivated professional who handles pressure well. I am extremely effective in molding groups of young people into productive, winning teams. For example, when I became the youngest 3A Head Coach in North Dakota at Evergreen High School in Fargo, I quickly produced a team with the most conference wins in the school's history.

I can provide a school system with a winning coach who is also an excellent teacher, administrator, and communicator. I will cheerfully relocate, and I can provide outstanding personal and professional references from all previous employers.

I hope you will call or write me soon to suggest a time convenient for us to meet and discuss your current and future needs and how I might serve them. Thank you in advance for your time.

Sincerely yours,

Jesse Underhill

JESSE UNDERHILL

1110½ Hay Street, Fayetteville, NC 28305   •   preppub@aol.com   •   (910) 483-6611

OBJECTIVE

To offer my positive and results-oriented leadership style, along with my experience in building and coaching winning teams, to an ambitious high school that can use an enthusiastic and intelligent professional with a reputation for the highest work and personal ethics.

EXPERIENCE

OFFENSIVE COORDINATOR & PHYSICAL EDUCATION TEACHER. Bismarck Senior High School, Bismarck, ND (2004-present). Hired as offensive coordinator for a football team which has built an impressive record of wins in a conference recognized as the toughest and most competitive in the state.

- Averaged 10 wins a year over the past two seasons while building teams that work well together under pressure. Contribute leadership as a member of a coaching staff which has been effective in winning "the big games."
- In my years here, guided the team to an impressive current streak of scoring in double figures for the last 21 games, a fact recently publicized by *High School Football News*.

HEAD FOOTBALL COACH & ATHLETIC DIRECTOR. Dakota Senior High School, Bismarck, ND (2001-03). Provided the management and guidance for a project in which three high schools combined and then coached the football program and directed all other sports for the consolidated school.

HEAD FOOTBALL COACH & ATHLETIC DIRECTOR. Fargo High School, Fargo, ND (1997-01). Led the state's smallest 3A school to four consecutive winning seasons in the state's toughest league; acted as administrator of the school's total athletic program.

- Coached four consecutive teams to state-level playoffs and record-setting years including the first time the school had reached the state playoffs since 1971.
- Supervised 20 coaches and administered a $75,000 athletic budget.
- Taught weight training and physical fitness to participants in all athletic programs.

HEAD FOOTBALL COACH. Evergreen High School, Fargo, NC (1994-97). Joined this organization as the youngest 3A high school head coach in the state and led the team to break several school records; supervised and trained an eight-person staff.

- Faced with a previous 1-9 record, turned the program around and in 1994 produced a team with the most conference wins in the school's history.
- Guided the 1996 team to the best overall record in the school's 18-year history.
- Scored in every game over a three-year period covering 30 games while playing against teams in the state's "Top 10" as the smallest 3A school in the state.

HEAD FOOTBALL COACH & INSTRUCTOR. Central High School, Fargo, ND (1991-94). Obtained my Master of Education degree in Physical Education while teaching classes and coaching three sports—football, wrestling, and track—at this 2A school.

- After two years of hard work, developed an 0-7 junior varsity football team into an 8-4 varsity playoff team. Coached track and wrestling teams to become conference champions.

EDUCATION

M.Ed. degree, Sports Administration, North Dakota State University, Fargo, ND, 1994.
B.S., Physical Education, Regents College, Albany, NY, 1989.

FOOTBALL COACHING EXPERTISE

In my coaching career, have gained experience in these areas:

offensive and defensive coordination   formulation of game plans
special team coordination fundamentals in all positions

PERSONAL

Was "MVP" of my high school football team. Won a Merit Scholarship to ND State University.

TWO-PAGE RESUME

GEORGE HOLMES
1110½ Hay Street, Fayetteville, NC 28305
preppub@aol.com   •   (910) 483-6611

OBJECTIVE

I want to contribute to an organization that can use an accomplished Health and Fitness Director who offers outstanding skills in program development and program management.

HEALTH & FITNESS DIRECTOR

EXPERIENCE

HEALTH & FITNESS DIRECTOR. The Alaska Club, Anchorage, AK (2000-present).

Major Responsibilities:
- Administration of physical building and supervision of physical and aquatic departments (2 professional staff members, 4 support staff members, 65 part-time staff members, and 280 volunteers).
- Oversee a budget of $320,000.

Program Responsibilities:
- Youth and adult sports
- Special population aquatic programs
- Youth and adult fitness
- Gymnastics, karate, ballet, tennis
- Corporate wellness
- Corporate cup
- Private school P.E. program
- Corporate membership
- Healthy back, weight management
- Rehabilitation programs
- Annual road race
- Learn to swim (youth and adult)

Key Accomplishments:
- Direct the revision of all policies and procedures governing operation of physical building (general operating procedures and staff performance standards).
- Increased annual operating budget in physical and aquatic departments from $170,000 in 2000 to $320,000 in 2004 (81% from increased program participation and 7% from sports sponsorships).
- Established and administered youth sports sponsorship program, raising $10,000 in 2003.
- Spearheaded program fund raisers which raised $5,000 in 2003.
- Assisted in increasing the annual support campaign from zero income in 1999 to $60,000 in 2003.
- Currently assisting in administration of Aurora Project to raise $1.5 million.
- Increased programs and participation in the following areas:
  Fitness classes: Established 10 off-site classes per week.
  Corporate wellness programs: Created four on-site corporate programs and 23 total corporate membership accounts.
  Youth sports: Improved participation from 690 total participants in 1999 to 1,675 total participants in 2003.
  Home School P.E. program: Pioneered a program which is now

used in numerous Alaska Clubs across the Southcentral Region.

Other programs: Develop and implement private school P.E. programs, Health Education, sports camps, and a Fit Kids summer camp.

YOUTH & FAMILY DIRECTOR. Anchorage YMCA, Anchorage, AK (1995-2000).
Major Responsibilities:
- Administration of youth and family programs consisting of preschool, youth sports, leaders club, youth in government, summer day camp, and special events.
- Supervised two support staff members and 15 part-time staff members.
- Oversaw a budget of $130,000.

Key Accomplishments:
- Established a Junior Leaders Club and youth volunteer program (65 youth participants within six months).
- Implemented Summer Day Camp weeks and increased participation by 65 percent.
- Boosted participation in youth soccer from 110 participants in the fall of 1995 to 265 in the spring of 2000.
- Created youth sport camps.
- Assisted in the administration of Aurora Project, which raised $900,000 in 2000.

ATHLETIC DIRECTOR & PHYSICAL EDUCATION TEACHER. Southcentral High, Eagle River, AK (1990-94).
Major Responsibilities:
- Administration of sports program and teaching P.E. classes for grades K-10.
- Coached the varsity basketball and soccer teams.

OTHER EXPERIENCE

BASKETBALL COACH/TRACK COACH, Wasilla Senior High, Wasilla, AK
COMMERCIAL FISHERMAN, Aleutian Islands, Dutch Harbor, AK

EDUCATION & TRAINING

Academic:
University of Alaska Anchorage, Anchorage, AK
B.A. in Physical Education, 1990.

Professional:
- Alaska Club Principals and Practices, 2003
- Alaska Club Pricing Seminar, 2003
- Alaska Club Program Planning Seminar, 2003
- Alaska Club Marketing Seminar, 2002
- Alaska Club Budget Planning, 2002
- Alaska Club Basic Principals, 2001
- Alaska Club Fitness Specialist, 2001
- Alaska Club Healthy Back Instructor, 2001
- Alaska Club Weight Management Instructor, 2000

INTERESTS
- Basketball
- Coaching basketball and soccer
- Antiques
- Family camping
- Fishing

Exact Name of Person
Title or Position
Name of Company
Address (no., street)
Address (city, state, zip)

HIGH SCHOOL STUDENT
SEEKING FOOTBALL
SCHOLARSHIP

Dear Exact Name of Person: (or Dear Sir or Madam if answering a blind ad):

With the enclosed resume, I would like to make you aware of my interest in applying for a football scholarship with your organization. I would like to obtain an engineering degree and establish a career in biomechanics with the long-range goal of becoming involved in the field of robotics.

As you will see from my resume, I have extensive involvement in sports. I have participated in football since I was in 3rd grade and have gained experience throughout the years. This senior year, I am both a fullback and middle line backer. In my junior year, I was given the Hero Award by the players and coaches in recognition of my dedication.

I hope you will call or write me soon to suggest a time convenient for us to meet to discuss my application to your scholarship. Thank you in advance for you time.

Sincerely yours,

Joel Roberts

JOEL ROBERTS

1110½ Hay Street, Fayetteville, NC 28305 • preppub@aol.com • (910) 483-6611

OBJECTIVE

To obtain an engineering degree and establish a career in biomechanics with the long-range goal of becoming involved in the field of robotics.

PSAT/SAT

SAT scores on the May 2002 test were 1290 (640 math; 650 verbal)

EDUCATION

Seabrook High School, San Jose, CA, 1999-2003; Top 15% of class.
Educational Scholar, American Classical League *magna cum laude* National Exam, 2001

SCOUTING

Rose to the rank of **Life Scout**

SPORTS

Football:
- 12th grade: Senior year positions are fullback and middle line backer.
- 11th grade: Received **Hero Award** given by players and coaches in recognition of my dedication despite an injury in which I tore ACL.
- 10th grade: Was one of seven 10th graders to make the Varsity team; started at **Center** on a team that made the state playoffs.
- 9th grade: **Team Captain,** Seabrook High School Junior Varsity team; started as fullback and middle line backer.
- 8th grader: **Team Captain** and **Defense MVP** on a team that was the undefeated conference champions, Dickenson Middle School.
- 7th grader: Only 7th grader to start on the Dickenson Middle School team and one of only five 7th graders to make the team.
- 3rd-6th grades: Played on City of San Jose Youth League, 3-year starter. Named **Defense MVP** and **City Champions.**

Wrestling:
- 11th grade: Wrestled at 160 lbs. **Team Captain.** Received the **Avery Hill Memorial Award** given by players and coaches in recognition of "outstanding courage and hard work" in finishing 3rd in the conference despite a grueling recovery from an ACL injury suffered during football practice.
- 10th grade: Received the **Coaches Award** given by the wrestling coaches to the player who most exemplifies the work ethic and positive attitude sought in dedicated wrestlers. Also received the **Outstanding 10th Grade Wrestler Award**. Wrestled for Seabrook Senior High School Varsity Team at 171 lbs. Was 28-6 overall on a varsity team which was the undefeated (7-0) conference champion.
- 9th grade: Lettered at 150 lbs.

OTHER AWARDS

8th grade: Received the **Ronald Dwyer Student-Athlete Award** given annually which singles out one student in the school who exemplifies the best combination of athletics and scholarship. A prestigious award which is considered one of the five major awards given annually at the school.

SERVICE

Contributed numerous volunteer hours on service projects as a Boy Scout
Volunteered at Salvation Army for pickup, sorting, and delivery of clothes to needy

WORK

WEB-BASED BUSINESS ENTREPRENEUR. San Jose, CA. (2001-present). Have established a web-based business which recruits web surfers who allow advertisers to send information to their computers.

Date

Exact Name of Person
Title or Position
Name of Company
Address (no., street)
Address (city, state, zip)

HIGH SCHOOL   Dear Exact Name of Person: (or Dear Sir or Madam if answering a blind ad.)
STUDENT
SEEKING   With the enclosed resume highlighting my tennis achievements, scholastic honors,
TENNIS   and personal qualities, I would like to formally introduce myself and tell you that I
SCHOLARSHIP   would like to explore the possibility of playing on your tennis team as an incoming
freshman in the class of 2005.

       Currently an Honor Roll junior with a straight-A average, I believe I will have the
grades and SAT score to be admitted to the school of my choice on academics alone. I
have already scored a 1280 on the SAT and am hoping to improve on that score when I
take the SAT again in the spring. A student at Dearborn Senior High School, I have a
class rank of #5 out of approximately 300 students.

       You will see from my resume that I offer a track record of accomplishments in
tennis, and I sincerely believe I have the talent and drive to become one of the world's
all-time best tennis players. My most recent rankings are #1 in NV, #1 in the Regional
Section, and #8 nationally.

       In this letter of introduction, I not only want you to know that I am a top scholar
and athlete but also that I pride myself on my strong character and personal reputation
for reliability, morality, and stamina. I am confident that I have the skills and personal
qualities needed to become one of the world's greatest tennis professionals.

       I will be playing in the Tennis League in Sacramento, CA, April 9-15, and in the
Nationals this summer. I enclose a detailed schedule of my upcoming tournaments in
the hope that I might have the opportunity to meet you during the months ahead.

       I am in the process of identifying the schools to which I will be applying, and I
would be appreciative if you could give me some indication, in writing or by phone, of
whether you would like to explore the possibility of my playing for you. I know of your
fine reputation and would be honored to talk with you about how my talents might fit
into your program.

Sincerely,

Victor Rodriguez

VICTOR RODRIGUEZ

1110½ Hay Street, Fayetteville, NC 28305   •   preppub@aol.com   •   (910) 483-6611

GOAL	To continue to develop my skills as a tennis player and to make a significant contribution to the reputation and winning record of a respected university.		

RANKINGS

	State (NV)	*Regional*	*National*
2004:	No. 1 (16s)	No. 1 (16s)	No. 8 (16s)
2003:	•	No. 4 (16s)	No. 59 (16s)
2002:	•	No. 2 (14s)	No. 7 (14s)
2001:	No. 1 (14s)	No. 8 (14s)	No. 70 (14s)
2000:	No. 1 (12s)	No. 1 (12s)	

- No NV ranking in 2002-03 because I did not play required number of tournaments.

GAME DATA

- *Right-handed* player
- *Best surface*: hard
- *Best shot:* forehand and serve
- *Style:* all court

SCHOLARSHIP

- Class rank: #5 out of approximately 300 students; am currently a junior
- Honor Roll student at Dearborn Senior High School, Reno, NV
- SAT scores: Verbal 610; math 670; am taking SAT again in spring 2004

SCHOOL LEADERSHIP

- National Honor Society
- Junior Class President
- Member of Spanish Club (Vice-President)
- Recipient of Athletic Scholarship Achievement Award
- Named Outstanding Freshman, 2002-03; faculty award

TENNIS HONORS

- *Invited by USTA to represent the U.S.* in the Flower Bowl in Spain and the International Junior Championships of France, 2004; unfortunately I was unable to compete because the U.S. was not issuing passports during the government shutdown.
- *Fourth Place in The National Indoors*, Nashville, TN, 2004
- *Third Place in The Nationals*, Philadelphia, PA, 2004
- *Finalist in The Nationals*, Charleston, SC, 2004
- Played in *Morrison International Championships*, 2004; one of only five Americans to reach Round of 32
- *Closed Singles Champion*: 2004, 02, 01
- NV State 3A High School *Singles Champion*, 2004
- Invited to participate in USTA National Training Camps, Salt Lake City, UT: 2004, 03,
- NV Qualifier *Singles Champion*: 2004, 00
- NV Qualifier *Doubles Champion*: 2004, 03, 02, 01, 00
- Played in *Tennis League Championships*, 2004, 03, 02, 01; finished in **top 16** in Boys 16s, 2004.
- Played in *Junior Tennis Bowl*, 2002
- *NV Junior Cup Team*, 2004, 03, 02, 01
- Recipient of *Junior Tennis Council Award* for contributions to NC Junior Tennis, 2004, 02
- Named *South 3A Conference Player of the Year*, 2004, 03
- Named *MVP, Dearborn Senior High School Tennis Team*, 2004, 03

COACHES

Personal coach: Bill Taylor; High school coach: Sal Burrows

Date

Exact Name of Person
Title or Position
Name of Company
Address
City, State, Zip

MARKETING DIRECTOR OF A PROFESSIONAL TEAM

Dear Exact Name of Person: (or Dear Sir or Madam if answering a blind ad.)

I am sending you the enclosed resume and the materials you requested in response to your recent advertisement in NCAA News for an Assistant Sports Information Director and Program Assistant.

After doing some research into the characteristics of your 2,400-person student body, I feel my background would be "tailor-made" to your needs.

As you will see from my resume, I am currently excelling as Marketing Director of a professional basketball team. In that capacity, I control marketing, sales, and public relations for a basketball team in its first year of operation in the new Global Basketball Association. I provide team statistical information, handle press conferences and press releases, and arrange public appearances for team members. My team has become recognized as one of the league's most effective marketing operations through the success of my management style.

On the technical side of sports information, I offer every qualification and skill your ad mentions. I am an expert at organizing and compiling statistical information, writing press releases, authoring comprehensive training camp booklets and media guides, and preparing game notes and other publications. With extensive experience in desktop publishing using PageMaker, I am skilled at using computers with word processing software. I offer proven supervisory abilities.

During the last 2 1/2 years I have demonstrated my "flair" for working with national and local media. Since public relations in professional sports requires diversified expertise in every aspect of sales and media relations, I am comfortable in all areas of media relations.

I am sending you the enclosed packet of materials to give you some idea of my capabilities. I send my sincere best wishes for the continued success of your fine college athletic program.

Sincerely yours,

Eric Bump

ERIC BUMP

1110½ Hay Street, Fayetteville, NC 28305   •   preppub@aol.com   •   (910) 483-6611

OBJECTIVE

To apply my education and my experience in the areas of marketing, public relations, and sales to an organization that can benefit from my specialized knowledge of sports marketing and my organizational and planning abilities.

EDUCATION

B.S. in Education with a major in Sports Management, University of Washington, Seattle, WA, 2002.
- Specialized in Sports Information, Marketing, and Promotion.
- Partially financed my education while gaining experience in these jobs:

Student Recreation Center Manager. (1999-02). In the highest position available to a student at the rec center, managed a $10 million complex.

Student Assistant to the Sports Marketing and Promotion Director. (1998-00). Gained experience in college-level sports marketing and promotion while writing promotional materials and developing advertising copy.

EXPERIENCE

MARKETING DIRECTOR. The Seattle Chinooks, Seattle, WA (2004-present). Control marketing, sales, and public relations for a basketball team in its first year of operation in the new Global Basketball Association.
- Sold season tickets and $132,000 in corporate sponsorships and small business packages in the franchise's first seven months of existence.
- Provide team statistical information, handle press conferences and press releases, and arrange public appearances for team members.
- Coordinate entertainment and promotions including booking halftime acts.
- Led the sales staff by accounting for 85% of all advance ticket sales: sold $14,000 in preseason small business packages in a 45-day period.
- Have led the team to become recognized as one of the league's most effective marketing operations through the success of my management style.

SPORTS MARKETING SPECIALIST. PRP, Inc., Seattle, WA (2003-04). Coordinated information from high school athletic directors and created the design for producing a sports calendar for local businesses.
- Generated $25,000 in sales of advertising space in a 4 1/2 month period.

PUBLIC RELATIONS ASSISTANT. The Portland Pirates, Portland, OR (2002-03). Earned rapid promotion from an entry-level job to assistant director of public relations for this professional basketball team while training three interns.
- Wrote press releases, organized press conferences, arranged public appearances, and maintained statistics.
- Made the year's largest group sale: 1,200 tickets for one game.
- Refined my ability to manage time and work under pressure as the assistant public relations director.

COMPUTER KNOWLEDGE

Use IBM and MacIntosh computers and software including PageMaker, Microsoft Word, MacPaint, and MacWrite.

PERSONAL

Am a licensed softball umpire, baseball umpire, and basketball official. Offer a willingness to work long, hard hours to ensure quality results. Excellent references.

Date

Exact Name of Person
Title or Position
Name of Company
Address (no., street)
Address (city, state, zip)

MARKETING TRAINEE

Seeking entry-level
position with a sports
team.

Dear Exact Name of Person: (or Dear Sir or Madam if answering a blind ad.)

Can you use a self-starter and fast learner who offers extensive computer knowledge and sharp math skills along with proven abilities related to management and marketing?

While earning my B.S. degree in marketing, I excelled in several "real-world" projects that involved setting up a minor league baseball team, establishing a new franchise "from scratch," and analyzing the financial condition of a major electronics corporation. I am skilled at using several popular software packages.

My mathematical abilities are considered top-notch: I was ranked in the highest percentile of high school students based on my superior math S.A.T. score. I also offer some experience in sales, business management, and customer service through jobs I held prior to earning my college degree.

I am seeking to make a long-term commitment and significant "bottom-line" contribution to a company that can use a versatile and creative young leader with a capacity for hard work.

I hope you will welcome my call soon to arrange a brief meeting at your convenience to discuss your current and future needs and how I might serve them. Thank you in advance for your time.

Sincerely yours,

Christopher Henderson

Alternate last paragraph:
I hope you will call or write me soon to suggest a time convenient for us to meet and discuss your current and future needs and how I might serve them. Thank you in advance for your time.

CHRISTOPHER HENDERSON

1110½ Hay Street, Fayetteville, NC 28305 • preppub@aol.com • (910) 483-6611

OBJECTIVE

To benefit an organization that can use a hard-working young professional who offers a proven ability to quickly learn and creatively apply information with a "bottom-line" orientation.

EXTENSIVE COMPUTER SKILLS

Have used software and programming languages including:

Adobe PageMaker   Excel

Access   Word

EDUCATION

Earned **Bachelor of Science (B.S.) degree in Marketing,** The Ohio State University, Columbus, OH, 2004.

EXPERIENCE

MARKETING TRAINEE. The Ohio State University, Columbus, OH (2004-present). As a successful candidate for the Bachelor of Science degree, excel in several "real-world" projects which enhanced my business administration and marketing skills.

- In a project for a **promotion** course, started up a Minor League baseball team for the city of Columbus: developed advertising, prepare schedules, prepared consumer literature and discount booklets, and determined logo/team colors.
- In a project for a **retail management** course, established "from scratch" a new franchise: performed extensive feasibility analysis and prepared in-depth oral/written presentations.
- For a **finance** course, performed extensive in-depth financial analysis, including ratio analysis, of the IBM Company: prepared five-year and 10-year projections.
- For a **marketing** project, collected information to help determine community banking needs and the public's perception of Bank of America.

FULL-TIME STUDENT. The Ohio State University, Columbus, OH (2000-04). Was a full-time student earning a B.S. degree in Marketing.

ACTING STORE MANAGER/MANAGER TRAINEE. Taco Bell, Cincinnati, OH (1997-2000). Was entrusted with occasionally managing this store after learning the internal workings of this fast-food preparation and delivery business serving the Cincinnati area.

Scheduled/directed drivers.   Ordered food/supplies.

Balanced daily receipts.   Answered phones/took orders.

Made bank deposits.   Prepared/delivered food.

SALES CLERK. Second Chance Pawn Shop, Cincinnati, OH (1997). Acquired excellent customer relations skills and learned valuable inventory control techniques while monitoring a diversified inventory including stereo equipment and firearms.

Other experience: Learned the importance of "attention to detail" as a dishwasher at a seafood restaurant and lifeguard at a country club pool.

MATHEMATICS KNOWLEDGE & ACADEMIC ABILITY

Scored a very high 700 on the math portion of Scholastic Aptitude Test (S.A.T).
- Was ranked in the top percentile of high school students in math mastery.

Was offered an academic scholarship by The Ohio State University.
- Received a Academic Fitness Award for academic excellence.

PERSONAL

Was elected pledge president in my college fraternity. Enjoy racquetball, golf (12-handicap), skiing, surfing, basketball, softball, and baseball. Excellent references on request.

Date

Exact Name of Person
Exact Title
Exact Name of Company
Address
City, State, Zip

MASSAGE THERAPIST   Dear Exact Name of Person (or Dear Sir or Madam if answering a blind ad):

With the enclosed resume, I would like to make you aware of my background as an educated and experienced Certified Massage Therapist with exceptional client relations skills who offers additional training in aromatherapy, alternative healing, and energy balancing techniques.

As you will see from my enclosed resume, I completed 1,000 hours of course work in Massage Therapy at the Grand Rapids Community College. Since completing my Certified Massage Therapist program, I have worked as an independent contractor, providing Massage Therapy to clients at Sports Center and Health and Fitness Gym in Grand Rapids, IL. I perform Swedish, shiatsu, Russian, and American sports massage as well as accupressure, reflexology, and other massage services. In addition, I offer aromatherapy and am knowledgeable in various forms of alternative healing. In Grand Rapids, I worked with one client who was suffering from extreme back problems, and was able to alleviate his pain even though the medical community had been unable to do so.

If you can use a motivated, caring Certified Massage Therapist, I hope you will contact me to suggest a time when we might meet to discuss your needs. I can assure you that I have an excellent reputation and could rapidly become an asset to your company.

Sincerely,

Candice Hall

CANDICE HALL

1110½ Hay Street, Fayetteville, NC 28305　　•　　preppub@aol.com　　•　　(910) 483-6611

OBJECTIVE

To benefit an organization that can use an experienced certified massage therapist with exceptional communication, organizational, and customer service skills who offers a background as a small business owner, independent contractor, and personal trainer.

EDUCATION

Completed 1,000 hours of course work in Massage Therapy, Grand Rapids Community College, Grand Rapids, MI, 2002.
Finished nearly three years of college towards a degree in Business Management, Wheaton College, Wheaton, IL, 1993-96.
Completed course work in Emergency Medical Rescue, which includes First Aid and CPR.

AFFILIATION & CERTIFICATION

Member, American Massage Therapy Association
Certified Massage Therapist; Qualified to perform Energy Balancing techniques

EXPERIENCE

CERTIFIED MASSAGE THERAPIST. Health and Fitness Gym, Grand Rapids, MI (2004-present). Work as an independent contractor, providing massage, aromatherapy, and other services to clients of the gym on an individual basis.

- Provide Swedish, shiatsu, accupressure, Russian, and American sports massage, reflexology, and other massage services.
- Worked with one client who was suffering from extreme back problems and was able to alleviate his pain even though the medical community had been unable to do so.
- Knowledgeable in a number of alternative health and common sense remedies for muscle sprains and related problems.
- Act as a nutrition and fitness consultant, frequently recommending yoga as a tool to aid muscle flexibility and reduce muscle-related pain.
- Develop and implement effective methods of promoting and advertising my services in order to build clientele. Manage all aspects of the operation, including contacting, scheduling, and billing customers as well as purchasing materials and supplies.

CERTIFIED MASSAGE THERAPIST. Sports Center, Grand Rapids, MI (2002-03). Was an independent contractor providing massage therapy to the gym's existing clients as well as the new clientele I developed through creative marketing strategies.

- Provided Swedish, shiatsu, accupressure, Russian and American sports massage, reflexology, and other massage services. Served as a nutrition and fitness consultant.
- Developed advertising and marketing tools that included the Sports Center's first official brochure.

CO-MANAGER. New Age Shop, Wheaton, IL (2000-02). Provided supervisory and administrative support to the operation of the city's largest gift shop; oversaw the in-processing, pricing, and shelving of items.

- Served on the Board of Directors, participating in strategic planning and playing a key role in organizing and coordinating special events. On my own initiative, reorganized the shop, instituting new controls that transformed it into a profitable enterprise.

Other experience: Worked as a **Personal Trainer** from 1996-1999, providing education and assistance related to proper nutrition and exercise to individuals seeking help.

PERSONAL

Excellent personal and professional references on request. Outstanding reputation.

Exact Name of Person
Title or Position
Name of Company
Address (no., street)
Address (city, state, zip)

MASSAGE THERAPIST

Dear Exact Name of Person: (or Dear Sir or Madam if answering a blind ad):

With the enclosed resume, I would like to make you aware of my interest in exploring employment opportunities with your organization.

As you will see from my resume, I am a graduate of the 525-hour massage therapy program from Champlain College in Burlington, VT, and I have been a distinguished member of the therapeutic massage field. I have been cited for professionalism and have become known for my high personal standards and ethics. With numerous certifications in this field, I serve as a board member for the Burlington Massage Therapy Association which I serve as the Secretary.

After graduation from the Massage Therapy Program in 2000, I founded a business which I manage as a Licensed Massage Therapist. I handle all business functions in addition to providing professional massage services integrated with the different modalities depending on muscle needs.

My husband and I are in the process of relocating to West Virginia, where we both grew up, and I am in the process of selling my business to my assistant. I am seeking an employer in the West Virginia area who can make use of my expertise in the field of massage therapy as well as my strong management abilities.

I hope you will call or write me soon to suggest a time convenient for us to meet to discuss your current and future needs. Thank you in advance for you time.

Sincerely yours,

Rachel Sutton

Alternate last paragraph:
I hope you will call or write me soon to suggest a time convenient for us to meet and discuss your current and future needs and how I might serve them. Thank you in advance for your time.

RACHEL SUTTON

1110½ Hay Street, Fayetteville, NC 28305 • preppub@aol.com • (910) 483-6611

OBJECTIVE

I want to contribute to an organization that can use a respected young massage therapist who offers experience in working with sports and trauma injuries.

CERTIFICATIONS

Certified Therapeutic **Massage and Bodywork Practitioner**
Member, Massage Therapy Association
Licensed by the State of Vermont and the city of Burlington to engage in the practice of therapeutic massage under the required business name "Sutton Corner."
Certified in CPR by American Red Cross.

EDUCATION

Graduated from the 525-hour massage therapy program, Champlain College, Burlington, VT, 2000; was cited for professionalism and high personal standards and ethics.
* Completed course work which included these areas of emphasis:
   Core curriculum: Anatomy and Physiology, Communications and Somatics, Swedish Massage, Sports Massage, and Deep Muscle Massage
   Secondary modalities: Joint Movement, Polarity, Lymphatic Drainage, and Introduction to Oriental bodywork
   Supportive curriculum: Business Practices, Hydrotherapy, Introduction to Touch, Observation and Analysis, Pathology, and Sensory/Motor Development

AFFILIATION

Board Member (Secretary), Burlington Massage Therapy Association

EXPERIENCE

LICENSED MASSAGE THERAPIST. Sutton Corner, Burlington, VT (2000-present). As the owner and founder of this business, handle all business functions in addition to providing professional massage services integrated with the different modalities depending on muscle needs. Provide massage to clients in various situations—some recovering from an accident, some with chronic muscular problems, and some who just want relaxation and stress relief.
* Have worked with various organizations and companies in these areas:
Sports massage clientele: For the Burlington Trackers Football Team, am in my second season of providing professional massage therapist services; work with the players before home games and occasionally in between the games.
Chiropractic clientele: For the Andrew Chiropractic Center, work as needed on accident victims and patients with chronic muscular problems experiencing aches and pains; have gained experience in working with patients who have insurance coverage for massage treatment. For the Burlington Family Chiropractic Center, provide massage therapy for insurance patients who were accident victims, and assist chiropractor in writing narratives.
Salon clientele: For a prominent hair and nail salon, provide massage for relaxation.
Spa clientele: For the Family Day Spa, work in the Massage Center; provide massages, facials, hot herbal bodywraps, and body polishing while also creating fliers and brochures describing the spa's services.

TEACHER'S ASSISTANT. Auburn Area Schools, Northfield, VT (1996-99). Displayed initiative while assisting teachers and filling in for absent teachers.

Other experience: Excelled in jobs as a Receptionist, Retail Assistant Manager, and Property Manager before deciding to embark upon a career in the message therapy field.

PERSONAL

Highly reliable individual who works well with medical professionals at all levels. Have a knack for reading and understanding others so that I can help them.

Date

Exact Name of Person
Title or Position
Name of Company
Address (no., street)
Address (city, state, zip)

OUTDOOR ACTIVITIES
INSTRUCTOR

Dear Exact Name of Person: (or Dear Sir or Madam if answering a blind ad):

With the enclosed resume, I would like to make you aware of my interest in exploring employment opportunities with your organization. I am aware of the fine reputation of your Wilderness Program, and I would like to explore the possibility of becoming associated with it.

As you will see from my resume, I hold a B.A. in Environmental Education and a Minor in communication and wilderness leadership from the University of Nevada. In numerous internships while earning my degree, I refined my ability to develop new programs, recruit and train participants, and assure the safety of people involved in strenuous outdoor activities. I am very proud of the fact that there has never been a single serious injury of anyone involved in programs which I have supervised. I am well known for my total commitment to safety at all times.

In my current position with Northwest Outdoor School, I provide logistical organization of 22-day mountaineering courses which involves organizing back country resupplies, coordinating staff pairings, reviewing student backgrounds, and dividing students into patrols in conjunction with instructor teams.

In previous employment, I worked as an instructor at the University of Nevada in the Wilderness Orientation Program and I planned and taught a 22-day raft trip down the Colorado River.

I hope you will call or write me soon to suggest a time convenient for us to meet to discuss your current and future needs. Thank you in advance for you time.

Sincerely yours,

William Nelson

WILLIAM NELSON

1110½ Hay Street, Fayetteville, NC 28305 • preppub@aol.com • (910) 483-6611

OBJECTIVE   To give quality instruction in the field of outdoor education and to teach a wide variety of introspective learners. To implement certain values of environmental education, leadership, and communication into my teaching and facilitation of course work and curriculum. To provide leadership, solid communication and judgement in the positions of coordinator or director for outdoor and environmentally based programs.

OUTDOOR   White Water Rafting, Class IV and V   Orienteering
SKILLS   Mountaineering   Glacier Travel
&   Rock Climbing, 5.8-5.9 Leader   Crevasse Rescue
TRAINING   Mountain Search and Rescue   Backpacking

INTERPERSONAL Interpersonal Communication/Counseling   Teaching
SKILLS &   Experiential Education   Group Processing
TRAINING   Working with Youth Conflict Resolution

EXPERIENCE   *Northwest Outdoor School, Bozeman, MT (2000-present)*: Handle multiple roles:
CHIEF INSTRUCTOR. (2004-present). Provide logistical organization of 22-day mountaineering courses; organize back country resupplies and staff pairings; review student backgrounds and divide students into patrols in conjunction with instructor teams.
- Provide field support for staff with course-related activities, student issues, and Outward Bound policies and operating procedures.

INSTRUCTOR. (2000-present). Work in diverse program areas: Ascent, 22-day mountaineering courses for youth at risk; Leadership, 22-day mountaineering courses for motivated teens; Standard 22-, 14-, and 8-day courses for adults; Venture, 22- and 14-day courses for teens.
- Instruct fundamentals of expedition travel in river and mountain settings.
- Facilitate group living skills, teamwork, and communication.
- Set up challenging outdoor activities for students and foster care for the environment.

Highlights of other education/instruction experience:
EDUCATION PROGRAM INSTRUCTOR. Adventure Center, Billings, MT (1999). Instructed and facilitated groups in environmental education and adventure-based activities, including caving, orienteering, teams challenge courses and low ropes, traditional evening programs, and outreach.
- Trained and supervised high school camp counselors, gave school presentations, and led teams in course and awareness activities; facilitated mobile team challenge courses and traditional programming.

INSTRUCTOR. Community College of Southern Nevada, North Las Vegas, NV (1996-98). Taught Wilderness Orientation, an introductory course at Community College of Southern Nevada; conducted rigorous three-week backpacking treks through canyons and mountains in Nevada. Focused on wilderness living skills, expedition travel, introduction to the southwest, and philosophy of Community College of Southern Nevada..

EDUCATION   **B.A., Environmental Education**. Minors in: communication and wilderness leadership,
&   University of Nevada-Las Vegas, Las Vegas, NV, 1996.
TRAINING   Have participated in numerous training programs that comply with teaching and instructing in both the Environmental and Outdoor Education Fields.

Date

Exact Name of Person
Title or Position
Name of Company
Address (no., street)
Address (city, state, zip)

PERSONAL FITNESS TRAINER

Dear Exact Name of Person: (or Dear Sir or Madam if answering a blind ad):

With the enclosed resume, I would like to make you aware of my interest in exploring employment opportunities with your organization.

As you will see from my resume, I am currently employed by Gold's Gym as a Personal Fitness Trainer. I am AAFA Certified, with nearly three years experience in overseeing fitness assessment, implementing programs, and performing consultations.

While attending Thomas Edison State College, I was highly involved in sports and was named co-captain of the National Champ Cross Country Team. I was also a specially selected member of the U.S. Developmental Cycling Team at the Essex County College.

Even though I originally became certified as a Fitness Trainer as a means of making a living and putting myself through college, I have truly bonded to the field and wish to make a career in some sports-related organization. I am certain that my Bachelor of Science degree in Communication would allow me to contribute in creative and managerial ways to an organization such as yours.

I hope you will call or write me soon to suggest a time convenient for us to meet to discuss your current and future needs. Thank you in advance for you time.

Sincerely yours,

Patrick Ferguson

PATRICK FERGUSON

1110½ Hay Street, Fayetteville, NC 28305 • preppub@aol.com • (910) 483-6611

OBJECTIVE   To offer exemplary personal attributes, extensive technical knowledge, and professional commitment to an organization that can use an experienced personal fitness trainer.

EDUCATION   **Bachelor of Science** in Communications with a concentration in Media Advertising and a minor in Marketing, Essex County College, Newark, NJ, May 2004.
Honors:
Dean's List, 2 semesters
Selected as member of U.S. Developmental Cycling Team
Graduated with 3.2 GPA
Related course work:

Public Speaking	Writing for Radio and TV
Journalism	Broadcast Production
Social Psychology	Desktop Publishing (IBM and Macintosh)
Consumer Behavior	Management/Sales

Advertising Practicum: Newark Convention & Visitor's Bureau, Newark, NJ (2000-01). Communicated, researched, created, and implemented an exciting ad campaign.

Completed **Associate of Arts degree**, Thomas Edison State College, Trenton, NJ, 2001.
Honors:
Dean's List, 3 semesters
Co-captain of National Champ Cross Country Team
Graduated 3.1 GPA

CERTIFICATION   Certified Personal Fitness Trainer, National Association of Certified Fitness Trainers, since 1999.
Completed ACE Personal Training Certificate, 2001.

EXPERIENCE   **PERSONAL FITNESS TRAINER.** Gold's Gym, Newark, NJ (2000-Present). Am an AAFA Certified Fitness Trainer with 2 1/2 years experience overseeing fitness assessment, implementing programs, and performing consultations.
- Have become skilled at varying my approach to fitness training, depending on the age and agility of the customer.
- Utilize a variety of diagnostic tools in performing fitness assessments.
- On my own initiative, developed a fitness workout that allows me to correctly diagnose potential cardiac problems.
- Developed a new program for seniors which nearly doubled the membership of this gym.

MEDIA MARKETING COORDINATOR. Cycletown, Newark, NJ (1999-00). Handled responsibilities for advertising sales, public relations events, and advertising development.
- Developed a new account which turned out to be the biggest-ever account for this organization.

COUNSELOR. Camp Rosemount, Lakewood, NJ (Summer 1998). Ensured a challenging, fun, Christian, and safe learning and growing environment.

PERSONAL   Outstanding references available upon request.

Date

Exact Name of Person
Exact Title
Exact Name of Company
Address
City, State, Zip

PERSONAL TRAINER   Dear Exact Name of Person (or Dear Sir or Madam if answering a blind ad):

With the enclosed resume, I would like to make you aware of my interest in exploring employment opportunities with your organization as a Personal Trainer. I have recently relocated to your area and am seeking an organization that can use my experience and credentials as a Personal Trainer.

In my previous employment in Hawaii, I worked in two jobs simultaneously. In one position as a Personal Trainer at a fitness center with 2,000 employees, I was the center's only female Personal Trainer and I rapidly cultivated a loyal clientele. I helped all my clients make significant improvements in fitness: all lost body fat ranging from 22% to 30%, most lost inches, and one quit smoking and adopted a healthier lifestyle. In addition to acting as a Personal Trainer, I also handled front desk and customer service responsibilities, and I became known for my gracious style of interacting with the public. In a simultaneous part-time at a facility, I worked as a Supplement Specialist as I prepared health drinks and protein shakes and sold supplements. The owner of the facility relied on me to open and close the facility when he was out of town or otherwise unavailable.

A Certified Fitness Trainer, I have studied with Amy Stuart and Morgan Ivey. I am currently completing the ACE Personal Training Certificate and have finished the Nutrition portion of that certificate.

You would find me in person to be a vivacious, outgoing individual who takes great pride in helping customers and co-workers. Known for my strong personal initiative and total reliability, I am a team player who understands the importance of working hard to ensure my employer's success and profitability.

I am confident that I could become a valuable asset to your organization, and I hope you will contact me if you can use a dedicated young Personal Trainer. I can provide outstanding personal and professional references from all previous employers as well as from my clients.

Yours sincerely,

Laverna Quinn

LAVERNA QUINN

1110½ Hay Street, Fayetteville, NC 28305　　•　　preppub@aol.com　　•　　(910) 483-6611

OBJECTIVE　　I want to contribute to an organization that can use a vibrant and enthusiastic young professional who offers strong sales and customer skills along with technical knowledge related to fitness, personal training, and nutrition.

EXPERIENCE　　**PERSONAL TRAINER & SUPPLEMENT SPECIALIST.** Gold's Gym and The Fitness Coral, Honolulu, HI (2002-04). Worked in these two part-time jobs simultaneously:

Personal Trainer, Gold's Gym. Was the only female personal trainer at this fitness center and gym catering to more than 2,000 members in a diversified community.

- Rapidly built up a regular clientele after only a few months; worked with females most of whom were aged 26-39. Also worked with elderly clients with various physical challenges. Provided fitness training to one client who gave up smoking and adopted a healthier lifestyle.
- All clients showed significant improvements: all lost body fat ranging from 22% to 30%, most lost inches, and one quit smoking and adopted a healthier lifestyle.
- Taught clients how to utilize a wide range of tools for personal fitness which included Hammerstrength, Cybex, Body Master, free weights, aerobics, saunas, and tanning beds.
- Handled front desk responsibilities which included answering the phone, making appointments for tanning and other services, signing membership contracts, and showing the facilities to prospective customers.
- Earned respect for my gracious manner of dealing with people, including customers with complaints.

Supplement Specialist, The Fitness Coral: Worked part-time as a Supplement Specialist at a facility which served a clientele that was 80% male; I prepared health drinks, protein shakes, and sold supplements.

- Became a valued employee, and was entrusted with the responsibility of opening and closing the facility on Saturdays and when the owner was out of town.

PHOTOGRAPHER'S ASSISTANT. Forever Photos, Honolulu, HI (2001-02). Traveled extensively to dozens of schools in HI to provide assistance to a professional photographer working under contract at schools to take formal photographs of high school students for yearbooks and other purposes. Photographed senior proms and other events.

- While working in the office, performed extensive telemarketing; set up appointments and sold various packages. Was entrusted with handling up to $4,000 in cash.

FRAGRANCE MODEL & SALES REPRESENTATIVE. (Part-time). Polo and Chanel, Nordstrom and Gottschalks Department Stores, Honolulu, HI (2001-03). Worked part-time at two of the city's most respected fashion stores as I represented the products of Polo and Chanel. Hired other fragrance models and trained them in all aspects of their jobs.

EDUCATION　　Completed one year of college studies in math and science, Hawaiian Pacific University, Honolulu, HI, 2000-01.

Graduated from Luau Senior High School, Honolulu, HI, 2000.

CERTIFICATION　　Certified Fitness Trainer, National Association of Certified Fitness Trainers.

- Studied with Amy Stuart, Vice President, and Morgan Ivey, President.

Currently completing the ACE Personal Training Certificate; have finished the Nutrition Supplement portion of the training.

PERSONAL　　Outstanding personal and professional references upon request.

CAREER CHANGE

Date

Exact Name of Person
Title or Position
Name of Company
Address (no., street)
Address (city, state, zip)

PHYSICAL EDUCATION TEACHER

Dear Exact Name of Person: (or Dear Sir or Madam if answering a blind ad.)

I would appreciate an opportunity to talk with you soon about how I could contribute to your organization through my superior motivational, leadership, and communication skills as well as my reputation as a mature and adaptable young professional.

As you will see from my enclosed resume, I am pursuing a degree in Elementary Education and have held summer jobs and volunteer positions in which I mentored and coached young people in settings including a college dormitory, high school sports team, and church camp. During several summers at a church-sponsored youth camp, I was effective in relating to the participants and provided a positive role model. More recently I volunteered as a coach for an American high school in Turkey where I worked with the cross country teams and used my academic prowess as well as my natural leadership skills to help them work together.

I have just completed four years of service with the U.S. Army and was consistently singled out for my performance as an Intelligence Analyst. I received several medals and awards for my professionalism, dedication to excellence, and ability to exceed expectations in demanding, time-sensitive environments filled with pressure.

Through my education, experience in working with people of many nationalities, and reputation as a fast learner, I have become known as a dedicated, mature, and articulate professional. I enjoy working with people and finding ways to help them grow and mature, and I believe I would be especially effective in positions where counseling and training others would be the prime goal.

I hope you will call or write me soon to suggest a time convenient for us to meet and discuss your current and future needs and how I might serve them. Thank you in advance for your time.

Sincerely,

Annie McDonald

ANNIE McDONALD

1110½ Hay Street, Fayetteville, NC 28305 • preppub@aol.com • (910) 483-6611

OBJECTIVE

To offer superior motivational, leadership, and communication skills along with a reputation as a self-disciplined and adaptable young professional to an organization that will benefit from my customer service orientation and ability to help and set an example for others.

EDUCATION

Completing a bachelor's degree in **Physical Education,** Jefferson Community College, Watertown, NY. Completed extensive coursework in Elementary Education.
- Contributed to the success of the college's cross country team and participated in indoor and outdoor track events where individual abilities were showcased.

Earned an A.A. degree, Liberal Studies, Dona Ana Branch Community College, Las Cruces, NM, 1991.

EXPERIENCE

Earned a reputation as an intelligent, mature, and reliable individual who could be counted on to give unselfishly to team efforts or individual tasks as an INTELLIGENCE ANALYST in the U.S. Army:

Ft. Drum, NY (2004-present). Recognized for my outstanding performance and dedication to excellence, was awarded a commendation medal for "exceptionally meritorious service" and technical knowledge.
- Awarded an achievement medal for athletic accomplishments which included being the fastest female in the 10th Mountain's ten-mile race. Was selected to compete at the 2004 All-Army Track Team Trials (for the second time) where I placed in the top five participants.
- Contribute time and efforts which made the Ft. Drum Vacation Bible School a success by demonstrating patience and my love for children while planning games and recreational activities.

Germany (2003). Was singled out for special assignments and praised for my technical knowledge and attention to detail while examining information and preparing reports.
- Selected to provide support during a four-month assignment with a special task force, was awarded a commendation medal in recognition of my dedication which increased the quality of intelligence information by preparing weekly briefings, providing data base analysis and seeing that information was disseminated to the appropriate personnel.
- Received Joint Service Achievement Medals for my achievements and contributions during task force operations in 2003.
- Earned the respect of school administrators for my volunteer work as a cross country team coach, mentor, and counselor at the American high school.

Ft. Richardson, AK (2001-03). Was recognized as a thoroughly knowledgeable technician while keeping management personnel and executives constantly updated on the latest information available to them so they could make correct decisions.

Gained experience in counseling, customer service, and project coordination in part-time and summer jobs in high school and then while financing my college education:

RESIDENT ASSISTANT. Jefferson Community College, Watertown, NY (1998-00). Provided guidance and supervision for dormitory activities for 20 female students.
- Was recognized as Resident Assistant of the Year for 2000.

CAMP COUNSELOR. Little Foot Summer Camp, Gallup, NM (summer 1995-00). Gained self-confidence in my ability to counsel and serve as a leader and example for campers while contributing my skills in several areas: as a lifeguard and medic while leading sports activities.

PERSONAL

Offer additional versatile skills including qualification as a sharpshooter and parachutist.

Date

Exact Name of Person
Title or Position
Exact Name of Company
Address (no., street)
Address (city, state, zip)

PHYSICAL EDUCATION TEACHER SEEKING POSITION IN ATHLETIC ADMINISTRATION

Dear Exact Name of Person: (or Dear Sir or Madam if answering a blind ad):

With the enclosed resume, I am making formal application for the position of Coordinator, Physical Education and Intramural Sports, for the Lexington Public School System.

As you will see from my resume, I recently completed my master's degree in Educational Administration. With a Teaching Certification in Physical Education and a Certification in Educational Administration, I offer extensive technical expertise in athletic administration.

Prior to earning my master's degree, I excelled as a Physical Education Teacher in the Lexington Public School System. I planned, implemented, and coordinated fitness programs and field days while acting as a resource to principals and teachers. As a Physical Education Teacher, I applied for and received a grant from the Junior League which enabled me to organize a PTA Family Walking Project as well as a 6th grade Walking Project that became the subject of a newspaper article. On my own initiative, I organized Fitness Clubs for jump rope, muscle development, and cardiovascular improvement through jogging.

Although I have extensive expertise in physical education, I feel that my strongest personal qualities are my leadership, initiative, and resourcefulness. For example, as a Teacher Assistant at Anderson Elementary School, I played a key role in organizing county and state organizations for teacher assistants and served as President of the Lexington Teacher Assistant Association for two years. I also served as President of the Lexington Junior High School PTA.

A hard worker known for perseverance, creativity, and a cheerful attitude, I sincerely love physical activities and have coached baseball, soccer, and flag football.

Please give me the opportunity to show you in person that I am the energetic, imaginative, and dedicated professional you are seeking. I can provide outstanding personal and professional references which will attest to my strong desire to contribute to the Lexington School System as its Coordinator of Physical Education and Intramural Sports.

Sincerely yours,

Renee Sanders

RENEE SANDERS

1110½ Hay Street, Fayetteville, NC 28305　•　preppub@aol.com　•　(910) 483-6611

OBJECTIVE　To serve the Lexington School System as its Coordinator, Physical Education and Intramural, through my proven abilities related to planning, implementing, and managing fitness programs while serving as a resource professional to teachers, principals, and staff.

EDUCATION　**Master of Arts in Education** majoring in Educational Administration, University of Kentucky, Lexington, KY, 2003.
Bachelor of Science in Physical Education, *Cum Laude,* University of Kentucky, 1999.
- Named to Kappa Chi Honor Society and Dean's List and inducted into *Who's Who Among Students in American Universities and Colleges.*
- Was President and Vice-President, Physical Education & Recreation Majors Club. Excelled in continuing education (CEU) courses offered by Lexington to enhance teaching skills: Cooperative Learning, Mastery Learning, and Elements of Instruction.

CERTIFICATIONS Teaching Certification in Physical Education and Certification in Educational Administration.

HIGHLIGHTS
OF
ATHLETIC
ADMINISTRATION
KNOWLEDGE
- Selected in 2003 as District Representative for Physical Education Committee which involved working with Lexington Board and fellow PE teachers.
- Invited to serve on the Family Health Committee.
- In 1999, received Athletic Scholarship Award, based on a vote of the Health, Physical Education, and Recreation Department, University of Kentucky.
- Worked as a coach and assisted in organizing University of Kentucky Wrestling and All Sports Summer Camp.

EXPERIENCE　**PHYSICAL EDUCATION TEACHER** (1999-present) & **PHYSICAL EDUCATION GRADUATE ASSISTANT** (2003-present). Southview Elementary School, Lexington, KY. Plan and implement programs of instruction in physical education while advising the principal on health/recreational matters.
- Have been commended for my innovative ideas while assisting teachers in planning and implementing lessons that reinforce physical education concepts; contribute to students' understanding of "a sound mind in a sound body."
- Act as Judge for Lexington's Super Fitness Field Day.
- Organize school field days; selected to attend State Wellness Workshops.
- Develop and organize 10-week Wellness Workshops for school/CEU credit.
- Applied for and received a grant from the Junior League; used the money to organize a 6th grade Walking Project which was the subject of a newspaper article.
- Organize Fitness Clubs for jump rope, muscle development, and jogging.
- Participate in Physical Education Mall Demonstration Week; organize PTA programs to promote physical education.
- In my spare time, coach T-ball and Peewee baseball teams, flag football, and soccer.

GRADUATE ASSISTANT. University of Kentucky, Lexington, KY (2003-04). Gained valuable experience working in the university environment while serving my assistantship.
- Assisted in coordinating and planning the Teaching Fellows Program.

OTHER
HONORS
&
AFFILIATIONS
- Served as President, Lexington Junior High School PTA
- Board Member and Secretary, Lexington Youth Association
- Kentucky Association of Educators
- Kentucky Association of Physical Education, Recreation, and Dance
- Current Member of University of Kentucky Teaching Fellows Advisory Committee

Date

Exact Name of Person
Title or Position
Name of Company
Address (no., street)
Address (city, state, zip)

**PROFESSIONAL
BASEBALL PITCHER.**

Dear Exact Name of Person: (or Dear Sir or Madam if answering a blind ad.)

I would appreciate an opportunity to talk with you soon about I could contribute to your organization through my versatile management experience and proven ability to find methods for improving productivity.

You will see from my resume that, during my time as a junior military officer in the U.S. Air Force, I have advanced in the field of transportation management and recreation management at Hill AFB, UT. In my current job I manage a $2.2 million annual operating budget while developing mobility plans and ensuring that when these plans are followed, personnel and equipment will be quickly loaded and transported wherever they are needed worldwide. In earlier jobs as a Vehicle Maintenance Manager and Transportation Operations Manager, I became known for my ability to locate sources for hard-to-find items and procure them at substantial cost savings.

You would find me to be a dynamic leader who easily takes my place as a manager and dedicated team member. I am a very athletically inclined and physically fit individual who has been active in sports as a player and as a coach for Little League and adult industrial league baseball teams. In 2000 I was a 29th round draft pick by the Seattle Mariners and was considered a key player in one farm team's league winning season as a pitcher with a 3.98 ERA. The War on Terrorism ended my playing career, however. I had financed my college career as a member of the National Guard and was called into active duty. I served with distinction in Iraq, and I am proud to have had the opportunity to serve my country.

I am confident that I could make valuable contributions to your organization, too, through my track record of success and reputation for integrity and honesty.

I hope you will welcome my call soon to arrange a brief meeting at your convenience to discuss your current and future needs and how I might serve them. Thank you in advance for your time.

Sincerely yours,

Phillip Riley

PHILLIP RILEY

1110½ Hay Street, Fayetteville, NC 28305　　•　　preppub@aol.com　　•　　(910) 483-6611

OBJECTIVE　　To benefit an organization that can use a dynamic, articulate, and aggressive leader who has excelled in managing people, services, and finances through creatively applying my problem-solving and motivational skills as well as my ability to build a winning team.

EDUCATION & TRAINING

College: Earned a **B.S.B.A. degree,** The University of Iowa, Iowa City, IA, 2000.
- Was honored as an **All-American in baseball** for 1999 and 2000: led the league in wins and strikeouts, and had the lowest earned run average (ERA).
- Set a **national collegiate record as a pitcher**: struck out 22 hitters in one game and had one "no hitter" during the 2000 season.
- During my senior year, was **captain** of the college's varsity baseball team.

Military: Excelled as a student at the Air Force's 398-hour program for transportation managers as well as in instructional techniques, team problem solving, and quality awareness.

EXPERIENCE　　*Advanced in the field of recreation management, U.S. Air Force, Hill AFB, UT, and Iraq:*

RECREATION OPERATIONS MANAGER. (2004-present). Managed a $2.2 million operating budget while in charge of developing and overseeing recreational programs for military professionals and their families on military bases in eight states.

VEHICLE MAINTENANCE MANAGER. (2002-03). During the War on Terrorism, was deployed to Iraq for nine months. Earned promotion to this job which involved the management of, and budgeting for, in excess of $20 million worth of vehicles, facilities, and equipment including 527 vehicles with a total value over $15 million; managed 45 people.
- Evaluated as an aggressive manager, was the force behind improvements including cutting in half the number of vehicles unavailable while waiting for parts.
- Significantly increased vehicle availability to 92.9%—3% above Air Force standards.
- Coordinated with officials to set up a joint program which brought civilian job training students to the base and gave the unit 576 additional man hours a month.
- Applied my creativity to find sources for hard-to-obtain equipment: saved $34,000 on aircraft towing tractor tires and $15,000 on flight suits to replace worn-out coveralls.

RECREATION OPERATIONS MANAGER. (2001-02). Evaluated as "a quality performer who quickly grasps management principles and concepts," was soon promoted to a position supervising 30 employees.
- Provided the leadership to personnel who processed and moved more than 21,000 line items weighing more than 17 tons.

PITCHER. Seattle Mariners, various locations (2000-01). Was drafted by the Seattle Mariners out of college. Learned to contribute to team efforts while playing an important role in the league championship: had the third lowest ERA in the league with a 7-3 record.
- Advanced within the Mariner's minor league organization and built a professional record of 15 wins and six losses with a 3.98 ERA and was a league leader in strikeouts and wins.
- Because I was in the National Guard, I was called into active duty to serve in the War on Terrorism in Iraq. This ended my professional baseball career.

PERSONAL　　Coached Little League; played/coached intramural golf, baseball, volleyball, and basketball. Placed second overall as one of six military personnel invited to participate in a civilian sports festival. Support community activities including blood drives.

Date

Exact Name of Person
Exact Title
Exact Name of Company
Address
City, State, Zip

**PROFESSIONAL
BASEBALL
PLAYER
& PITCHER.**

This individual is taking
careful aim at the Boston
Red Sox, the team for
which he really wants to
work.

Dear Exact Name of Person (or Dear Sir or Madam if answering a blind ad):

I would like to take this opportunity to make you aware of my desire to become a part of your pitching staff. I grew up in Boston, and it has long been my dream to become a part of the Red Sox organization.

As you will see from my enclosed resume, I received my B.S. in Recreational Management from Marywood University, Scranton, PA, which I attended on an athletic scholarship.

During spring semester 2004, I had the opportunity to work as the pitching coach for the college baseball team. That internship refined my abilities as a mentor, instructor, and role model as I played a major role in transforming an average pitching staff into one of the top ten college pitching staffs in the country.

Currently I am excelling as a Pitching Coach for a minor league team. I have helped pitchers refine their techniques related to the fast ball and curve ball, and I have helped pitchers acquire a solid third pitch--the change-up, slider, split-fingered fast ball, and screwball. Although I am held in high regard in my current position, it has long been my desire to become a part of the coaching staff of the Boston Red Sox, and I am confident that I can make a significant contribution to this great team.

You will notice that I was an award-winning athlete both at the college level and earlier in high school and was consistently named to All-Conference, All-State, and All-Region teams as well as being honored with the Best Pitcher Award two years in college. Through sports, I have learned how to compete, how to win, and how to persist.

If you can use a skilled pitching coach with the ability to help the Red Sox become the best pitching team in the country, I hope you will contact me to suggest a time when we might meet to discuss your needs.

Sincerely,

Scott McNeill

SCOTT McNEILL

1110½ Hay Street, Fayetteville, NC 28305 • preppub@aol.com • (910) 483-6611

OBJECTIVE   To contribute to an organization that can use an articulate young professional with exceptional leadership and human relations skills along with a talent for teaching and motivating others to improve their technical skills in every aspect of pitching.

EXPERIENCE   **PROFESSIONAL BASEBALL PITCHING COACH.** The Tacoma Lynx, Tacoma, WA (2004-present). Was recruited as a pitching coach for this minor league team.
- Helped pitchers refine their techniques related to the fast ball and curve ball. Taught pitches including the change-up, slider, split-fingered fast ball, and screwball.

Refined time management skills and gained experience in leadership and training in a college internship and in part-time jobs while attending college full time:
PITCHING COACH. Marywood University, Scranton, PA (2003-04). Applied my ability to mentor, instruct, train, and serve as a role model for others and was credited with turning an average pitching staff into one of the top ten in the country at the collegiate level.
- Was recognized by coaching personnel for my ability to tailor activities and my coaching style for each player's individual strengths and skills.
- Served as a model for players while encouraging them to improve their skills as well as their mental attitude so they could accomplish individual and team goals.
- Sharpened written communications skills producing a report each week for the head of the Recreation Department on what I had accomplished.
- Planned and scheduled daily activities so that players had the opportunity to work on their running and fielding skills on a regular basis.

EDUCATION   **College:**
Earned a **Bachelor of Science degree** in **Recreational Management**, Marywood University, Scranton, PA, 2003.
- Completed a program which included a 440-hour internship with an emphasis on the development of college baseball pitching staff workout plans and proper techniques for field maintenance.
- Assisted the baseball coach at Plainview High School in Scranton: this part of my course work allowed me to help high school players develop and improve skills.
- Participated in community service activities as a recipient of an athletic scholarship: coached and umpired for Scranton Boys and Girls Club baseball; served as captain of the college baseball team; and assisted ground crew members in field maintenance.
- As a senior, was All-Conference in baseball. As a junior, placed on the All-Conference team in baseball.
- As a sophomore, won the Best Pitcher Award and placed on the baseball All-Conference and All-Region teams. As a freshman, was recognized with the Best Pitcher Award and placed on the All-Conference and All-Region teams.

High school:
Graduated from J.B. Hall High School, Pittsburgh, PA, 1994.
- As a senior, earned honors including playing in the East-West All-Star Game and recognition on All-State, All-Conference, and All-Area baseball teams; was voted as Most Valuable Player; was recognized as an All-Conference player in basketball.
- As a junior, earned honors on the All-Conference, All-Area, and All-State baseball teams; was a Gold Medal recipient in State Games as a baseball player.
- Received 100 hours of training in business operations and computers.

PERSONAL   Thrive on challenges. Enjoy learning new ideas and ways to get things done.

Date

Exact Name of Person
Title or Position
Name of Company
Address (no., street)
Address (city, state, zip)

PROFESSIONAL SKI PATROLLER

Dear Exact Name of Person: (or Dear Sir or Madam if answering a blind ad):

With the enclosed resume, I would like to make you aware of my interest in exploring employment opportunities with your organization.

As you will see from my resume, I was a licensed as a Professional Ski Patroller by the National Ski Patrol. As a Professional Ski Patroller, I perform a wide variety of tasks related to keeping mountains skiable at this fast-growing resort near Anchorage. While working in this winter paradise, I have become knowledgeable of environmental issues regarding wildlife endangerment, air pollution, overpopulation, diminishing scarce resources, and the disposal of hazardous wastes and toxic substances.

Extensively trained in Search and Rescue with the National Association of Search and Rescue, I participate in avalanche patrols and work with explosives. I have refined my decision-making skills handling numerous emergencies, including organizing the medical rescue of a skier who broke his femur.

I hope you will call or write me soon to suggest a time convenient for us to meet to discuss your current and future needs. Thank you in advance for you time.

Sincerely yours,

Terry Samson

TERRY SAMSON

1110½ Hay Street, Fayetteville, NC 28305 • preppub@aol.com • (910) 483-6611

OBJECTIVE

To contribute my strong communication, management, and public relations skills to an organization that can use a versatile and energetic professional.

COLLEGE EDUCATION

Bachelor of Arts (B.A.) degree, Political Science and Political Philosophy, The Colorado College, Denver, CO, 2003.
- Was awarded a $1,000 scholarship to attend Fort Lewis College; worked every summer to finance my education.
- As a senior, took a graduate course in International Law.
- Was elected Senator, Student Government Association, freshman year.

HIGH SCHOOL EDUCATION

Graduated from Rocky Senior High School, Denver, CO, 2000.
- Was inducted into the Key Club, a service organization.
- Member, German Club.
- Member, Drama Club, and was chosen for several lead roles; gained a reputation as a talented public speaker, and was selected as Master of Ceremonies of the Miss Rockies Beauty Pageant.
- Played football freshman year; played soccer sophomore, junior, and senior years and was **All Conference** my junior and senior years.

LANGUAGE

Speak and read German with moderate ease

LICENSES

- National Registry of Emergency Medical Technicians (EMT)
- Winter Emergency Care Technician
- Completed the Tahoe Outdoor School, Mountaineering Course
- Professional Ski Patroller, licensed by National Ski Patrol, 2003
- Extensively trained in the Search and Rescue, National Association of Search and Rescue.

EXPERIENCE

PROFESSIONAL SKI PATROLLER. Alyeska Ski Resort, Girdwood, AK (2003-present). Am one of 28 ski patrollers who perform a wide variety of tasks related to keeping mountains skiable at this fast-growing resort near Anchorage.
- Participate in avalanche patrols and work with explosives as required.
- Have refined my decision-making skills handling numerous emergencies, including organizing the medical rescue of a skier who broke his femur.
- While working in this winter paradise, have become knowledgeable of environmental issues regarding wildlife endangerment, air pollution, overpopulation, diminishing scarce resources, and the disposal of hazardous wastes and toxic substances.

CARPENTER. Frontier Construction, Co., Denver, CO (Summers 2000-03). In summer jobs during college, worked in construction companies performing trim work, constructing concrete form, and setting reinforcing steel and wire.

SENIOR COUNSELOR. Creekfield Park Boys Summer Camp, Denver, CO (Summer 1999). At this 60-year-old boys camp on the Creekfield Park, supervised 14 boys full time.

LANDSCAPE TECHNICIAN/NURSING HOME WORKER. Rocky Mountain House Nursing Home, Denver, CO (Summers 1994-98). Worked on the grounds crew and in plant maintenance for a large medical facility with 7 1/2 acres of lawns.

PERSONAL

Congenial personality and desire to help others. Traveled extensively in Europe and Asia.

CAREER CHANGE

Date

Exact Name of Person
Title or Position
Name of Company
Address (no., street)
Address (city, state, zip)

Dear Exact Name of Person: (or Dear Sir or Madam if answering a blind ad.)

I would appreciate an opportunity to talk with you soon about how I could contribute to your organization through my education as well as my experience in working with abused and exceptional children. I am especially interested in becoming associated with the Special Olympics in some management capacity. I had the privilege of working as a volunteer with the Special Olympics for two summers while in college, and I feel I have much to offer this fine organization now that I possess a degree along with considerable sales and customer service experience.

As you will see from my resume, I am a recent graduate of Boise State University where I earned a B.A. degree in Psychology. I completed specialized courses including child development, personality, social psychology, the family and society, and exceptional children (autistic, learning disabled, and mentally challenged).

My actual experience with these children includes tutoring a child with reading disabilities and low self-esteem as well as working with another child who is autistic. Working with these children allowed me to help them through positive reinforcement and my strong wish to reach them. This experience enabled me to appreciate the advantages I grew up with and strengthened my desire to help others with special needs.

While a student at Boise State University, I volunteered through the Campus Corner service organization as Program Coordinator and Advocate. I cared for children whose parents were receiving counseling, helped set up a program in Twin Falls, conducted regular business and training meetings, and participated in presenting educational programs to local and campus groups.

I hope you will welcome my call soon to arrange a brief meeting at your convenience to discuss your current and future needs and how I might serve them. Thank you in advance for your time.

Sincerely yours,

Julia Barker

JULIA BAKER

1110½ Hay Street, Fayetteville, NC 28305   •   preppub@aol.com   •   (910) 483-6611

OBJECTIVE
I want to apply my "newly minted" degree in psychology, as well as my empathy and experience in relating to children and adolescents, to an organization that can use a mature and dependable young professional.

EDUCATION
B.A., Psychology, Boise State University, Boise, ID, 2004.
- Learned to manage time and coordinate a busy schedule while working a minimum of 20 hours a week to help pay for my college expenses as well as participating in numerous volunteer activities.
- Completed specialized course work including:

  family life and society   child development
  social psychology   personality
  exceptional children: autistic, learning disabled, and mentally challenged

Internship. Worked with two students in a Smith Elementary School program for "exceptional children."
- Provided positive reinforcement and feedback for a child with reading disabilities and low self-esteem. Worked closely with a crisis intervention counselor and supervised the schoolwork for an autistic child.
- Learned the importance of providing positive reinforcement at every opportunity when working with children with disabilities.

EXPERIENCE
ASSISTANT MANAGER. Soccer/Lacrosse Supply, Twin Falls, ID (2002-present). Polished my management, bookkeeping, and inventory control skills while overseeing numerous aspects of sales and operations.

RETAIL SALES ASSOCIATE. Wal-Mart, Twin Falls, ID (1999-2002). Excelled in providing outstanding customer service while handling daily functions including customer sales and service, inventory control, stocking, and closing out the register.
- Consistently received "superior" performance evaluations in every area.

Volunteer experience: Excelled in these positions in college, Boise, ID (2000-04).
PROGRAM COORDINATOR & ADVOCATE AND CARE GIVER. Campus Corner, Boise State University. Provided care for abused children while their parents attended counseling and conducted biweekly meetings to provide information to, and training for, volunteers.
- Gained a broad base of "hands-on" experience with abused children and became familiar with the types of situations they endured.
- Played a major role in setting up the program in Twin Falls. Was effective in passing my knowledge and observations on to less experienced workers in order to educate them.

MEMBERSHIP CHAIRMAN. Campus Corner, Boise State University. Refined my organizational skills through attention to the details of coordinating activities with 32 other committees. Handled the collection of, and accounting for, membership dues from approximately 750 students. Set up an automated system to simplify accounting.

VOLUNTEER, SPECIAL OLYMPICS. Excelled for two summers while working in entry-level roles with the Special Olympics.

PERSONAL
Am an enthusiastic and outgoing person. Have a desire to work with disadvantaged children and adolescents. Offer superior communication skills. Familiar with Excel and Word.

CAREER CHANGE

Date

Exact Name of Person
Exact Title
Exact Name of Company
Address
City, State, Zip

Dear Exact Name of Person (or Dear Sir or Madam if answering a blind ad):

With the enclosed resume, I would like to make you aware of my interest in exploring employment opportunities with your organization.

While earning my college degree in Interdisciplinary Studies, I worked part-time for four years in jobs which refined my counseling skills. As a Recreational Activities Coordinator with the Boys and Girls Club of America, I coordinated activities for kids aged 5-12 while also performing administrative tasks related to membership services. At two different camps, I worked with children challenged mentally and physically by afflictions such as cerebral palsy. I am skilled at organizing activities related to sports, fine arts, enrichment, and other areas.

I was a member of the National Guard Reserve during college, and I was called into active duty after graduation in order to participate in the War On Terrorism.

Most recently I have excelled in supervisory positions while serving in the U.S. Air Force. Promoted ahead of my peers to middle management, I managed eight employees in a section handling maintenance and production duties, and I became known as an outstanding motivator, supervisor, and counselor. Although the U.S. Air Force has aggressively recruited me to remain in military service, I decided to leave the U.S. Air Force and enter civilian employment. I am seeking a situation in which I can utilize my abilities to help, educate, and motivate others.

If my background and skills interest you, I hope you will contact me to suggest a time when we could meet in person to discuss your needs. Thank you.

Yours sincerely,

Dylan Lund

DYLAN LUND

1110½ Hay Street, Fayetteville, NC 28305 • preppub@aol.com • (910) 483-6611

OBJECTIVE   I want to contribute to an organization that can use a skilled manager of people, financial resources, and physical assets who offers a proven ability to produce outstanding results through applying my strong planning, organizational, and leadership abilities.

EDUCATION   **Bachelor of Arts (B.A.)** degree in Interdisciplinary Studies, South Dakota State University, Brookings, SD, 2002. Was a member of the Air Force National Guard.
- Completed numerous courses in Management and Business Administration.
- Excelled academically with a 3.5 GPA.

Completed numerous leadership development and technical courses sponsored by the U.S. Air Force; received training in production operations, maintenance management, quality assurance, hazardous materials control.

Graduated from Brookings Senior High School, Brookings, SD, 1997; ran cross country (named All-Conference for three years) and track.

COMPUTERS   Utilize computer software including Microsoft Word, PowerPoint, and Excel.

EXPERIENCE   **SECTION CHIEF.** U.S. Air Force (2004-present). Manage up to eight maintenance technicians who are members of a crew which maintains and operates equipment used in military training projects.
- Was promoted ahead of my peers to the rank of E-5 and was aggressively recruited to remain in military service; I have decided, however, to leave the military and enter the civilian work force.
- Accounted for an inventory of equipment which includes cannons and military equipment.
- Refined my supervisory skills in the process of training, motivating, and managing multiple employees.
- On an continuous basis, resolved numerous problems related to maintenance management; have earned a reputation as a resourceful problem solver.

MAINTENANCE TECHNICIAN. U.S. Air Force (2002-04). Was called into active duty after college graduation. After excelling in several months of training related to production management, was chosen for a job as part of a maintenance crew.

RECREATIONAL ACTIVITIES COORDINATOR. Boys and Girls Club of America, Brookings, SD (1997-02). Worked up to 20 hours a week while in college and was involved in coordinating after school activities for kids 5-12; organized games, sports, and other activities. On the weekend, worked in membership services.

COUNSELOR. Rapid City Parks & Recreation, Rapid City, SD (summer 1999). During one summer while in college, worked with impaired children in a camp environment.

COUNSELOR. Camp Holmes, Vermillion, SD (summer 1998). Worked with kids aged 5-12 who were mentally and physically challenged because of cerebral palsy and similar afflictions. Coordinated sports, nature, and fine arts activities.

PERSONAL   Received several medals and awards while serving in military service. Can provide outstanding references on request.

Exact Name of Person
Title or Position
Name of Company
Address (no., street)
Address (city, state, zip)

RECREATION ASSISTANT

Dear Exact Name of Person: (or Dear Sir or Madam if answering a blind ad):

With the enclosed resume, I would like to make you aware of my interest in exploring employment opportunities with your organization.

Currently a Recreation Assistant at the Family Center, I monitor daily operations of a recreation center and restaurant. I inspect equipment and food items to ensure optimum conditions while planning programs, activities, decorations, and menus for special events. Public relations is my responsibility, and I provide the community with information about upcoming events. On my own initiative, I have enabled my organization to secure extensive free advertising and public service announcements.

An experienced and reliable professional, I would like to explore the possibility of using my management, supervisory, and administrative skills to benefit your organization. Although I am held in high regard by my current organization and am being groomed for further advancement, I have decided to selectively investigate opportunities in other organizations which can use an ambitious individual who enjoys the challenge of handling multiple tasks.

I hope you will call or write me soon to suggest a time convenient for us to meet to discuss your current and future needs. Thank you in advance for you time.

Sincerely yours,

Abigail Curtis

ABIGAIL CURTIS

1110½ Hay Street, Fayetteville, NC 28305 • preppub@aol.com • (910) 483-6611

OBJECTIVE   To use my management, supervisory, and administrative skills to benefit an organization in need of an experienced, reliable professional with a proven ability to handle multiple tasks.

EXPERIENCE   **RECREATION ASSISTANT.** The Family Center, Providence, RI (2004-present). Monitor the daily operations of a recreation center and restaurant.
- Plan programs, activities, decorations, and menus for special events/ banquets; provide the community with information about upcoming events.
- Inspect equipment and food items to ensure optimum conditions.
- Inventory stock, assist with inventory report, and order over $1,000 monthly in items for the restaurant/recreation center programs.
- Fill out daily activity reports on cash flow, verify cash register receipts, make deposits, and secure the building.
- Supervise and train snack bar employees and cashiers.
- Act as chairman of the Christmas Bazaar, coordinating with 50 vendors and collecting and accounting for more than $36,000.

EMERGENCY RELIEF ASSISTANT. Providence Family Services Center, Providence, RI (2002-03). Coordinated office operations while assisting clients to schedule appointments and fill out paperwork to receive loans.
- Maintained files. Credited payments and kept a monthly record of payments received.

SUMMER SCHOOL DIRECTOR. New Port YMCA, New Port, RI (2000-02). In this elected position, organized a campaign to get more parents and youth involved in after-school programs and created all activities for all age groups.
- Researched the costs of programs, materials, special trips, and menus and purchased supplies, staying within budgetary guidelines.
- Raised funds from community members through a public relations campaign.
- Recruited and trained employees and volunteers.

ADMINISTRATOR & HOUSEPARENT. House of Care, New Port, RI (1998-99). Performed custodial and administrative duties in caring for 10 foster children for the state; provided round-the-clock care.
- Instructed children to perform daily chores, prepare meals, and develop good personal hygiene habits; aided in homework and crafts.
- Assessed behavior, emotional needs, and conduct in a variety of environments to prepare monthly progress reports on each child.
- Met with each child's social worker to chart the best plan for progress.
- Managed the facility's financial operations, tracking bank deposits and withdrawals and documenting all gifts received.
- Drafted proposals to board members for special projects.

TRAINING   Attended Johnson and Wales University, Providence, RI (1990-91) and Rhode Island College, Providence, RI (1997-98). Have completed a course in desktop computers, learning the basics of Word, Adobe PageMaker, and Microsoft software.

PERSONAL   Am a detail-oriented hard worker. Enjoy working with the public.

Date

Exact Name of Person
Title or Position
Name of Company
Address (no., street)
Address (city, state, zip)

**RECREATION BOARD
CHAIRMAN**

Dear Exact Name of Person: (or Dear Sir or Madam if answering a blind ad.)

I would appreciate an opportunity to talk with you soon about how I could contribute to your organization through my experience and personal qualities.

As you will see from my resume, I have earned a BS in Leisure Systems Studies with a concentration in Community Recreation. As you will see from my resume, I offer administrative and programming skills which would benefit any recreation program.

In my current position as Recreation Board Chairman, I schedule and oversee programs for the Nelson Schools and provide area children with quality organized leisure activities. I plan, organize, and supervise intramural basketball and softball leagues, and I am accustomed to the discipline of working within a strict budget.

In my previous position, I programmed and provided age-related activities to increase the cognitive and social skills of children K-2 which included arts and crafts, games, events, and special projects. Part of my job was to account for all financial transactions, and I have earned a reputation for "attention to detail."

I hope you will call or write me soon to suggest a time convenient for us to meet and discuss your current and future needs and how I might serve them. Thank you in advance for your time.

Sincerely yours,

Bryan Reese

BRYAN REESE

1110½ Hay Street, Fayetteville, NC 28305 • preppub@aol.com • (910) 483-6611

OBJECTIVE
To benefit an organization that can use an enthusiastic young professional who offers strong expertise in public recreation, management, and customer service.

EDUCATION & TRAINING
Bachelor of Science degree in Leisure Systems Studies with a concentration in Community Recreation, University of West Alabama, Livingston, AL, 2002.
Hold certification in CPR and First Aid, Underwater Scuba Training I; received programming exposure to arts and crafts as well as weight training and the weight room.
Graduated from Little Rock High School, Little Rock, AR.
• Received varsity sports letters in tennis and wrestling.

EXPERIENCE
RECREATION BOARD CHAIRMAN & RECREATION COORDINATOR. Nelson Area Schools, Livingston, AL (2004-present). Schedule and oversee programs for the Nelson Schools and provide area children with quality organized leisure activities.
• Plan, organize, and supervise sports, arts and crafts, and special programs, including the intramural basketball and softball leagues.
• Conduct board meetings.
• Plan and work within a strict budget.

DIRECTOR/PROGRAM MANAGER. SunShine, Livingston, AL (2003). Programmed and provided age-related activities to increase the cognitive and social skills of children K-2 which included arts and crafts, games, events, and special projects.
• Provided weekly lesson plans and master schedules for staff; organized staff-parent activities that promote parented involvement.
• Accounted for all financial transactions and completed ledger statements.

RECREATION ASSISTANT. Gardenia Community Recreation, Livingston, AL (2002).
• As *Activity Club Attendant*, provided administrative support including typing, running daily errands, and inputting spreadsheet applications in addition to adhering to maintenance regulations.
• As *Riding Stables Attendant*, operated heavy equipment including tractors and tractor trailers in addition to ensuring upkeep of horses, stalls, and outdoor areas.
• As *Ice Rink Attendant*, provided music as DJ and performed indoor and outdoor maintenance.

RECREATION ASSISTANT. University of West Alabama, Livingston, AL (1998-02). Monitored and supervised weight room and gymnasium, ensured facility maintenance, and provided instruction including individual training programs, weight room orientation sessions, and general programming.
• Earned an outstanding performance certificate from University of West Alabama.

Highlights of other experience:
• Programmed activities and provided supervision and counseling to campers as a **Camp Counselor** and **Volunteer** at various camps nation wide.
• Supervised art room and study room in addition to monitoring various activities as a **Volunteer** at the Boys and Girls Club.

PERSONAL
Enjoy running, weight lifting, painting, tennis, aerobics, and cooking.

Date

Exact Name of Person
Title or Position
Name of Company
Address (no., street)
Address (city, state, zip)

RECREATION DIRECTOR   Dear Exact Name of Person: (or Dear Sir or Madam if answering a blind ad):

With the enclosed resume, I would like to make you aware of my interest in exploring employment opportunities with your organization.

As you will see from my resume, I am a Certified Clinician through the National Sports Coaches Association. Known for my ability to work effectively with and motivate others, I have a real love of track and a strong desire to be associated with an excellent sports program.

Currently I am a Recreation Director at the Moscow Parks & Recreation Department, where I was promoted from Program Assistant to Director because of my knowledge, hard work, and dedication. I conduct aggressive and highly effective public relations by publicizing events and special activities while conducting promotions through various community organizations.

My program management and financial management skills have been refined through experience in the U.S. Army and National Guard. As a Supply Supervisor in the U.S. Army, I controlled $3 million in assets with perfect accountability.

I hope you will call or write me soon to suggest a time convenient for us to meet to discuss your current and future needs. Thank you in advance for you time.

Sincerely yours,

Alice Wendler

ALICE WENDLER

1110½ Hay Street, Fayetteville, NC 28305   •   preppub@aol.com   •   (910) 483-6611

OBJECTIVE

To contribute to an organization that can use an excellent trainer, motivator, and manager who has benefited employers through strong planning and communication skills.

EDUCATION & TRAINING

Received credit for a Supervisor Training Program from University of Idaho, Moscow, ID, 2002.
Certified Clinician through National Sports Coaches Association, Detroit, MI.
Received Certificate from Training Institute, 2001.
Graduated from the U.S. Army's Basic Training, 1999-2003.
Attended an Athletic Director's Workshop, Moscow, ID, 2000.
Attended Wayne County Community College, Detroit, MI, 1988.

AFFILIATIONS

Drug Task Force, Moscow, ID, 2004
Member of ID Recreation & Parks Society, Moscow, ID, 1998-02
Idaho Recreation Parks Society, Moscow, ID, 2000

EXPERIENCE

Excelled in the following track record of promotion:
2004-present: RECREATION DIRECTOR. Moscow Parks & Recreation Department, Moscow, ID. Was promoted from Supervisor to Director due to my knowledge, hard work, and dedication.
- Assign supervisors to specific athletic programs.
- Conduct public relations by publicizing events and special activities.
- Coordinate with various community groups and organizations.
- Provide specialized programming and assistance to the elderly or handicapped.
- Manage a budget of $200,000 while coordinating 32 different programs.
- In a part-time position with the National Guard as an **Assistant Supply Supervisor,** supervise up to 286 personnel while accounting for supplies. Account for requests, receipts, and storage of expendable supplies and equipment on individual, organizational, and installation levels.

1998-04: PROGRAM ASSISTANT. Moscow Parks & Recreation Department, Moscow, ID. Served as the Director of the recreation center in the supervisor's absence.
- Organized, planned, and conducted recreation programs for all ages from preschoolers through senior citizens.
- Planned and prepared leisure activity scheduling and local league rules.
- Supervised athletic events.

Other experience:
SUPPLY SUPERVISOR. U.S. Army (1992-98). Maintained inventory accountability for more than $3 million of equipment while supervising a staff of five employees.
- Received a Top Secret security clearance.

ASSISTANT GYM SUPERVISOR. Twin Falls Parks & Recreation Department, Twins Falls, ID (1990-92). Assisted in the overall operations of the gym and its various programs.
- Planned and promoted athletic events, leisure play, and tournaments.
- Promoted and provided new programs for the entire complex.
- Opened and closed the gymnasium.

PERSONAL

Am known for my good "way" with people and thrive on working with and motivating others. Have a real love of track and a strong desire to be associated with an excellent sports program.

Date

Exact Name of Person
Title or Position
Name of Company
Address (no., street)
Address (city, state, zip)

RECREATIONAL
DIRECTOR

Dear Exact Name of Person: (or Dear Sir or Madam if answering a blind ad.)

Can you use a bright and hard-working young professional who offers unusually strong oral and written communication skills along with proven leadership ability, an enthusiastic personality, as well as unlimited personal initiative and drive?

A recent graduate of Hesser College, I refined my natural "people skills" while working every summer since I was 17 years old as well as some semesters during college in order to finance my degree. As you will see from my resume, I have gained valuable skills in jobs ranging from management trainee, to recreational director, to swim instructor and lifeguard, to special projects coordinator and wine steward!

After college graduation, I was recruited by Alcon Pool to become its Recreational Director. Although I am excelling in the position, I am selectively exploring other opportunities. I worked for Alcon in a part-time position while in college and can provide outstanding references.

Even before I entered Hesser College, I had demonstrated my leadership, scholastic, and social skills. During my senior year of high school, I was elected president of the student body and was inducted into the National Honor Society while excelling in playing football and baseball. I offer a talent for "juggling" numerous simultaneous activities, all of which require hard work and "attention to detail" as well as getting along with people.

I feel certain that you would find me to be a warm and flexible person who would take great pride in making contributions to your organization.

I hope you will write or call soon to suggest a time convenient for us to meet and discuss your current and future needs and how I might serve them. Thank you in advance for your time.

Sincerely yours,

Ryan Townsend

Alternative last paragraph:
I hope you will welcome my call next week in order to try to arrange a brief meeting at your convenience to discuss your needs and goals and how I might serve them. Thank you in advance for your time.

RYAN TOWNSEND

1110½ Hay Street, Fayetteville, NC 28305   •   preppub@aol.com   •   (910) 483-6611

OBJECTIVE

To contribute to the success of an organization that can use a self-motivated and hard-working young professional who offers excellent written and oral communication skills along with a creative problem-solving style and the ability to get along well with all types of people.

EDUCATION

Bachelor of Arts degree in English, Hesser College, Manchester, NH, 2004.
- Inducted into Alpha Phi fraternity and was active for four years.

Graduated from Willowbrook High School, Willowbrook, NH, 2000.
- Elected Student Body President in 2000 at one of New Hampshire's largest and most diversified high schools.
- Was inducted into the National Honor Society in 1998.
- Played varsity football and baseball in high school while simultaneously excelling academically and in leadership roles.

EXPERIENCE

RECREATIONAL DIRECTOR. Alcon Pool, Jersey City, NJ (2004-present). Develop and implement recreational programs for youth and adults at this private resort while training/ directing lifeguards.
- Became skilled in performing advanced planning weeks ahead of program implementation in order to identify and organize needed resources.
- Credited with transforming an historically troubled recreational program into a smooth functioning, well-organized operation.
- Apply my communication skills in soothing dissatisfied customers, training employees, counseling both youth and adults, and motivating program participants to excel.

MANAGEMENT TRAINEE. Panda Express, Manchester, NH (2003-04). While working in this part-time job to finance my college education, began as a delivery boy and was promoted to handle increasing responsibilities related to operations management.
- In an organization where a heavy "bottom-line' price was paid for any late order, learned the importance of "doing it right the first time."
- Gained valuable experience in managing a small business.
- In the manager's absence, frequently supervised other employees and was commended for my ability to coordinate many personalities into a unified team.

LIFEGUARD. Alcon Pool, Jersey City, NJ (summers, 2002 and 2003). Refined my planning and time management skills and learned the importance of "constant vigilance" on the job while ensuring the safety of swimmers.

SPECIAL PROJECTS COORDINATOR & WINE STEWARD. Manchester's Best, Manchester, NH (summer 2001). Applied my organizational skills managing special projects which required me to plan and coordinate the activities of many people involved in activities such as organizing and setting up ballrooms for functions attended by more than 1,000 guests. Completed training in wine stewarding and learned the etiquette and techniques related to serving patrons in a 5-star resort.

SWIM INSTRUCTOR. YMCA, Hanover, NH (2001). Taught swimming and other activities to groups of up to 15 boys.

PERSONAL

Have a knack for establishing warm relationships with others. Offer "natural" sales/marketing abilities. Have been certified by the Red Cross in First Aid, Lifesaving, and CPR. Can provide outstanding references upon request.

Date

Exact Name of Person
Exact Title
Exact Name of Company
Address
City, State, Zip

RECREATION THERAPIST   Dear Exact Name of Person (or Dear Sir or Madam if answering a blind ad):

With the enclosed resume, I would like to make you aware of my interest in exploring employment opportunities with your organization for a Recreational Therapist.

As you will see from my resume, I am state certified and nationally certified in Recreation Therapy, and I have also become certified in TACT and CPR. I hold a B.S. degree in Therapeutic Recreation and an Associate of Applied Science in Recreation.

Since 1998, I have excelled as a Recreational Therapist with Behavioral Family Health Care, and I have worked with a variety of client populations. Since 2003 I have worked primarily with adult psychiatric patients suffering from depression as well as a wide range of other psychiatric ailments. Between 1998-2003, I primarily served the needs of a population of adolescents.

While in college, I financed most of my college education by working as a Fitness Consultant with Big Apple Gym, and I became skilled in coordinating personalized exercise programs and training individuals on aerobic fitness and strength improvement.

In volunteer positions, I have worked with high- and low-functioning mentally challenged clients as well as with stroke, amputee, and head injury patients.

I can provide excellent references at the appropriate time, and I would appreciate your contacting me to suggest a time when we might meet in person to discuss your needs. Thank you in advance for your interest in my skills and qualifications.

Yours sincerely,

Nathaniel Jack

NATHANIEL JACK

1110½ Hay Street, Fayetteville, NC 28305   •   preppub@aol.com   •   (910) 483-6611

OBJECTIVE   I want to contribute to an organization that can use an accomplished Recreational Therapist who offers strong skills related to administration and patient care.

EDUCATION   **Bachelor of Science (B.S.) degree in Therapeutic Recreation,** Columbia College, New York, NY, 1997.
- Course work included philosophical foundations, processes, and techniques related to therapeutic recreation service delivery; special courses focused on outdoor activities as vehicles for human growth and development.
- Learned activities and skills for special populations, therapeutic recreation processes and techniques, and therapeutic recreation services for the elderly.

Associate of Applied Science, Recreation, New York University, New York, NY, 1995.

CERTIFICATIONS   Nationally certified in Recreational Therapy
State certified in Recreational Therapy
Certified in Targeted Aggression Control (TACT) training
Cardio-Pulmonary Resuscitation (CPR) Certified

EXPERIENCE   **RECREATIONAL THERAPIST.** Behavioral Family Health Care, New York, NY (1998-present). Began as an Assistant and was quickly promoted to Recreational Therapist; have worked with a variety of client populations.
- From 2003-2004, have worked primarily with adult psychiatric patients suffering from depression and a wide range of disorders. Perform group counseling. Also perform assessments and work with an interdisciplinary treatment team to assure quality patient care.
- From 1998-2003, worked with adolescents suffering from psychiatric disorders; also filled in for other professionals and worked with children.

RECREATIONAL THERAPIST (Intern). New York Regional Hospital, New York, NY (1997). In a 12-week internship, assessed capabilities of brain injured, CVA, and SCI patients; devised individualized activities schedule.
- Accurately and proficiently completed detailed evaluation reports.
- Worked with patients in community reintegration.
- Assisted in coordinating a seat belt safety check.

FITNESS CONSULTANT. Big Apple Gym, New York, NY (1993-96). While in college, worked during the summers and during semester/holiday breaks.
- Coordinated personalized exercise program and trained people to improve on their strength and aerobic fitness. Conducted various fitness contests and ensured cleanliness of facility, to include maintaining the whirlpool.

AFFILIATION   Therapeutic Recreation Association; attended NY Therapy Association Annual Conference.

VOLUNTEER ACTIVITIES   Worked with high- and low-functioning mentally disabled, New York, NY, 1997.
Worked with stroke, amputee, and head injury patients, Rosalie Ruth Rehabilitation Center, Albany, NY, 1995.
Worked with the Junior League, New York, NY, 1994 and 1995.
Worked with the Junior League Bowling Program, New York, NY, 1994 and 1995.

PERSONAL   Highly skilled individual. Proven ability to provide quality care to clients. Excellent references.

CAREER CHANGE

Date

Exact Name of Person
Exact Title
Exact Name of Company
Address
City, State, Zip

REGIONAL MANAGER, OUTWARD BOUND

is seeking to transition into corporate sales.

Dear Exact Name of Person (or Dear Sir or Madam if answering a blind ad):

With the enclosed resume, I would like to make you aware of my interest in exploring employment opportunities with your organization.

As you will see from my resume, I am excelling in my current position and am believed to be the youngest person in the history of the company to assume the job as Regional Manager. I was recruited for my position during my senior year of college and have made numerous contributions to the organization while managing 12 individuals as well as a budget of approximately half a million dollars. After stepping into my position, I took over an underperforming operation which had experienced chronic sluggish performance for 13 years. Through innovative marketing, bulldog persistence, and skillful management, I have created one of the company's most profitable and efficient operations.

Although I am highly regarded in my current position and am being groomed for further rapid promotion, I am selectively exploring other opportunities. I am confident that I will be very successful in the sales arena as I have been in management. With strong communication and motivational skills, I offer natural sales abilities as well as the drive and determination which are critical to success.

Recently I used my sales skills in a volunteer role when I assumed the position as coach of a basketball team which had not won a game in two years. I completely transformed the skills and attitudes of boys aged 15-18, and the team I coached ended up second in the conference. I credit my own background as a basketball player with providing me with valuable leadership and teamwork experience. As a shooting guard in high school, I played a key role in leading my team to become the state champions and I was named Player of the Year and MVP for two years. In college at University of Portland, where I majored in Business Administration, I led my team to become the Intramural Basketball Champions. I recently played on an over-21 men's team which won the city championship. Through sports, I have learned how to compete, how to win, and how to persist.

I believe a career in sales would require the same highly disciplined and highly motivated attitude which has led me to be successful in sports and management. If you can use a hard charger with unlimited personal initiative and a drive to become a part of a winning team with a championship company, I hope you will contact me to suggest a time when we might meet to discuss your needs.

Yours sincerely,

Aaron Silver

AARON SILVER

1110½ Hay Street, Fayetteville, NC 28305   •   preppub@aol.com   •   (910) 483-6611

OBJECTIVE

To contribute to a company that can use a resourceful and dynamic young professional with strong sales and communication skills along with an aggressive bottom-line orientation.

EDUCATION

Bachelor of Science (B.S.) degree in Business Management, University of Portland, Portland, Oregon; graduated 2002. Sports leadership accomplishments:
- Was recruited by numerous colleges and offered scholarships to play collegiate basketball, but I declined the offers in order to attend UP's fine Business Management program.
- As a shooting guard, led my intramural team at University of Portland to become the **2001 Intramural Basketball Champions.**

Professional Training: Outward Bound Training Program, 2002.
Graduated from high school at Wright Senior High, Portland, OR, 1999.
Sports leadership accomplishments:
- Was named Player of the Year, 1998 and 1999, in basketball.
- As a shooting guard, led my team become the State Champions in 1997.
- Named All Conference and All Tournament and MVP in 1998 and 1999.

LANGUAGES

Strong working knowledge of **Spanish** (two years of college courses, three years in high school).

COMPUTERS

Highly proficient in operating computers with software including Microsoft Word; spreadsheets including Excel, and PowerPoint software for professional presentations.

EXPERIENCE

REGIONAL MANAGER. Outward Bound, Portland, OR (2002-present). Was recruited for a management trainee position by this organization which provides outdoor experiences for all age groups during my last semester of college; after three months of intensive on-the-job and hands-on training, was promoted to Regional Manager.
- Am the youngest person ever placed in this management role within a company which operates camp experiences and adventure training in sites worldwide; am being groomed for future rapid promotion.
- Supervise 12 employees who include site managers and support service coordinators; handle hiring, training, and employee supervision and terminate employees when necessary.
- Handle extensive financial management responsibilities including providing oversight for a budget of nearly ½ million dollars a year; am responsible for assuring tax credit management according to strict government guidelines.
- Handle financial planning which includes analyzing the previous fiscal year's expenses and calculating the budget for the next year; analyze trends and make projections for the upcoming year while estimating occupancy rates, payroll costs, and determining profitability projections.

BASKETBALL COACH (Volunteer). Mosely School, Portland, OR (2003-04). Volunteered to coach a local team of 15-18 year old boys who had not won a game in two years; coached them so that they ended up in 2nd place in their conference.
- Created a team that exhibited winning skills and a winning attitude.

PERSONAL

Highly motivated person with a talent for forming effective relationships. Excellent references.

CAREER CHANGE

Date

Exact Name of Person
Exact Title
Exact Name of Company
Address
City, State, Zip

SALES ASSOCIATE, SPORTING GOODS.

This young person is approaching elected state and national officials in hopes of becoming a staff member for a legislator.

Dear Exact Name of Person (or Dear Sir or Madam if answering a blind ad):

With the enclosed resume, I would like to make you aware of my interest in becoming a member of your fine staff.

As you will see from my resume, I earned a B.S. degree in Political Science in 2003 and subsequently accepted a management trainee/sales position with a prominent chain of stores. I have excelled in the job and have been aggressively encouraged to remain with the company and enjoy rapid promotion into management.

While earning my college degree, I became a respected leader on my college campus as I served as President, Vice President, Treasurer, and Scholarship Director of my fraternity. I refined my problem-solving skills in those positions as I learned to motivate young college students who needed practical help in acquiring adequate study skills and managing personal finances. I am proud of the fact that I led my fraternity to become involved in numerous community service activities including tutoring at-risk elementary students, helping youthful cancer patients, and participating in the Ronald McDonald House.

I am confident that I offer the "raw materials" needed to become a valuable member of your staff, as I am a dedicated hard worker, strong problem solver, and congenial individual who excels in working with others at all organizational levels. My analytical abilities, communication skills, and organizational talents are top-notch.

I am seeking to make a contribution to an organization that can use an articulate and dedicated young leader known for attention to detail as well as strong personal initiative. I can provide outstanding personal and professional references. I hope you will contact me soon to suggest a time when we might meet in person to determine if and how I could become a vital part of your team. I know it would be a pleasure meeting you, and I would sincerely appreciate your time.

Yours sincerely,

Jeffery Moses

JEFFERY MOSES

1110½ Hay Street, Fayetteville, NC 28305   •   preppub@aol.com   •   (910) 483-6611

OBJECTIVE

To benefit an organization that can use an enthusiastic, articulate young professional with a reputation as a strong and dedicated leader who possesses high personal standards along with an ability to motivate and inspire others to work toward common goals.

EDUCATION

B.A. in Political Science, Delaware State University, Dover, DE, 2004.

- **Campus leadership:** Was elected to leadership roles including President, Vice President, Treasurer, and scholarship director as a member of Alpha Sigma Phi fraternity. Gained maturity as I succeeded in helping college students acquire better study skills. As Treasurer, was in charge of collecting $9,000 in dues and in handling accounts receivable and payable for the organization.
- **Community service:** Organized, scheduled, and personally conducted tutoring for students at an area elementary school. Volunteered with organizations dedicated to helping childhood cancer patients. Volunteered with the Ronald McDonald House.
- **Club involvement:** Active member of the Political Science Club.

Graduated from Duplin Senior High School, Newark, DE, where I was active in the Key Club and Spanish Club; played junior varsity basketball.

COMPUTERS

Familiar with Microsoft Word, Excel, and PowerPoint

EXPERIENCE

SALES ASSOCIATE & MANAGEMENT TRAINEE. The Sporting Goods, Newark, NJ (2004-present). After college, accepted a job with a major sporting goods chain.

- **Management skills:** Have been encouraged to remain with this large regional sporting goods company and pursue management training because of my outstanding performance.
- **Inventory control:** Became familiar with the full inventory of sports, camping, and hunting equipment while pricing, selling, and stocking inventory. Gained the respect of my superiors for my attention-to-detail in pricing merchandise and controlling stock.
- **Public relations:** Became known for my ability to assist customers in finding appropriate merchandise and in tactfully resolving difficult customer problems.

WAIT STAFF MEMBER. Seashore Oyster Bar, Dover, DE (2003-04). Worked in a popular Dover restaurant while partially financing my education.

- **Cross training:** Became skilled in performing numerous jobs in this restaurant including acting as a Bartender, Barback, and Server. Rapidly mastered new tasks.
- **Customer relations:** Was commended for my poise in dealing with customers.

LEGAL COURIER & RESEARCH ASSISTANT. Smith and Smith Law Firm, Dover, DE (2002-03). While earning my degree in Political Science, worked part-time during college terms and full-time during the summer for a prominent law firm; was a trusted courier of documents intended for use by federal and state courts.

- **Supervision:** Supervised the training of new couriers.
- **Office management:** Assumed responsibility for assuring adequate office supplies.
- **Research and analysis:** Became a respected employee; was involved in researching specific topics and evidence related to a variety of cases. Acquired extensive knowledge of environmental and labor law and earned praise for my strong analytical skills.

Other experience: Involved in sales and collections, U.S. Alarm Systems (summer 2001).

PERSONAL

Highly motivated young professional who is skilled in handling multiple responsibilities. In my spare time, enjoy running, golf, and basketball. Outstanding references on request.

CAREER CHANGE

Date

Exact Name of Person
Exact Title
Exact Name of Company
Address
City, State, Zip

**SEMIPROFESSIONAL
FOOTBALL PLAYER**

is seeking administrative
position with a sports
team.

Dear Exact Name of Person (or Dear Sir or Madam if answering a blind ad):

I would appreciate an opportunity to talk with you soon about how I could contribute to your organization through my experience as well as my reputation as a physically and mentally tough professional who excels in working with others. I am responding to your recent advertisement for an Associate General Manager with the Carolina Panthers.

As you will see from my enclosed resume, I recently left military service after successfully advancing in supervisory and leadership roles with an emphasis on inventory control, warehousing and distribution, customer service, and quality control. Since January I have been a member of the new semiprofessional football team, the Missoula Mountaineers. As a Linebacker/Tight End I have contributed a positive attitude and leadership skills as well as my talents as an athlete. Although I love the playing field and am an accomplished athlete, I believe I would be a valuable asset to the administrative operation of the Carolina Panthers.

While serving in the U.S. Army from 1996 to 2004, I was the recipient of numerous honors and several medals for my professionalism and leadership abilities. I was also selected to attend an advanced professional leadership development course to help sharpen and refine my skills. During my last assignment, I supervised eight people while ensuring the quality and reliability of parachutes and related equipment used by specialists from Ft. Campbell, KY.

I am confident that, through my versatile experience and training, I offer a track record of accomplishments and abilities which would allow me to rapidly become an asset to your organization. I hope you will contact me soon to suggest a time when we might meet to discuss your needs and how I might contribute. Thank you in advance for your time.

Sincerely,

Darren Joseph

DARREN JOSEPH

1110½ Hay Street, Fayetteville, NC 28305　　•　　preppub@aol.com　　•　　(910) 483-6611

OBJECTIVE　　To benefit an organization that can use a dedicated and mature young professional with experience in inventory, warehousing, and quality control/quality assurance operations along with a reputation for outstanding customer service and leadership skills.

TRAINING　　Excelled in more than 1,200 hours of training which included advanced and basic professional leadership development courses and other programs which emphasized military customs operations, load planning, and advanced trauma life support techniques.

EXPERIENCE　　**SEMIPROFESSIONAL FOOTBALL PLAYER.** The Missoula Mountaineers, Missoula, MT (2004-present). Am contributing a positive attitude and strong leadership skills as a member of a newly organized professional athletic team; play Linebacker/Tight End.

Excelled in supervising and leading teams of well-trained specialists, U.S. Army:
QUALITY CONTROL INSPECTOR & SUPERVISOR. Ft. Campbell, KY (2003-04). Polished leadership and supervisory skills while overseeing the performance of eight specialists entrusted with properly packing parachutes for personnel.
- Achieved a perfect record of seven months with no malfunctioning products.
- Completed daily equipment inventories; oversaw issuing, processing, and receiving.

SPECIALTY TEAM LEADER. Ft. Campbell, KY (2001-03). Was promoted on the basis of my professionalism in supervising a team of up to six people and seeing that their equipment was prepared in order to meet exacting standards.

SECURITY SPECIALIST & INVENTORY CONTROL SPECIALIST. San Juan, Puerto Rico (2000-01). Contributed knowledge of security operations and procedures which ensured the safety of local community members as a member of an international task force; participated in aircraft load planning in order to balance loads and meet weight requirements.
- Learned to develop mutual trust and respect with people from other countries and to perform in a manner which reflected favorably on the United States.

INVENTORY CONTROL SUPERVISOR & TEAM LEADER. Ft. Drum, NY (1998-00). Directed a team of six specialists involved in preparing ammunition supplies for shipping and storage as well as for issuing, receiving, and destroying ammunition supplies.
- Provided guidance during a period of 18-hour days required to process millions of tons of ammunition for shipment. Was singled out from a pool of 20 well-trained and qualified candidates for Supervisor of the Quarter (1999).

WEAPONS RANGE SAFETY AND AMMUNITION CONTROL SPECIALIST. Ft. Hood, TX (1996-98). Gained experience in ensuring the high quality of customer service and the vital importance of enforcing safety rules on weapons firing ranges.
- Provided support and enhanced training. Was recognized with a "High Performance Award" and named "Soldier of the Quarter" from a group of 38 candidates in 1998.

Highlights of other experience: As a Security Specialist/Bartender for a nightclub, provided a physical presence and security for employees and customers.

PERSONAL　　Was entrusted with a Secret security clearance. Received honors including the National Defense Service, Humanitarian Service, and three Army Achievement Medals.

CAREER CHANGE

Date

Exact Name of Person
Title or Position
Name of Company
Address (no., street)
Address (city, state, zip)

**SOCIAL STUDIES
TEACHER & COACH**

is seeking a coaching
role.

Dear Exact Name of Person: (or Dear Sir or Madam if answering a blind ad.)

With the enclosed resume, I would like to make you aware of my interest in becoming a member of your fine coaching staff.

As you will see from my resume, I have excelled as an educator since earning my B.S. degree in History from the University of New Hampshire. I was aggressively recruited by the college to play basketball, and as a captain I led the college to the first semifinals in its history. For three years in high school, I was named Player of the Year in New Hampshire.

Since graduation, I have excelled as an educator and coach and have earned the respect of peers, students, and parents for my creativity as well as my strong communication and problem-solving skills. Although I am held in the highest regard within the teaching community, I have come to the realization that a long career in teaching is not for me. I have, however, thoroughly enjoyed the challenge of teaching social studies, government, and history to preteens, and I have been successful in 8th grade, 9th grade, as well as exceptional children's classrooms. I have become particularly respected for my highly inventive nature and for my ability to apply my creativity in practical ways to help students; for example, I created and implemented end-of-grade practice tests which prepared students for an exam which can count up to 20% of their final grade. I offer a proven ability to walk into an established situation and, on my own initiative, develop and implement effective new approaches without alienating veterans in the field.

I am confident that I could become an enthusiastic and committed member of your staff, and I offer hands-on knowledge related to coaching. I have exceptionally strong written and oral communication skills, and colleagues have told me that I possess an unusually strong ability to motivate and influence others. In my previous job, I coached a middle school basketball team to second place finish in the county. I would enjoy utilizing my knowledge and motivational skills in helping you accomplish your goals.

If you can use a dedicated, congenial, and enthusiastic hard worker known for the ability to produce the highest quality results under the pressure of long hours and tight deadlines, I hope you will contact me to suggest a time when we might meet to discuss your needs and goals. With an outstanding personal and professional reputation, I can provide superior references.

Sincerely,

Jason Revels

JASON REVELS

1110½ Hay Street, Fayetteville, NC 28305 • preppub@aol.com • (910) 483-6611

OBJECTIVE

To benefit an organization that can use an articulate communicator, strong problem-solver, and talented organizer with extensive knowledge of government and the legislative process along with a desire to apply that knowledge for the benefit of an elected official.

EDUCATION

Bachelor of Science (B.S.) degree in History, University of New Hampshire, Durham, NH, 1998.
- Inducted into Beta Gamba Chi; recognized in the top 10% in the Social Science Department of the Association of Northeastern Colleges.
- As a captain, led the college to the first semifinal game in its history.
- Named **All-Region NCAA**, a respected college basketball honor.

Graduated from Portsmouth High School, Portsmouth, NH, 1994.
- Named **Player of the Year** in New Hampshire, 1994.
- Named to New Hampshire All-Star High School Basketball Team.

AFFILIATIONS

Member, Northern Historical Society; National Educators Association (NEA).

EXPERIENCE

SOCIAL STUDIES TEACHER & COUNSELOR. Strafford County Schools, Portsmouth High School, Portsmouth, NH (2003-present). As a 9th grade teacher, teach social studies to 110 students and prepare them for the end-of-grade writing, reading, and math tests.
- On my own initiative, teach remediation classes in the morning and afternoon in order to ensure that every student has an opportunity to achieve mastery learning.
- Played an organizational and leadership role in the Drama Teamsters.
- Counsel students/parents about matters related to student achievement and well-being.
- Coach the varsity basketball team.

COMMUNICATIONS SKILLS TEACHER & COACH. Strafford County Schools, Strafford Middle School, Portsmouth, NH (2000-02). As an 8th grade teacher, taught English and reading skills to 142 students while also administering end-of-grade tests and exams.
- On a daily basis, counseled 28 children and helped them set high personal goals.
- Became respected by other teachers for my ability to develop creative materials which helped prepare students for high school.
- Coached the basketball team to the second place finish in the county.
- On my own initiative, created and administered end-of-grade practice tests which helped children ready themselves for a test which counts up to 20% of their total yearly grade.

EXCEPTIONAL CHILDREN'S TEACHER. Strafford County Schools, Northwood School, Portsmouth, NH (1998-00). As an 8th grade teacher, taught social studies skills to children who could not attend public schools; became a valuable part of the intervention process for children with extreme discipline problems, and helped many of them return to mainstream classrooms.

SUPERVISOR, SUMMER PLAYGROUND. Hillsborough County Parks and Recreation, Manchester, NH (1996-98). As a college student, invented and planned daily activities for children aged 5-14; supervised a staff of three professionals overseeing up to 50 children.
- Refined my organizational skills while resourcefully administering summer activities.

PERSONAL

Highly motivated individual who desires to apply my knowledge of government, social studies, and the educational process. Strong computer skills. Excellent references.

Exact Name of Person
Title or Position
Name of Company
Address (no., street)
Address (city, state, zip)

**SOFTBALL TEAM
MANAGER
FOR A COLLEGE**

is seeking her first
full-time position
after college
graduation.

Dear Exact Name of Person: (or Dear Sir or Madam if answering a blind ad):

With the enclosed resume, I would like to make you aware of my interest in exploring employment opportunities with your organization.

As you will see from my resume, I received a B.S. in Exercise Science and Wellness with a minor in Nutrition from the University of Nebraska-Lincoln. Currently a softball team manager for the University of Nebraska softball team, my duties include designing, implementing, and supervising the training program which includes weight training and conditioning drills.

While attending college, I was a Sports Official and officiated more than 100 high school-level volleyball matches per season as well as youth basketball and soccer games. I was also a Softball Umpire for the Nebraska Softball Association and officiated over 200 games per season which included charity games at a nearby city installation. I was selected out of several hundred umpires by the State of Nebraska's Umpire-in-Chief as one of 20 umpires to officiate a national tournament.

In previous employment, I was an instructor and personal trainer at a local gym where I assisted members in establishing and attaining personal goals through one-on-one instruction.

I hope you will call or write me soon to suggest a time convenient for us to meet to discuss your current and future needs. Thank you in advance for you time.

Sincerely yours,

Ruth Godwin

RUTH GODWIN

1110½ Hay Street, Fayetteville, NC 28305 • preppub@aol.com • (910) 483-6611

OBJECTIVE   I want to contribute to an organization that can use a talented coach, motivator, and manager.

EDUCATION   **Bachelor of Science** degree in Exercise Science and Wellness, with a minor in Nutrition, University of Nebraska-Lincoln, Lincoln, NE, April 2004.
- Dean's List, 2003-04.

EMPLOYMENT   **SOFTBALL TEAM MANAGER.** University of Nebraska Softball Team, Lincoln, NE (2004-present). Became the trusted "right arm" of the head coach while assisting with the design, implementation, and supervision of the training program during the fall and spring which included weight training and conditioning drills.
- Am responsible for accountability, maintenance, and preparation of all uniforms and equipment.
- Excelled in this job while carrying a full college load and excelling in my studies; learned to manage my time for maximum efficiency.
- Worked as a Lifeguard for the Franklin Splashers in Lincoln; ensured pool area safety, sanitation, and that all chemical levels were strictly maintained.

SPORTS OFFICIAL. Lincoln, NE (2000-03). Simultaneous with the job below and while earning my college degree in Exercise Science and Wellness, officiated more than 100 high school-level volleyball matches per season as well as youth basketball and soccer games.

SOFTBALL UMPIRE. Nebraska Softball Association, Lincoln, NE (2000-03). Officiated over 200 games per season which included charity games at a nearby city installation.
- Was selected out of several hundred umpires by the State of Nebraska's Umpire-in-Chief as one of 20 umpires to officiate a national tournament.

RESEARCHER. University of Nebraska-Lincoln, Lincoln, NE (2000). Conducted a nutritional study on the effect of diet deficits in the performance of a college athlete; after extensive research, authored a report which was reviewed by my college professor and which led to my receiving an "A" in a college course.

INSTRUCTOR/PERSONAL TRAINER. Highland Center, Lincoln, NE (2000-01). Assisted members in establishing and attaining personal goals using proper techniques for using equipment through one-on-one instruction.

PRIOR MILITARY EXPERIENCE: TEAM LEADER. U.S. Air Force (1994-99). Provided combat support operations in various locations in the United States and overseas.
- Received numerous awards for outstanding performance, dedication, and initiative.
- Was recognized for participation in U.S. Air Force community sports programs.

LICENSES   Hold the following American Red Cross certifications:
Standard First Aid Certified
CPR Certified
Lifeguard Certified

PERSONAL   Proficient with Windows. Can provide outstanding references from all previous employers. Offer a reputation as a hard worker with a cheerful personality who prides myself on doing every job to the best of my ability.

Date

Exact Name of Person
Title or Position
Name of Company
Address (no., street)
Address (city, state, zip)

**SPECIAL PROGRAMS
INSTRUCTOR & COACH**

Dear Exact Name of Person: (or Dear Sir or Madam if answering a blind ad):

With the enclosed resume, I would like to make you aware of my interest in exploring employment opportunities with your organization.

As you will see from my resume, I am currently a Special Programs Instructor and a coach for the Orange County Schools. I oversee and develop teaching materials for a number of special learning programs for Pensacola Senior High School in addition to coaching several award-winning athletic teams. I led the girls' softball team to district and conference championships for three consecutive years as the head coach. I was also selected as the Pensacola Coach of the Year for three years. Through a vote of my colleagues, I received the annual Excellence in Coaching Award. I have cultivated good sportsmanship and a winning attitude as head coach for the junior varsity football team and as assistant coach for the varsity football team.

I am credited with building Pensacola High School's "softball dynasty;" the team has won conference championships for five consecutive years as well as the state championship. I have been honored with multiple Coach of the Year awards for girls' softball and basketball.

I hope you will call or write me soon to suggest a time convenient for us to meet to discuss your current and future needs. Thank you in advance for you time.

Sincerely yours,

Jared Fields

JARED FIELDS

1110½ Hay Street, Fayetteville, NC 28305 • preppub@aol.com • (910) 483-6611

OBJECTIVE

To benefit an organization in need of a well-rounded professional with excellent motivational skills as well as abilities in adapting to changing situations, learning new concepts quickly, and building individuals with varied backgrounds into cohesive and successful teams.

EDUCATION

Bachelor of Science degree in Health and Physical Education, Florida State University, Tallahassee, FL, 1994.
- Actively served in Kappa Beta fraternity; was elected to the offices of Vice President and President.
- Participated in college-level athletics as a member of the soccer and wrestling teams.

EXPERIENCE

SPECIAL PROGRAMS INSTRUCTOR & COACH. Orange County Schools, Pensacola, FL (2001-present). Oversee and develop teaching materials for a number of special learning programs for Pensacola Senior High School in addition to coaching several award-winning athletic teams.
- Direct the Saturday Academy program, the first of its kind in the county; give Saturday instruction to students in danger of dropping out or falling behind in course work.
- Create presentations for the drug awareness program and provide guidance and supervision to troubled students in the dropout and in-school suspension programs.
- Was handpicked to attend the Florida Center for Advancement in Teaching.
- Led the girls' softball team to district and conference championships for three consecutive years as head coach.
- Was selected as the Pensacola Coach of the Year for three years and as Basketball Coach of the Year for three years as the head coach of the girls' team. Through the vote of my colleagues, received the Excellence in Coaching Award.
- Cultivate good sportsmanship and a winning attitude as head coach for the junior varsity football team and as assistant coach for the varsity football team.

TEACHER/DEPARTMENT CHAIRMAN & COACH. Pensacola High School, Pensacola, FL (1996-01). Handled multiple responsibilities while providing instruction in world, U.S., and Florida history.
- Maintained high standards as chairman of the social studies department.
- Guided seniors through their final year as senior class advisor.
- Built a "softball dynasty," winning conference championships for five consecutive years and the state championship in 2001.
- Was honored with multiple Coach of the Year awards for girls' softball and basketball.
- Acted as the head coach of the junior varsity football team and assistant coach of the varsity football team.

SURVEY CHIEF. Carey & Associates, Tampa, FL (1994-96). Earned rapid promotion from an entry-level to a supervisory position based on qualities of adaptability and versatility in the highly technical field of surveying.
- Received two promotions in one year. Advanced to supervise teams of up to four workers; oversaw operations during field projects including title, land and boundary, topographic, construction, and route surveying.

PERSONAL

Enjoy the opportunity to learn new concepts and ideas. Pride myself on my accomplishments in instilling pride and self-confidence in young people.

CAREER CHANGE

Date

Exact Name of Person
Exact Title
Exact Name of Company
Address
City, State, Zip

SPORTS MEDICINE INTERNSHIP.

This individual is writing to a professional sports team in hopes of securing an internship related to his degree program.

Dear Exact Name of Person (or Dear Sir or Madam if answering a blind ad):

With the enclosed resume, I would like to make you aware of my interest in obtaining an internship in Sports Medicine. This internship will be a part of my degree program in Physical Therapy with Sports Medicine concentration. I am particularly interested in pursuing an internship with the New Hampshire Hockey Wizards because it is my hope to be associated with a sports team after graduation from the program.

As you will see, I have been pursuing my degree part-time while excelling in various positions with the New Hampshire Department of Transportation. While completing my general studies requirements, I have maintained a 3.85 GPA and was elected to the Vocational-Technical Honor Society. I hold current certifications in Community CPR and First Aid, and I have completed a number of courses related to the health sciences.

In ten years of service to the New Hampshire Department of Transportation, I have shown myself to be an articulate communicator and persuasive leader as well as a dedicated and reliable team player who applies imagination and ingenuity to problem-solving. Highly regarded by my present employer, I can provide outstanding references and letters of recommendation at the appropriate time.

I would appreciate the opportunity to speak with you about your needs and how I could serve them. I assure you in advance that I have an excellent reputation and could quickly become an asset to your organization.

Sincerely,

Andrew Haye

ANDREW HAYE

1110½ Hay Street, Fayetteville, NC 28305 • preppub@aol.com • (910) 483-6611

OBJECTIVE

To benefit an organization that can use an accomplished young professional with a strong desire to make a contribution in the health care field.

EDUCATION

Completing a **Physical Therapy Degree with concentration in Sports Medicine**, Keene State College, Keene, NH, 2004.
- Named to the Vocational-Technical Honor Society, currently maintaining a 3.85 GPA. Courses related to the medical field which I have completed or am currently completing include:

Sports Injuries	Basic Chemistry I & II
Health Sciences Physics	General Psychology
Developmental Psychology	First Aid & CPR
Anatomy & Physiology I & II	General Microbiology

Completed a **Bachelor of Science in Business Administration,** Dartmouth College, Hanover, NH, 1995.

CERTIFICATION

Hold current certifications in First Aid and Community CPR (adult, child, and infant).

AFFILIATIONS

Member, Vocational-Technical Honor Society, 2004.

COMPUTERS

Familiar with many popular computer operating systems and software programs, including Windows XP and Microsoft Word, Excel, Access, and PowerPoint.

EXPERIENCE

PHYSICAL THERAPY (SPORTS MEDICINE CONCENTRATION) STUDENT. Keene State University, Keene, NH (2002-present). Demonstrate exceptional time management skills by excelling in my part-time college studies while working full-time for the New Hampshire Department of Transportation.

New Hampshire Department of Transportation: advanced in the following "track record:"
2003-present: **AUDITOR.** Hanover, NH. Promoted to this job from a position as Transportation Technician II; excelled in this difficult position requiring careful attention to detail while simultaneously pursuing my college education.
- Audit all records and reports submitted to the DOT in relation to the $32 million highway construction project managed by S & R Engineering Consultants.
- Verify accuracy of all documentation, ensuring that all records and reports are in compliance with applicable New Hampshire standards and specifications.

2001-03: **TRANSPORTATION TECHNICIAN II.** Hanover, NH. Oversaw the work of a survey crew, organizing and planning survey work to be done on various road construction projects throughout New Hampshire.
- Supervised and provided training to three employees in the correct operation of survey equipment and performing intermediate field calculations.
- Served as liaison between various contractors and DOT officials.

Highlights of earlier experience (1995-01): Excelled in earlier positions with the NH Department of Transportation as a **Transportation Technician I** and **Engineering Aide.**

PERSONAL

Am known as a reliable and dedicated team player who applies imagination and ingenuity to problem-solving. Excellent personal and professional references are available upon request.

Date

Exact Name of Person
Title or Position
Exact Company Name
Address (no., street)
Address (city, state, zip)

**SPORTS THERAPIST
& REHAB MANAGER**

Dear Exact Name of Person: (or Dear Sir or Madam if answering a blind ad):

With the enclosed resume, I would like to make you aware of my interest in the position as Vencor's Regional Rehabilitation Director or, in the event that the position is filled, the Director of Occupational Therapy position. As I believe you will see from my resume, I meet all your criteria and would welcome the opportunity to show you in person that I am the candidate you are seeking.

With extensive experience as an Occupational Therapist and Sports Therapist, I have excelled in hospital corporate management for 13 years and most recently I have been involved in sports therapy for college and professional athletes. Clinically my expertise is in orthopedics, orthotics, hand therapy, and contracture management. My experience in Rehab Services Management has afforded me the opportunity to oversee large departments, programs, volumes, and revenues with significant fiscal responsibility related to budgeting, productivity analysis, cost accounting, and marketing.

You will notice from my resume that I held a couple of my jobs for rather short durations. This was due to the fact that my husband was an airline executive and we were relocated frequently. I am proud of the fact, however, that I made significant contributions to all organizations which employed me, and I can provide outstanding references from all of them. My husband is now retiring, and we are interested in relocating permanently to Colorado where our families live.

My management skills are extensive. At Triangle Medical Center in Colorado Springs, I was Director of Occupational Therapy for four years and supervised a staff of 25 while overseeing departmental gross revenue of $2 million. I was cited as a major program developer as I initiated a new Cancer Rehabilitation Program, a new Hand & Upper Extremity Clinic, and numerous other programs.

I hope I will have an opportunity to meet with you in person, as I would very much enjoy having the opportunity to see your facility and meet your staff. I am aware of your fine reputation, and I am certain I could become a valuable asset to you. Please contact me if my considerable talents and skills interest you.

Yours sincerely,

Cheryl Hall

CHERYL HALL

1110½ Hay Street, Fayetteville, NC 28305 • preppub@aol.com • (910) 483-6611

OBJECTIVE   To contribute to an organization that can use a skilled Occupational Therapist with extensive experience in supervising occupational therapy and managing rehabilitation services.

EDUCATION   **Masters of Occupational Therapy (M.O.T.) degree**, University of Colorado at Denver, Denver CO, 1992.
Bachelor of Arts (B.A.) degree in Psychology with a minor in Biology, University of Denver, Denver, CO, 1990.

EXPERIENCE   **SPORTS THERAPIST & REHAB MANAGER.** Colorado Medical Center, Denver, CO (2004-present). While traveling extensively throughout Colorado, am responsible for providing occupational therapy (OT) clinical services to athletes.
- Supervise OT assistants. Clinical focus: orthotics/contracture management.

DIRECTOR, INPATIENT REHABILITATION SERVICES. San Diego Medical Center, San Diego, CA (2002-04). Responsible for supervising PT, OT, and SLP departments in HVH, including administrative and fiscal management.
- Was praised in writing for skillfully working with the directors of the hospital's outpatient rehabilitation programs in providing the leadership necessary to develop a coordinated team approach for all rehab services.
- Significantly expanded occupational therapy services, specifically to patients needing hand therapy while also developing dedicated coverage of home health patients and planning therapy services for a new 21-bed skilled nursing unit.

MANAGER, REHABILITATION SERVICES. Providence Hospital, Providence, RI (2001-02). Was accountable for the planning, direction, and operation of inpatient and outpatient Physical Therapy, Occupational Therapy, and Speech/Language Pathology Services.
- Managed administrative activities and for all fiscal management of Rehabilitation Therapy Services.

SUPERVISOR, OCCUPATIONAL THERAPY. Denver Medical Center, Denver, CO (1996-2000). Managed the Occupational Therapy Department's operations and provided direct supervision to six Occupational Therapists.
- Responsible for monthly and annual financial and statistical fiscal reports.
- Clinically treated a variety of inpatients and outpatients including: CVAs, neurological diagnoses, hand injuries, as well as industrial and orthopedic injuries.

DIRECTOR, OCCUPATIONAL THERAPY. Triangle Medical Center, Colorado Springs, CO (1992-96). Responsible for managing the Occupational Therapy Department at Triangle Medical Center, including the effective planning, organizing, directing, controlling, and evaluating of department operations.
- Supervised a staff of 25 employees which included two Occupational Therapy Supervisors, four Senior Occupational Therapists, eight Staff Occupational Therapists, three Certified Occupational Therapy Assistants, and Occupational Therapy students in clinical placements.
- Was cited for major program development and revenue volume growth which resulted in departmental gross revenue of $2 million.

AFFILIATIONS American Occupational Therapy Association; Colorado Occupational Therapy Association.

Date

Exact Name of Person
Exact Name of Organization
Exact Address
City, State zip

**SPORTS PROGRAM
DIRECTOR**

Dear Exact Name: (or Dear Sir or Madam if answering a blind ad):

Can you use an enthusiastic self-starter who offers a proven "track record" of being promoted rapidly to greater and greater responsibilities in every job I have ever held?

In my current position as Sports Director and Programs Manager for the Montgomery Youth Services, I have excelled in managing a community center with extreme staff shortages. I have organized programs for youth which ranged from team sports such as soccer and baseball, to dance and karate, to scouts and other activities. I handle extensive responsibility for financial management and accounting, and I am continuously involved in developing monthly budgets that identify costs for each program.

I have been commended in writing for my "consistent cheerfulness and positive attitude" while working in a busy and understaffed organization. I am known for my willingness to "pick up the slack" and can always be relied upon to make sure office operations and organizational programs are the best they could be.

You would find me to be a hard worker who has the ability to rapidly master new skills. I can provide excellent personal and professional references at the appropriate time.

I hope you will call or write me soon to suggest a time when we might meet to discuss your needs and goals and how I might serve them. Thank you in advance for your time.

Yours sincerely,

Pearl White

PEARL WHITE

1110½ Hay Street, Fayetteville, NC 28305 • preppub@aol.com • (910) 483-6611

OBJECTIVE
To contribute to the success of an organization that can use a hard-working and self-motivating young professional who offers excellent communication and customer service skills along with an ability to rapidly master new tasks.

EXPERIENCE
PROGRAMS MANAGER & SPORTS DIRECTOR. Montgomery Youth Services, Montgomery, WV (2004-present). Was commended in writing for my "consistent cheerfulness and positive attitude" while working in a community center with extreme staff shortages; could always be counted on for my "team spirit" and for my willingness to "pick up the slack."
- Organize programs for youth which ranged from team sports such as soccer and baseball, to dance and karate, to scouts and other activities.
- On my own initiative, assumed responsibility for monthly status/progress reports and for accounting reports; developed monthly budgets that helped identify costs for each program.
- Register members for all programs and collected fees; recruited volunteers.
- Repeatedly handle a heavy work load with minimal supervision.
- Was praised in writing upon my departure for "setting a precedent and an example for others to follow."
- Learned valuable administrative skills while mastering the "art" of juggling numerous ongoing programs.
- Acted as the "right arm" of the center's general manager in arranging special events, gathering information, and representing Youth Services at community meetings.

CASHIER/INVENTORY CONTROLLER. Target, Montgomery, WV (2002-03). Learned how to serve customers graciously while operating a cash register, and was handpicked for increasing responsibilities involving inventory control and ordering.

SUPERVISOR & MECHANIC. Pep Boys, Montgomery, WV (2000-02). Trained and supervised up to two other employees while performed repairs and maintenance on diesel trucks and ordering parts for a wide range of trucks.

Other experience:
NANNY & CHILD CARE WORKER. Have taken care of children ranging in age from two to eight years old.
- Learned to understand the varying needs of children at different ages.

EDUCATION & TRAINING
Was selected for technical and leadership training while in military service.
Became CPR qualified and completed extensive first aid training.
Completed "hands-on" training in bookkeeping at Montgomery Youth Services.

PERSONAL
Have excellent public relations skills. Offer a proven ability to remain calm and productive under pressure. Will provide outstanding references on request. Am known for my reliability and flexibility during peak work loads.

Date

Exact Name of Person
Title or Position
Name of Company
Address (no., street)
Address (city, state, zip)

**SPORTS
PROGRAMMING
DIRECTOR**

Dear Exact Name of Person: (or Dear Sir or Madam if answering a blind ad):

With the enclosed resume, I would like to make you aware of my interest in exploring employment opportunities with your organization.

As you will see from my resume, I obtained my Master's in Sports Administration from Southern Connecticut State University, where I was selected from 300 applicants for one of the 25 positions in this "premier" program. I have excelled in more than 170 "practicum" hours in three areas of emphasis: the Sport's Director's office, sports and NCAA compliance, and ticket office procedures.

I now utilize my education as a Marketing & Sales/Sports Programming Director for Coppin's, where I develop and manage key promotions and timely advertisements while selling advertising options to businesses in an entertainment atmosphere.

In previous employment with the Atlantic Arena as an Event Coordinator, I coordinated the staffing and trained employees, processed receipts for all-season tickets, coordinated playoffs, and managed financial recordkeeping.

I hope you will call or write me soon to suggest a time convenient for us to meet to discuss your current and future needs. Thank you in advance for you time.

Sincerely yours,

Heidi Vines

HEIDI VINES

1110½ Hay Street, Fayetteville, NC 28305   •   preppub@aol.com   •   (910) 483-6611

EDUCATION

Master's degree in Sports Administration, Southern Connecticut University, New Haven, CT, 2001.
- Selected from 300 applicants for one of the 25 positions in this "premier" program.
- Excelled in more than 170 "practicum" hours in three areas of emphasis: the Sports Director's office, sports and NCAA compliance, and ticket office procedures.

B.S. degree in Communications, Southern Connecticut University, New Haven CT, 1994.

EXPERIENCE

MARKETING/SALES/SPORTS PROGRAMMING DIRECTOR. Coppin's, Bridgeport, CT (2004-present). Develop and manage key promotions and timely advertisements while selling advertising options to businesses in an entertainment atmosphere.
- Direct nightly sports programming utilizing satellite, video tape, cable and communications systems, stressing interesting and popular programming.

EVENT INFORMATION COORDINATOR. Atlantic Arena, Bridgeport, CT (2002-03). Coordinated the staffing and training of employees in addition to preparing and presenting Arena event information and schedules.
- Processed sales and cash receipts for all-season tickets, mini-plans, groups, playoffs, and batch orders, ensuring that discounts, prices, and payments were accurate.
- Prepared box office sales reports for presentation to top-level management.
- Ensured all company, state, and federal personnel and business regulations and laws were followed, including the American Disabilities Act.

SALES REPRESENTATIVE. New Haven Wildcats, New Haven, CT (2001-02). Generated, renewed, and maintained accounts for season tickets, partial plans, and group outings for the Wildcats, NHL hockey, and other Coliseum events. Contacted key decision makers regarding executive suites and club seats for Riverside Arena.

MARKETING/SALES REPRESENTATIVE. Fairfield Jaguars, Fairfield, CT (2001). As an intern, gained knowledge in functional areas including special program development and in planning a ticket sales promotion emphasizing regional sales growth.

NEWS AND SPORTS VIDEOGRAPHER. WKAR-TV, Waterbury, CT (2000). Taped, edited, and satellite-fed news and sports footage from the Waterbury, CT, area.

PUBLIC AFFAIRS OFFICER. U.S. Army, Ft. Campbell, KY (1997-00). As a military officer, gained extensive media, community, and public relations experience as the "voice" and "face" of the famed 101st Airborne Division.
- Coordinated FOX "Family Show" broadcasts; earned award for best "special" Family Show of all time.
- Coordinated VIP/media visits and international, national, and local television broadcasts.
- Managed the 101st Airborne Sports Parachute Club/Demonstration Team and Chorus.

SPORTS PRODUCER & DIRECTOR. Haven Video, New Haven, CT (1994-96). Supervised 10 people as the producer and director of all Southern Connecticut State University sports coverage with an emphasis on football and basketball: responsible for pre-production coordination, setup, production quality, and post-production editing.

PERSONAL

Member of 10-person committee bringing minor league baseball to New Haven, CT. Secret security clearance. Expert parachutist who has earned jump "wings" from three countries.

Real-Resumes Series edited by Anne McKinney **141**

Date

Exact Name of Person
Exact Title
Exact Name of Company
Address
City, State, Zip

SPORTS PROGRAMS DIRECTOR

Dear Exact Name of Person (or Dear Sir or Madam if answering a blind ad):

With the enclosed resume, I would like to express my interest in exploring employment opportunities with your organization. My husband and I have relocated to your area, and I am seeking an employer who can use a highly intelligent and totally reliable young professional with an outstanding work history.

In my most recent position, I programmed and managed a variety of youth services at a military base in North Carolina, where I handled the responsibility of creating written flyers and newsletters while also training and managing youth counselors. I was promoted to handle senior management responsibilities because of my strong communication and problem-solving skills.

In prior positions with the Seattle Police Department in Washington as well as with the Logistic Support Division in North Carolina, I excelled as a Communications Operator and Dispatcher. I became skilled at handling emergency situations with common sense and insight. At the Seattle Police Department, I monitored the activities of more than 30 officers per shift as I performed liaison with 911 and various elements of the Police Department.

If you can use a dedicated young professional who offers the proven ability to produce quality results in any type of work environment, I hope you will contact me soon to suggest a time we might meet to discuss how I could contribute to your organization. I can provide excellent professional and personal references at the appropriate time. Thank you for your time and consideration.

Sincerely,

Tracey Meyers

TRACEY MEYERS

1110½ Hay Street, Fayetteville, NC 28305   •   preppub@aol.com   •   (910) 483-6611

OBJECTIVE
I want to contribute to an organization that can use an experienced young professional who offers strong problem-solving and communication skills along with an enthusiastic customer service attitude.

EDUCATION & TRAINING
Completed two years toward Bachelor's degree with a concentration of course work in human resources and sociology, Methodist College; finishing my degree in my spare time.

EXPERIENCE
SPORTS PROGRAMS DIRECTOR. Pope AFB, NC (201-2004). For youth programs at a military base in North Carolina, was the lead counselor for up to 233 school-age children K-12; supervised up to 12 caregivers.

- Programmed daily activities in a variety of areas including academics, art, science, and physical education; managed several new programs. Was Coordinator of Project Learn, and Program Liaison for the YMCA.
- Coordinated activities that enhanced learning and growth; played a key role in organizing and implementing community activities such as carnivals, Halloween and Santa Claus events, military appreciation activities, talent shows, Easter egg hunts, and others.
- Conducted parents' meetings and handled accounts receivables; have been praised for keen negotiating skills.
- Became very knowledgeable of children's anger disorders and worked closely with children diagnosed with ADHD, ODD, autism, bipolar disorders, and physical challenges.
- Created flyers, calendars, and newsletters while also writing reports.

DISPATCHER. Logistic Support Division, Pope AFB, NC (1999-01). Was recruited as a Dispatcher for the Logistic Support Division, and was rapidly promoted to Manager of the Protocol Division, which involved organizing and managing arrangements for VIPs visiting North Carolina.

- Dispatched vehicle operators to military flightline and various other places on and off the base. Provided customer service by phone and in person.
- Was commended for my attention to detail while tracking statistics related to aircraft, vehicle fuel, and service records.
- On my own initiative, created a filing system which greatly improved efficiency.

POLICE DEPARTMENT DISPATCHER & COMMUNICATIONS OPERATOR. Seattle Police Department, Seattle, WA (1990-98). Established an excellent reputation within the Seattle community and participated in many emergency situations.

- Processed emergency and non-emergency information to officers.
- Was promoted to train new dispatchers; monitored the activities of more than 30 officers per shift while also monitoring and operating seven police channels using CAD (Computer Aided Dispatch) system.
- Acted as the liaison among 911, SPD, and the Seattle Sheriff's Department.

Other experience: Became a part of the workforce in North Carolina by becoming a temporary worker with a temporary service in Charlotte.

- Performed data entry and utilized Microsoft Word to write letters and reports.
- Read blueprints; handled filing; answered phones.
- Processed orders from business customers. Processed bulk mail.

PERSONAL
Outstanding references on request. Thrive on solving problems through people. Held one of the nation's highest security clearances: Top Secret/SBI.

RUSSELL KLEIN

1110½ Hay Street, Fayetteville, NC 28305
preppub@aol.com   •   (910) 483-6611

OBJECTIVE

To utilize my skills and experience working in a communications position.

JOURNALISTIC

SPORTS REPORTER, 1999-present
New Orleans Chronicle, New Orleans, LA
- Reported on 2003 Masters golf tournament
- Reported on Tulane University throughout men's 2001, 2002, 2003, and 2004 NCAA basketball tournaments
- Became knowledgeable of the Metro-Atlantic Athletic Conference
- Reported on University of New Orleans during men's 2000 and 2003 NCAA basketball tournaments
- Reported on various Conference basketball games during 2000-03 seasons
- Reported on Conference USA football games during 1999-04 seasons
- Reported on New Orleans Bluebirds baseball, 2001-04 seasons
- Reported on New Orleans Jaguars minor league basketball, 2001 and 2002 seasons
- Reported on 2004 NCAA Track and Field Championships
- Reported on high school and recreational sports

COPY EDITOR, 1998
New Orleans Chronicle, New Orleans, LA
- Designed page layouts for news desk on two-edition deadline
- Monitored news wire and recommended stories in daily budget meetings
- Selected and cropped color photos
- Edited staff and wire copy
- Wrote headlines and cutlines

SPORTS REPORTER, 1997
Loyola News, Loyola University, New Orleans, LA
- Reported on 1998 Loyola University football season for daily student newspaper
- Traveled to five road games for event coverage
- Interviewed former coaches and players for feature stories
- Wrote sports column

EDUCATION

Loyola University, New Orleans, LA
Bachelor of Arts, August 1997
Major: Journalism
GPA: 3.0/4.0 Major GPA: 3.5/4.0

HONORS

Dean's List: Loyola University, New Orleans:
1996, 1997, 1999

REFERENCES

Available upon request

MELVIN GOMEZ

1110½ Hay Street, Fayetteville, NC 28305   •   preppub@aol.com   •   (910) 483-6611

OBJECTIVE
To contribute to an organization that can use an astute thinker and writer who offers an ability to bring events to life through insightful and creative writing.

EDUCATION
Golden Gate University, San Francisco, CA
B.S. in Political Science, 1991

EXPERIENCE (Journalism)
Sports Correspondent, *San Francisco Chronicle,*
San Francisco, California
Responsible for event coverage, also conceive and write sports features.
2004-present

Sports Writer, Copy Editor, *The Berkeley News,*
Berkeley, California
Event coverage, features, column writing; page design and copy editing.
1998-2004

Assistant Sports Editor, *Berkeley Daily News,*
Berkeley, California
Sports writer, conceive and write sports features. Page design and layout.
1994-98

Sports Consultant, *San Francisco News,*
San Francisco, California
Responsible for area high school football coverage.
1994

Staff Reporter, *Golden Gate Area News,*
San Francisco, California
General assignment reporter and sports columnist. Also responsible for some photography.
1991-94

EXPERIENCE (General)
Maintenance/Painter, San Francisco County School System,
San Francisco, California
Maintained school facilities.
1988

Plastics Mold Injection Operator, Davis Corporation,
San Francisco, California
Operated textile machinery.
1986-87

ACTIVITIES
Pacific Coast Conference Sports Writers Association, 2001-present
California Press Association, 1991-present

PERSONAL
Outstanding references upon request.

Date

Exact Name of Person
Title or Position
Exact Name of Company
Address (no., street)
Address (city, state, zip)

**SPORTS TEAM
GENERAL MANAGER**

Dear Exact Name of Person: (or Dear Sir or Madam if answering a blind ad.)

I am sending you a confidential resume in response to your advertisement for a General Manager.

In my current job as General Manager of The Charlotte Soccer Pros, I have led the team to become recognized as one of the best managed teams in sports history. This is not just my personal opinion! I have been the subject of numerous newspaper articles discussing effective leadership styles.

I have adeptly handled all the areas you mention in your ad—fundraising, marketing, public relations, business management, ticket sales, and event operations. In addition to initiating exciting national press coverage in respected media for The Charlotte Soccer Pros, I have been the "voice and face" of The Pros.

Although I am held in high regard in my current position and can provide outstanding references at the appropriate time, I would appreciate your keeping my interest in your team in the strictest confidence at this time.

I hope you will write or call me soon to suggest a time when we might meet in person to discuss the objectives you have for the General Manager and how I might help you achieve them. Thank you in advance for your time.

Yours sincerely,

Dean Snipes

DEAN SNIPES

1110½ Hay Street, Fayetteville, NC 28305 • preppub@aol.com • (910) 483-6611

OBJECTIVE

To apply my education and my experience in the areas of marketing, public relations, and sales to an organization that can benefit from my specialized knowledge of sports marketing as well as my organizational and planning abilities.

EDUCATION

B.S. in Education with a major in Sports Management, Fordham University, New York, NY, 1990.
- Specialized in Sports Information, Marketing, and Promotion.
- Partially financed my education while gaining experience in these jobs:

EXPERIENCE

GENERAL MANAGER. The Charlotte Soccer Pros, Charlotte, NC (2001-present). Was promoted to oversee all budgeting, marketing, public relations, advertising, and supervisory operations for the Charlotte Soccer Pros, a professional soccer team in the Global Soccer Association.
- Entrusted with the management of an investment totaling $5 million.
- Control expenses, payroll, and bookkeeping of a $2 million operating budget.
- Develop marketing, advertising, and public relations campaigns to enhance visibility and popularity of team.
- Coordinate sales of season tickets, group and small business packages, and corporate sponsorships.

MARKETING DIRECTOR. The Charlotte Soccer Pros, Charlotte, NC (1998-01). Control marketing, sales, and public relations for a basketball team in its first year of operation in the new Global Soccer Association.
- Sold season tickets and $250,000 in corporate sponsorships and small business packages in the franchise's first seven months of existence. Provided team statistical information, handled press conferences, and arranged appearances for team members.
- Coordinated entertainment and promotions including booking halftime acts.
- Led the sales staff by accounting for 85% of all advance ticket sales: sold $14,000 in preseason small business packages in a 45-day period.
- Have become recognized as one of the league's most effective marketing operations through the success of my management style.

SPORTS MARKETING SPECIALIST. XYZ Advertising, New York, NY (1995-98). Coordinated information from high school athletic directors and created the design for producing a sports calendar for local businesses.
- Generated $25,000 in sales of advertising space in a 4 1/2 month period.

PUBLIC RELATIONS DIRECTOR. The Yorker Horizon, New York, NY (1991-94). Earned rapid promotion from assistant director to handle public relations duties for this professional basketball team while training three interns.
- Wrote press releases, organized press conferences, arranged public appearances, and maintained statistics.
- Made the year's largest group sale: 1,200 tickets for one game. Refined my ability to manage time and work under pressure as the assistant public relations director.

COMPUTERS

Use PageMaker, Microsoft Word, MacPaint, and MacWrite.

PERSONAL

Offer a willingness to work long, hard hours to ensure quality results.

Exact Name of Person
Exact Title
Exact Name of Company
Address
City, State, Zip

SWIM COACH   Dear Exact Name of Person (or Dear Sir or Madam if answering a blind ad):

With the enclosed resume, I would like to make you aware of my interest in joining your swim team coaching staff.

With more than 17 years of collegiate coaching experience, I enjoy the respect of my colleagues throughout the college coaching community. I have been specially recruited for every job I have ever held, including the Head Swim Coach position I held at University of New Mexico when the university wanted to establish a varsity swimming program "from scratch." For ten years, I served with distinction as Head Coach of the Women's and Men's Swim Teams at Arizona State University West. While at ASU West, I was named Metro Conference Women's Coach of the Year for two years. Prior to ASU West, I worked as Assistant Swimming Coach of the Men's and Women's Teams at The University of Arizona, and I played a key role in coaching the men's team to become PAC 10 Champions.

In my most recent college coaching experience, I was recruited to be Assistant Coach for the Swim Team at Arizona State University. Only six months after I arrived at ASU, however, the university decided to terminate the head coach's contract over issues with his coaching style, and the university's policy requires termination of all members of the coach's staff in such a situation. After leaving ASU, I decided to spend some time in my hometown with my mother and extended family, and I accepted employment coaching aquatic activities at Tucson, AZ. I am now ready to return to college coaching, and I have particular interest in your program. I can provide outstanding references from ASU as well as from all institutions at which I have coached.

With a Master's degree in Education as well as a B.S. in Physical Education and Health, I have taught a variety of college courses related to physical education, golf, tennis, and other subjects. During my own undergraduate career as a varsity swimmer, I was named Western Conference Outstanding Swimmer and Western Conference Outstanding Athlete, was All-Conference for four years, and was a Senior National Qualifier. As a coach, I have played a key role in producing a PAC 10 championship team, a Junior National Champion, numerous Olympic Trials Qualifiers, Men's and Women's All-Americans, Senior National Qualifiers, and Junior National Qualifiers. In addition to being a coach, I continue to be a strong athlete. I can provide outstanding references throughout the university world and college coaching community, and I hope you will contact me if you feel you can make use of my leadership ability and coaching experience.

Yours sincerely,

Bernard Swanson

BERNARD SWANSON

1110½ Hay Street, Fayetteville, NC 28305 • preppub@aol.com • (910) 483-6611

OBJECTIVE To contribute to an organization that can use an experienced swim coach who offers college coaching experience along with proven skills in developing champion swimmers and teams.

EDUCATION **Master's degree in Education,** The University of Arizona, Tucson, AZ, 1990.
B.S., Physical Education and Health, University of Phoenix, Phoenix, AZ, 1988.
- Received numerous honors, including these, as an undergraduate and Varsity Swimmer:

Team Captain, two years	Western Conference Outstanding Swimmer, three years
Four-year letterman	Western Conference Outstanding Athlete, one year
Four-year All-Conference	Senior National Qualifier

AFFILIATIONS Member, College Swim Coaches Association; American Swim Coaches Association, Past Chairman, Arizona Senior Swimming and Arizona Age Group Swimming.

EXPERIENCE **SWIM COACH.** YMCA, Tucson, AZ (2004-present). Coach aquatic activities for all ages.

ASSISTANT COLLEGE SWIM COACH. Arizona State University, Tempe, AZ (2004). Was aggressively recruited by the head coach to assist with the varsity swim team, played a key role in grooming four NCAA All-Americans and four Olympic Trial qualifiers.
- Within six months after I arrived, the university made a decision to terminate the head coach because of issues with his coaching style; in that situation, university policy requires termination of all member of the head coach's staff. I can provide excellent references.

HEAD COLLEGE SWIM COACH. University of New Mexico, Albuquerque, NM (2002-04). Was vigorously recruited by University of New Mexico to start its varsity swimming program "from scratch." Aggressively recruited athletes and established the foundation of a successful program. Taught courses related to physical activity, golf, tennis, and other areas.

ASSISTANT COACH. Arizona Aquatics, Phoenix, AZ (2000-01). Was recruited by the head coach to provide leadership to the senior swimming and junior developmental programs.
- Played a key role in producing three All-American swimmers, three Senior National Qualifiers, nine Junior National Qualifiers, and one Junior National Champion.

HEAD COLLEGE COACH, MEN'S AND WOMEN'S SWIM TEAMS. Arizona State University West, Phoenix, AZ (1990-00). Molded and shaped talented athletes into award winners during this decade; the program at Arizona State University West went through a period when swimming scholarships and budgets were slashed and the university actually tried to eliminate varsity swimming. Alumni support rescued the program, but varsity swimming subsequently did not enjoy strong support in the athletic department.
- Accomplishments during this period included 36 Senior National Qualifiers, one Olympic Trials Qualifier, the college's first Women's All-American, NCAA Championship Qualifiers (three years), and top three finish at Conference Championships (men, three years; women, four years).

ASSISTANT COLLEGE SWIMMING COACH, MEN'S AND WOMEN'S TEAMS. University of Arizona, Tucson, AZ (1985-90). Earned my Master's degree in my spare time at University of Arizona while recruiting and coaching the male and female individual medley and distance freestyle swimmers. Played a role in producing 64 Senior National Qualifiers, eight Olympic Trials Qualifiers, and 20 NCAA All-Americans. The Men's Team became **Men's ACC Champions** in 1990.

Date

Exact Name of Person
Title or Position
Name of Company
Address (no., street)
Address (city, state, zip)

SWIM PROGRAM INSTRUCTOR

Dear Exact Name of Person: (or Dear Sir or Madam if answering a blind ad.)

Can you use an enthusiastic and hard-working young professional who offers a "newly minted" degree and a reputation as an effective manager of time along with natural leadership and sales talents?

As you will see from my resume, I recently received a B.S. in Sports Management from Northern State University in Aberdeen, SD. Throughout my youth, I worked in jobs as a lifeguard, pool manager, and swim instructor in order to finance my college education. I am a strong swimmer and have taught swimming to all age groups.

I have excelled in a number of areas ranging from college athletics and academics, to professional sales and recreation-related jobs. I have always been effective through my determination to do my best at whatever I attempt and my ability to inspire respect and confidence in others.

I hope you will welcome my call soon to arrange a brief meeting at your convenience to discuss your current and future needs and how I might serve them. Thank you in advance for your time.

Sincerely yours,

Paul Waters

Alternate last paragraph:
I hope you will call or write soon to suggest a time convenient for us to meet and discuss your current and future needs and how I might serve them. Thank you in advance for your time.

PAUL WATERS

1110½ Hay Street, Fayetteville, NC 28305 • preppub@aol.com • (910) 483-6611

OBJECTIVE

I want to apply my aggressive and energetic personality for the benefit of an organization that can use a responsible, hard-working young professional who offers a reputation for working well with others and not being afraid to take an active leadership role.

EDUCATION

B.S. in Sports Management, Northern State University, Aberdeen, SD, 2004.

- Successfully completed an internship as a **Recreational Programmer** for Horizon Rec Center (January-May 2004).
- Placed on the university's Honor Roll in 2004, the Dean's List in 2002, and the Athletic Dean's List in 2003.
- Was a member of the varsity football team from 2000-2002.
- Am very athletic and was active in intramural sport including softball, basketball, co-ed football, and football.
- Completed a 10-hour Project Wild training program with an emphasis on outdoor recreation teaching skills.

PROFESSIONAL AFFILIATIONS

Hold current membership in the Leisure Systems Society and the Resort and Commercial Recreation and Parks Association.

EXPERIENCE

Helped finance my education while learning to manage my time effectively by attending college and gaining practical work experience in a variety of full-time and summer jobs:

MANAGER and **SWIM INSTRUCTOR**. Family Community Center, Rapid City, SD (2004-present). Am learning how to manage the financial aspects of running a small business while successfully dealing with people of all ages at a popular recreational site.

- Have become known for my ability to easily establish rapport with young children and gain their trust so that they can learn to swim and be comfortable in the water.

WAITER. Zack's, Rapid City, SD (2004-present). Simultaneously with my job as a pool manager/instructor, am a member of a well-trained staff of waiters and waitresses who provide quality service in a fine dining environment.

SALES ASSOCIATE. Best Buy, Aberdeen, SD (2002-03). Developed my sales style and learned to work as part of a team of sales professionals.

- Learned to develop a strong customer base and built a successful repeat sales record.
- Earned a reputation as a "natural" in sales while gaining an awareness of the importance of earning the trust and confidence of my customers.

SWIM INSTRUCTOR. The Center, Aberdeen, SD (summer 2002). Became aware of the business aspects of running a small business while excelling in teaching people of all ages and learning to deal assertively with parents of young students.

POOL MANAGER. Dakota Splash, Co., Aberdeen, SD (summer 2001). Ensured that pool maintenance was properly completed and supervised a staff of lifeguards/instructors.

Highlights of other experience: Contributed to the spirit of the holiday season by playing Santa Claus for Aberdeen Parks and Recreation, Christmas 1998 and 2000.

PERSONAL

Have been active in volunteer organizations including the South Dakota Country Boys' & Girls' Club, and a university "Big Brother"-type program. Will relocate. Will travel.

Date

Exact Name of Person
Title or Position
Name of Company
Address (no., street)
Address (city, state, zip)

SWIMMING POOL MANAGER & AQUATICS EXERCISE INSTRUCTOR

Dear Exact Name of Person: (or Dear Sir or Madam if answering a blind ad):

With the enclosed resume, I would like to make you aware of my interest in exploring employment opportunities with your organization.

As you will see from my resume, I currently manage the pool and snack bar area, supervise the lifeguards, prepare the lifeguards' work schedules, and provide rigorous oversight of their activities at a popular club. I am skilled at planning and communicating the rules and regulations so that pool safety is vigilantly maintained.

I am certified in many fields such as Certified Aquatics Exercise Instructor and Certified Pool Operator. With years of experience in the aquatics field, I would like to apply my professional skills within your organization.

If we meet in person you will see that I am an outgoing individual who excels as a team leader and motivator. I am confident that I would be an asset in your aquatics program.

I hope you will call or write me soon to suggest a time convenient for us to meet to discuss your current and future needs. Thank you in advance for you time.

Sincerely yours,

Eileen Taylor

EILEEN TAYLOR

1110½ Hay Street, Fayetteville, NC 28305   •   preppub@aol.com   •   (910) 483-6611

OBJECTIVE

I want to contribute to an organization that can use a skilled aquatics professional who offers strong management, communication, and interpersonal skills.

**EDUCATION &
TRAINING**

Associate of Science degree, Leisure Studies, Bemidji State University, Bemidji, MN, 2000.
Certified Aquatics Exercise Instructor; completed six-month training program, AEA, Minneapolis, MN, 2000.
Certified Pool Operator (CPO), National Swimming Pool Foundation, Minneapolis, MN.
Certified Lifeguard; completed Lifeguarding training, Northwest Technical College, Bemidji, MN, since 2001.
Completed Professional Rescuer CPR, Northwest Technical College, Bemidji, MN, 2001.
Completed First Aid training, Northwest Technical College, Bemidji, MN, 2001.

EXPERIENCE

SWIMMING POOL MANAGER. Seasons Club, Bemidji, MN (2004-present). Manage the pool/snack bar area and supervise the lifeguards; prepare the lifeguards' work schedules and provide rigorous oversight of their activities.
* Am involved in hosting parties. Plan and conduct exercise and swim classes.
* Am skilled at planning and communicating the rules and regulations so that pool safety is vigilantly maintained and future problems are avoided.

AQUATIC THERAPY AIDE. Bemidji Wellness Center, Bemidji, MN (2001-04). Acted as Pool Operator for this rehab organization; scheduled patients, changed and bathed patients, assisted in aquatic exercises. Planned games and activities for the Wellness Program.
* Through my training as a Pool Operator, saved the organization considerable money by applying my expertise and resourcefulness.

AQUATIC INSTRUCTOR. Sellers Center, Bemidji, MN (2001). Taught aquatic exercise classes to individuals of all ages. Received a plaque for exemplary professionalism.

OFFICE MANAGER. New Life, Bemidji, MN (2000). Managed the office for an organization to which individuals with drug and alcohol problems were referred for counseling and treatment; functioned as Drug & Alcohol Manager.
* Conducted classes for people who had received DWIs and DUIs.
* Conducted urinalysis tests; managed clients' case histories; counseled clients and their families on drinking and driving.
* On my own initiative, organized the company's files to boost efficiency and productivity.

FULL-TIME COLLEGE STUDENT. Bemidji State University, Bemidji, MN (1997-00). Earned Associate of Science degree in Leisure Studies.

MOVER. Smart Moving and Storage, Minneapolis, MN (1995-97). Loaded and unloaded boxes; packed furniture and household goods for military families.
* Greatly increased my upperbody strength.

DATA ANALYST & OFFICE MANAGER. U.S. Army, locations worldwide (1988-94). Was promoted to manage other individuals in office environments while serving my country in the U.S. Army. Completed extensive training. Received Army Commendation Medals.

PERSONAL

Can provide outstanding personal and professional references. In my spare time, enjoy swimming, fishing, hiking, horseback riding, and teaching.

Date

Exact Name of Person
Title or Position
Name of Company
Address (no., street)
Address (city, state, zip)

TENNIS COACH   Dear Exact Name of Person: (or Dear Sir or Madam if answering a blind ad.)

Can you use a well-trained tennis professional who offers outstanding teaching and motivational skills?

As you will see from my enclosed resume, I have gained coaching experience in a variety of settings including camps, clinics, and individual lessons in the U.S. and abroad. Most recently I spent July to September as a Teaching Professional and Private Coach at the Swank Tennis Academy in Houston. That experience gave me a chance to coach several top-ranked young players including preparing Kristy Yen for the Junior Tour.

I enjoy a reputation as a very outgoing and friendly individual who offers strong leadership skills and the ability to get along with people of all ages. I have helped players ranging from absolute beginners, to those competing internationally in professional tournaments. My motivational skills and patient attitude have allowed me to succeed as a champion college player, as a singles player, in doubles competition with my teammate, and as a teacher and coach.

I hope you will welcome my call soon to arrange a brief meeting at your convenience to discuss your current and future needs and how I might serve them. Thank you in advance for your time.

Sincerely yours,

Allen Harrington

Alternate last paragraph:
I hope you will call or write me soon to suggest a time convenient for us to meet and discuss your current and future needs and how I might serve them. Thank you in advance for your time.

ALLEN HARRINGTON

1110½ Hay Street, Fayetteville, NC 28305   •   preppub@aol.com   •   (910) 483-6611

OBJECTIVE

To contribute to an organization that can use a well-trained tennis professional who offers outstanding teaching and motivational skills along with related experience in clay court maintenance and equipment selection and stringing.

EXPERIENCE

In addition to experience in both singles and doubles competition, have gained coaching experience in settings including camps, clinics, and individual lessons:
TEACHING PROFESSIONAL and **PRIVATE COACH.** Swank Tennis Academy, Houston, TX (2004). Taught tennis classes to students at all levels — beginners, intermediate, advanced, tournament, and professional.
- Coached Kristy Yen, ranked as high as #87 on the Junior Tour in 2004.
- Set an example for children attending the academy classes while taking them on daily excursions and overseeing their activities throughout the day.

TEACHING PROFESSIONAL and **COACH.** Tennis Academy, Houston, TX (2003). Worked with players from all over U.S. and gained experience in teaching/coaching at all levels from beginners, to intermediate, to advanced, to tournament and professional players.
- Helped coach the #2 junior player in U.S. in the 18-year-old bracket.

ASSISTANT TENNIS PRO. Gateway Country Club, Dallas, TX (2001-02). In addition to my main duty of maintaining clay courts, taught tennis to pee wees, juniors, and adults.
- Played a main role in organizing special men's night and ladies night tennis programs.
- Contributed to the organization and running of a pro-am tournament.

EDUCATION

Completed approximately three years of college course work in pursuit of a Bachelor's degree in Business and Physical Education, North Harris College, Houston, TX.

Highlights of playing experience: As a singles player and in doubles with my teammate, Eric Paul, offer these career highlights as a player:
2004—Singles champion and doubles runner-up, Southcentral Indoor Championship, Houston
2003—Played Italian club tennis in Rome, Italy; Played the Professional American Tour
2002—Played on a segment of the American Tournament: Won the Summer Rain Tournament at Wingate Racquet Club in Houston, and the Texas Tennis Championship in Austin
Played the All-Amateur Tournament (July-August): Was Champion at Classic Racquet Club, New York, and ranked no lower than quarter-finalist in all eight tournaments. Finished #4 in the country on the Amateur Tournament and almost got a wild card in the U.S. Open Qualifying. Was singles and doubles champion at the Herring Park Adult Open in Tampa
2001—As a player for North Harris College, helped lead the school team to its second-ever winning season. Won All-Conference honors and finished #2 in the region. Was a finalist in a regional tournament at North Harris College, Houston. Was ranked #18 in the national college rankings for Division II colleges.
2000—Played during the fall season for North Harris College
1999—During my first year at North Harris led the team to its first-ever winning season with a 21-1 record. Was named to the All-Conference team and rated #1 in singles
1997-98—Bowled professionally and semiprofessionally while out of school for two years
1996—Played for the nation's #1-ranked tennis team, Tyler Junior College, Tyler, TX

PERSONAL

Am a very outgoing, friendly, and even-tempered individual. Offer strong leadership and motivational skills along with the ability to get along with people of all ages.

Date

Exact Name of Person
Title or Position
Name of Company
Address (no., street)
Address (city, state, zip)

**TENNIS COACH
& EDUCATOR**

Dear Exact Name of Person: (or Dear Sir or Madam if answering a blind ad.)

I am sending you a resume which describes the management ability, finance and budgeting skills, and "track record" of accomplishments I have established while earning a reputation as a powerful motivator and communicator.

What I believe you will see revealed on the attached resume is a life of accomplishment based on hard work, persistence, and unlimited initiative. The accomplishments I am proudest of are my achievements in transforming tentative young talents into self-confident winners through my expertise in teaching/coaching tennis.

With proven entrepreneurial abilities, I have established many successful "new ventures." Although many people had tried to establish a Pro Shop at Liberty Racquet Club, I was the first to succeed in setting up and managing what is now a thriving retail operation. In a previous job, I established a new tennis program emphasizing juniors development, and I learned the process of putting investors together to build a new tennis club.

I believe my creativity, "bottom-line" orientation, and management skills have been refined to extremely high levels, and my drive to succeed is exceptionally strong. I couple that deep-rooted desire to excel in all things with the highest principles of honesty, integrity, courage, and loyalty. Managing a profitable business that is helping people is my ultimate goal, and I believe I have demonstrated all the skills, experience, and qualities required to achieve that objective.

You would find me personally to be a kind and caring individual who thinks of myself as a "go-giver" rather than a classic "go-getter."

I hope you will write or call me soon to suggest a time when we might meet to discuss my strategic plans and I propose to benefit your organization through implementing those goals.

Sincerely yours,

Gene Gibson

GENE GIBSON

1110½ Hay Street, Fayetteville, NC 28305   •   preppub@aol.com   •   (910) 483-6611

OBJECTIVE

To benefit an organization that can use a hard-working and imaginative business manager who offers a reputation as a powerful motivator, resourceful administrator, effective strategic planner, and skillful budget controller.

EDUCATION

B.S. degree in Natural Science, Concord College, Athens, WV, 1988.

PROFESSIONAL TRAINING

Was trained at University of Virginia, Charlottesville, VA, 1993.
Studied environmental affairs and world issues at West Liberty State College, West Liberty, WV, 1997-2002.

LEADERSHIP HONORS & AWARDS

- Was named U.S.T.A. Area Training Center Coach, 2001-02, based on my outstanding track record in developing top WV junior players.
- Was named U.S.T.A. Scout, 2002-04, for ability to detect superior talents.
- Was voted Captain and Most Valuable Player, Men's Tennis Team, Concord College, 1988, based on outstanding leadership on and off the court.
- Am a member, United States Professional Tennis Registry (U.S.P.T.R.) and WV Association of Tennis Professionals.

EXPERIENCE

Have excelled in these often-simultaneous positions:
1998-present. SCIENCE INSTRUCTOR and **DEPARTMENT CHAIRMAN.** Public Schools of Athens, Athens, WV. Have earned a reputation as an exceptionally strong administrator and motivator while teaching chemistry, biology, and human anatomy and physiology. Co-authored and received a research grant from the Alliance Foundation.
- Was honored by having the 2004 yearbook dedicated to me.
- Was named "Coach of the Year" four times in six years! Coached men's tennis.

1997-02: DIRECTOR OF JUNIOR TENNIS and **DIRECTOR OF TENNIS.** Liberty Racquet Club, Athens, WV. In a job simultaneous with the one above, refined my business management skills while significantly increasing club membership.
- Designed and implemented tennis activities including the promotion and management of U.S.T.A.-sanctioned tournaments and other events.
- Produced state champions in the junior and adult divisions. Took great pride in teaching, coaching, motivating, and managing a junior player who became a national champion.

1997-present: PRO SHOP OWNER/MANAGER. My Pro Shop, Athens, WV. Succeeded in establishing a Pro Shop at Liberty Racquet Club which became a thriving retail operation; although my predecessors had attempted this, I was the first person to succeed in this effort.
- Learned how to open business accounts with dozens of companies.
- Refined my skills in buying merchandise, controlling inventory, and managing a business.

Highlights of other experience;
TENNIS PRO. West Virginia Racquet Club, Athens, WV (1995-97). Played a key role in "pulling together" investors in order to build a tennis club; developed plans for selling memberships and maintained clay courts.
TENNIS DIRECTOR. City of Athens, WV (1988-94). Maintained the city courts while organizing sanctioned tournaments.

PERSONAL

Am known for courage, honesty, and loyalty. Am ambitious but believe in a patient, steadfast, disciplined, and persistent approach to achieving goals.

Date

Exact Name of Person
Title or Position
Name of Company
Address (no., street)
Address (city, state, zip)

**TRACK ATHLETE &
RECREATION ASSISTANT**

Dear Exact Name of Person: (or Dear Sir or Madam if answering a blind ad):

With the enclosed resume, I would like to make you aware of my interest in exploring employment opportunities with your organization.

As you will see from my resume, I earned a B.A. in Psychology from the University of Portland. During the summers, I have worked as a Recreation Assistant at the local YMCA where I planned, organized, and managed children's activities. I tutored children in math and reading while also counseling children with developmental and emotional problems.

In my previous employment while attending college, I was an Act Mentor involved in motivating, counseling, and assisting freshmen athletes. I became a trusted counselor to younger college students and advised them about every area including financial, personal, and academic.

I am very athletic and was named an All-American many times nationally. Among the top 50 United States Track Athletes, I hold records in the 100, 200, and 4x100. I was awarded the Most Valuable Player in 2004 and Scholar Athlete in 2003.

I hope you will call or write me soon to suggest a time convenient for us to meet to discuss your current and future needs. Thank you in advance for you time.

Sincerely yours,

Robyn Matthews

ROBYN MATTHEWS

1110½ Hay Street, Fayetteville, NC 28305   •   preppub@aol.com   •   (910) 483-6611

OBJECTIVE

I want to contribute to an organization that can use a caring young professional who offers superior communication and motivational skills as well as a genuine desire to help others.

EDUCATION

Bachelor of Arts in Psychology, University of Portland, Portland, OR, 2003.
- Completed course work in Child Psychology, Written and Oral Communications, Research, and other areas.
- Trained in CPR, First Aid, and Water Safety.

DISTINCTIONS

Considered a Scholar-Athlete and have achieved many distinctions:
- Am among the Top 50 United States Track Athletes
- Record holder in 100, 200, and 4x100
- Most Valuable Player (MVP) Award 2004
- Scholar Athlete Award 2003
- Went to Olympic Trials in 2002
- Named All American many times

EXPERIENCE

RECREATION ASSISTANT. YMCA, Eugene, OR (Summers 2001, 2002, and 2003). Planned, organized, implemented and managed children's activities for the YMCA during the summers while earning my college degree.
- Tutored children in math and reading.
- Counseled children with developmental and emotional problems.
- Transported children to and from various sites for planned activities.
- Performed light office work including typing, filing, and other tasks.
- Worked with the parents of nearly all the students I supervised.

ACT MENTOR. University of Portland, Portland, OR (2001-03). Earned a reputation as a dynamic leader with outstanding motivational skills while counseling and assisting freshmen athletes in adjusting to college life.
- Taught freshmen how to manage their time and trained them to utilize good study habits.
- Became a trusted counselor to younger college students, and advised them about every area including financial, personal, and academic.

CUSTOMER SERVICE REPRESENTATIVE. T & E Company, Portland, OR (Summer 2000). Assisted customers seeking information about catalog items, and answer their questions in a professional manner.
- Sharpened my telephone skills while serving customers of varying levels of sophistication.
- Confirmed the status of orders already placed. Performed data entry.

COMPUTERS

Familiar with programs including Word, Excel, Access.

PERSONAL

Am a good talker and listener who relates well to others. Am very friendly. Familiar with Microsoft Word, and Excel.

CAREER CHANGE

Date

Exact Name of Person
Title or Position
Name of Company
Address (no., street)
Address (city, state, zip)

TRACK COACH & CROSS COUNTRY COACH

Dear Exact Name of Person: (or Dear Sir or Madam if answering a blind ad.)

I would appreciate an opportunity to talk with you soon about how I could contribute to your organization through my management and communication skills which have been refined through teaching and coaching experience.

As you will see from my resume, I have excelled as a high school teacher and coach since earning my B.S. degree in Biology Education. Although I love working with youth and take pride in the fact that I have made a difference in the lives of many teenagers, I have decided to transition out of the teaching profession.

With outstanding personal and professional references, I am seeking an opportunity where I can make a contribution to an organization that can use a talented motivator, communicator, and manager who works well with people at all levels.

If you can use a vibrant and hard-working young professional with versatile abilities and skills, I hope you will contact me soon to suggest a time when we can meet in person to discuss your needs and how I might meet them.

Sincerely yours,

Jonathan Wallace

JONATHAN WALLACE

1110½ Hay Street, Fayetteville, NC 28305   •   preppub@aol.com   •   (910) 483-6611

OBJECTIVE
To become a valuable member of an organization that can use a creative and highly motivated young professional who offers outstanding management and communication skills along with strong planning, organizational, and marketing abilities.

EDUCATION
Bachelor of Science (B.S.) degree in Biology Education, University of New England, Biddeford, ME, 2002.

EXPERIENCE
Am excelling as a Track & Cross Country Coach and Teacher with North Atlantic Senior High School, Orono, ME, 2004-present:
TRACK & CROSS COUNTRY COACH. With a reputation as a tireless and selfless coach, am supervising assistant coaches while acting as Head Coach for boys and girls **Cross Country, Indoor Track,** and **Outdoor Track.**
- Have derived great satisfaction in my ability to help teenagers learn about life and strengthen their values through sports; try to instill in youth the concept that they can improve themselves every day and aim for being the best they can be.
- Created and implemented a program that in two years has resulted in a dramatically transformed and strengthened program; have produced teams which have gone farther in regional and state competitions than any of the school's previous teams.
- Counsel student athletes about their personal lives, academic problems, and other areas.

TEACHER. Have earned the respect and admiration of students, parents, faculty, and administrators because of my excellent performance in teaching:
Teach science courses to students in grades 9-12.
- Play a key role in developing the curriculum and physical science laboratory activities.
- Provide tutoring to students who need extra help; have also become a mentor to many of my colleagues.
- Have used my leadership skills to organize a team approach and esprit de corps among physical science teachers who had previously worked in an independent and isolated fashion; this team approach has increased science mastery in our academic area.
- Have learned much about management from the creative way in which my principal leads his staff to produce outstanding results within a lean budget.

Other experience:
TEACHER/COACH. Orono Schools, Orono, ME (2002-04). Excelled in the dual roles of teacher and coach at New England Senior High School. As Assistant Coach for **Football** as well as for **Baseball** and **Track**, worked with head coaches to improve their programs.
- Instructed wide receivers and quarterbacks in safe and proper football skills.
- Handled a variety of administrative and organizational activities related to sports programming and tournaments; authored practice guides, game write-ups and plans.
- Learned how important it is to have coaches that get along with each other in order for the youth they coach to be successful and develop a "winning attitude."
- Developed and implemented both short-term and long-range goals and showed youth how to use targets and milestones in accomplishing their overall objectives.

CHRISTIAN CAMP COUNSELOR (summers 2001 and 2002). Instructed youth in rock climbing, spelunking, white water rafting, ropes course, and other areas.

PERSONAL
Excellent references upon request.

Exact Name of Person
Title or Position
Name of Company
Address (no., street)
Address (city, state, zip)

**TRACK COACH
& TEACHER**

Dear Exact Name of Person: (or Dear Sir or Madam if answering a blind ad.)

I would appreciate an opportunity to talk with you soon about how I could contribute to your organization through my versatile background in the areas of teaching, coaching, sales, and management.

As you will see from my resume, I have a history of coaching track at the Oxnard County Schools. I started out as an Assistant Track Coach at the Oxnard High School coaching both boys and girls, jumpers and sprinters, and officiating track meets for high school and college level athletes. I was recruited to become the Head Track Coach at the Oxnard Middle School because of my popularity with students. I was able to increase students involved in track from eight to 45 within two years! My hard work, relentless training, and persistent discipline took the team from last to second place!

I have a reputation for being able to deal with people at all levels, from community and civic leaders, to parents, to children and youth, to supervisors, to my associates. I get along well with others and can be counted on to get the job done.

I hope you will welcome my call soon to arrange a brief meeting at your convenience to discuss your current and future needs and how I might serve them. Thank you in advance for your time.

Sincerely yours,

James Smith

Alternate last paragraph:
I hope you will call or write me soon to suggest a time convenient for us to meet and discuss your current and future needs and how I might serve them. Thank you in advance for your time.

JAMES SMITH

1110½ Hay Street, Fayetteville, NC 28305   •   preppub@aol.com   •   (910) 483-6611

OBJECTIVE   To contribute to an organization that can use an experienced and resourceful coach and teacher with strong communication skills that have been refined in previous positions in teaching, coaching, sales, and management.

COMPUTERS   Experienced with Windows, Word, Publisher, Outlook, PowerPoint, FrontPage, PaintShop, PhotoShop, and many other programs/software.

EDUCATION   **Bachelor of Science in History**, San Diego City College, San Diego, CA, 2001.
Associate of Arts in General Studies, San Diego City College, San Diego, CA, 1999.
Effective Teacher Training, San Diego State University, San Diego, CA, 2001.

EXPERIENCE   *Have excelled as teacher and coach in the Oxnard School System, Oxnard, CA:*
2002-present: **HEAD TRACK COACH.** Oxnard Middle School. Through aggressive recruiting and because of my popularity with students, increased students involved in track from eight to 45 within two years!
- Hard work, relentless training, and persistent discipline took the team from last to second place! On my own initiative, established and implemented a track team and became their first track coach.

2001-present: **ASSISTANT TRACK COACH.** Oxnard High School. Coached both boys and girls, jumpers and sprinters, and officiated track meets for High School and College level students.
- Provided team leadership as well as individual attention to large groups of 50 students and more. Organized numerous track meets, and chaperoned large groups of students on out-of-town trips.

2000: **SUBSTITUTE TEACHER.** In popular demand as a Substitute Teacher, substituted in every grade from K-12 and taught nearly every subject ranging from World History, to Band, to PE.
- Worked with parents from different social and economic backgrounds.
- Learned the inner workings of a school system, from classroom to district-level operations.
- Was featured in California's *New Day Herald*, 2000, for my historical research paper.

Other experience: Financed my college education in the jobs below while earning my degrees at San Diego City College in San Diego, CA:
SERVER Olive Garden. Handled prep cooking, reservations, serving fine wines and catering to customers of fine dining.
SALES ASSOCIATE. Became skilled at sales and customer service as a Sales Associate for Walgreens Drug Store, Ski Technician for a ski rental shop, and Produce Sales Coordinator.
- From September-October in college, worked on a farm to harvest pumpkins and then transported pumpkins to markets where they were sold; established the pumpkin lot and sold the product.
- At the ski resort, advanced into responsibilities related to teaching and equipment maintenance; Certified Ski Technician.

PERSONAL   Can provide outstanding personal and professional references. Offer a highly refined ability to deal with people in a gracious and well mannered way. In my spare time, compete in track events and in mountain bike racing. Volunteer my time to coach three Division I track athletes.

Date

Exact Name of Person
Title or Position
Name of Company
Address (no., street)
Address (city, state, zip)

**VARSITY SOCCER &
BASEBALL COACH
& TEACHER**

Dear Exact Name of Person: (or Dear Sir or Madam if answering a blind ad.)

With the enclosed resume, I would like to initiate the process of being considered for employment as a teacher and coach.

As you will see from my enclosed resume, I graduated from Savannah High School, where I was a star athlete and student leader, and from Savannah State University, where I earned my B.S. degree in Physical Education with an emphasis in Sports Management.

Since 2004 I have excelled as a teacher and coach with the Augusta Area Schools. While teaching students in grades 9-12, I have earned a reputation as a well organized teacher while also becoming known as a coach who is successful in developing teams respected for their motivation and discipline.

I am highly regarded in my current position. I am single, have been certified to teach K-12 in GA, and can provide excellent personal and professional references.

You will notice from my resume that I gained valuable experience in a variety of part-time jobs while working to help finance my college education. For example, I instructed youth soccer, basketball, and swim programs at the Boys and Girls Club, acted as Aquatic Director and Adult Fitness Instructor, and also worked with a social services agency counseling troubled youth on safety and riding skills for minibikes.

You would find me in person to be a congenial individual who prides myself on my high personal and professional standards. If you can make use of my strong teaching and coaching talents, please contact me to suggest a time when we might talk in person or by phone about your needs. Thank you very much in advance for your consideration.

Sincerely,

Clinton Roscoe

CLINTON ROSCOE

1110½ Hay Street, Fayetteville, NC 28305   •   preppub@aol.com   •   (910) 483-6611

OBJECTIVE   I want to contribute to a school system that can use a high-energy, action-oriented teacher and coach with outstanding written and oral communication skills along with a gift for motivating students to excel both in the classroom and on the sports field.

EDUCATION   **Bachelor of Science degree in Physical Education** with an emphasis in Sports Management, Savannah State University, Savannah, GA, 1999.
- Member, Beta Phi Sigma National Fraternity and was Intramural Chairman.
- Played intramural sports and in summer softball and golf leagues.
- Served as Senior Representative, Interfraternity Council.

Graduated from Savannah High School, Savannah, GA; served on Student Council.
- Played varsity baseball; was 1st team All Star. Played varsity baseball; was 1st team All Star on a team that finished 16th in the state; ran track and qualified for districts.

CERTIFICATION   Certified to teach K-12 in GA

EXPERIENCE   *Have established myself as a dedicated and hard-working teacher as well as a dynamic and enthusiastic coach who is known for my style of setting a strong personal example while helping each player develop to his/her fullest potential:*
TEACHER & VARSITY COACH. Rockmount Senior High School, Augusta, GA (2003-present). Teach special topics, math, and physical education to students in grades 9-12 while acting as Varsity Soccer Coach for the boys and girls' teams as well as Junior Varsity Boy's Baseball Coach. Improved results of all teams I coached; for example, the varsity soccer team improved from the previous year and made it to the second round in 2004.

STUDENT TEACHER. Atlanta School District, Atlanta, GA (2002). Was involved in a variety of teaching activities as a student teacher.
- **Kindergarten:** Designed health lessons and activities to encourage individual, group, and whole class instruction.
- **Kindergarten, First Grade, and Second Grade:** Designed and presented physical education lessons directed toward developmentally appropriate practices.
- **Seventh Grade and Eighth Grade:** Designed health lessons and activities to encourage hands-on learning; designed and presented basketball unit which incorporated psychomotor, cognitive, and affective domains.
- **Ninth and Tenth Grade:** Designed and presented football units.
- **Eleventh Grade:** Designed and presented a unit on nutrition.

FIFTH-GRADE TEACHER (PRACTICUM). Mary Lou Elementary School, Atlanta, GA (2002). Taught 73 fifth grade students; prepared and presented health and physical education lessons on gymnastics, floor hockey, rope jumping, track and field, CPR.

Other experience (1999-2002):
Boys and Girls Club Instructor/Facility Supervisor (Intern). Instructed and refereed for Boys and Girls Club youth soccer, basketball, and swim programs; taught preschool physical education, swim, and creation classes; selected and trained volunteer coaches.
Junior High Basketball Coach. Coached 40 junior high school boys.
Physical Director. Served as Aquatic Director; developed and instructed youth sport classes while also supervising adult fitness classes. Organized youth sport camps.

PERSONAL   Excellent references on request.

Date

Exact Name of Person
Title or Position
Name of Company
Address (no., street)
Address (city, state, zip)

VOLLEYBALL COACH

is writing to high school principals seeking teaching and coaching opportunities.

Dear Principal:

With the enclosed resume, I would like to make you aware of my interest in exploring employment opportunities with your school.

As you will see from my resume, I am currently a Volleyball Coach and played an important part in the development of successful high school and middle school girls' volleyball teams. I have assumed the responsibility for holding tryouts, making decisions on the potential of each candidate, and teaching sports skills when no faculty member was familiar enough with the sport to take charge. I selected the 16 members of the high school team which came in fourth place in state finals competition—a major accomplishment for a first-year team in a school which had gone seven years with no team!

I offer enthusiasm, energy, and drive to an organization that can use a dedicated professional who can provide proven managerial and administrative skills. Prior to teaching, I excelled in business environments as an Administrative Assistant and Legal Clerk.

I am confident that I could become a valuable teaching and coaching resource for your school.

I hope you will call or write me soon to suggest a time convenient for us to meet to discuss your current and future needs. Thank you in advance for you time.

Sincerely yours,

Shelia Gold

SHELIA GOLD

1110½ Hay Street, Fayetteville, NC 28305   •   preppub@aol.com   •   (910) 483-6611

OBJECTIVE
To offer my enthusiasm, energy, and drive to an organization that can use a dedicated professional who can provide managerial and administrative skills along with a very strong commitment to helping young adults and contributing to their growth.

EDUCATION
Earned **Bachelor of Science** in **Physical Education**, University of Cheyenne, WY, 2002.

EXPERIENCE
VOLLEYBALL COACH & PHYSICAL EDUCATION TEACHER. Cheyenne, WY (2002-present). Play an important part in the development of successful high school and middle school girls' volleyball teams.
- Was chosen to take on the responsibility for holding tryouts, making decisions on the potential of each candidate, and teaching basic skills when no faculty member was familiar enough with the sport to take charge.
- Work with students at Wagner Middle School and Easton High School from seventh grade through seniors in high school.
- Select the 16 members of the high school team which came in fourth place in state finals competition—a major accomplishment for a first-year team in a school which had gone seven years with no team!
- Was successful in teaching the middle school team members the skills which would enable them to advance to the high school team and help it continue to grow.
- Learned the importance of treating young adults with respect in order to earn respect.

ADMINISTRATIVE ASSISTANT. Blend Heating, Inc., Cheyenne, WY (2002). Originally hired as a Clerk/Typist, became known for my attention to detail while tracking the progress of new projects and keeping work flowing smoothly.

POSTAL SUPERVISOR. United States Postal Service, Rock Springs, WY (2001-02). Trained and directed seven mail clerks involved in the metering section of the main post office where all mail was processed and then turned over to the U.S. Postal Service for final processing.
- Gained experience in quality control operations as an inspector.

ADMINISTRATIVE SPECIALIST. Hannah & Associates, Rock Springs, WY (2001). Was selected to provide clerical support for a highly confidential project to obtain bids and oversee development of a software product.

PERSONNEL RECORDS CLERK. J&B Enterprises, Inc., Rock Springs, WY (1995-00). Processed and maintained the personnel records for people attending training programs; serviced approximately 175 people attending each of several 90-day training programs.

LEGAL CLERK. Law Offices of Redwood, Rock Springs, WY (1993-95). Provided a supply services organization with clerical and office administration support.

TRAINING
Completed training programs including courses for postal operators, administrative specialists, and a leadership development course.

SPECIAL SKILLS
Offer experience with IBM, Microsoft Word and processing programs.

PERSONAL
Received several awards and medals for professionalism and dedication. Completed one semester of general studies at the college level. Excellent references.

CAREER CHANGE

Date

Exact Name of Person
Exact Title
Exact Name of Company
Address
City, State, Zip

**VOLLEYBALL COACH &
ENGLISH TEACHER**

Dear Exact Name of Person: (or Dear Sir or Madam if answering a blind ad):

With the enclosed resume, I would like to make you aware of my background as a dynamic and articulate professional whose exceptional skills in developing, coordinating, and marketing have been proven in challenging environments.

Although I have recently excelled as an English teacher in the Providence County School system, you will see from my resume that I have previously marketed my skills in a number of different venues, achieving success through my natural leadership and exceptional sales ability. While simultaneously running a prosperous business as a private instructor in music, language arts, and gymnastics, I planned, developed, coordinated, and marketed the "Jump the Gun" athletic readiness program. In addition to producing the fliers and other marketing materials, I made "cold calls" to local child care center directors and civic officials, as a result of which I "sold" the program to a number of child development centers and to the Providence Parks & Recreation Department.

Although I am highly regarded as an educator and can provide exceptional personal and professional references at the appropriate time, I am very interested in exploring career opportunities in the areas of sales and marketing. When we have the opportunity to meet in person, I think you will agree that my outgoing personality, strong bottom-line orientation, and "take charge" attitude would be well suited to a selling environment.

If you can use a motivated professional with exceptional problem-solving skills along with the proven ability to sell ideas and services, I hope you will welcome my call soon to arrange a brief meeting to discuss your goals and how my background would serve your needs.

Sincerely,

Robert Isaac

Alternate Last Paragraph:
If you can use a motivated professional with exceptional problem solving skills and the proven ability to sell ideas and services, I hope you will write or call me soon to suggest a time when we might meet to discuss your needs and goals and how my background might serve them.

ROBERT ISAAC

1110½ Hay Street, Fayetteville, NC 28305   •   preppub@aol.com   •   (910) 483-6611

OBJECTIVE
To benefit an organization that can use an articulate, experienced professional with exceptional planning and organizational skills who offers a background in sales and marketing, public relations, and project management.

EDUCATION
Bachelor of Science in **Education**, with a major in Language Arts, Providence College, Providence, RI, 1996.

CERTIFICATION
Hold Rhode Island Class-B Teaching Certificate in Language Arts.

EXPERIENCE
ENGLISH TEACHER and **VOLLEYBALL COACH.** Regina High School, Newport, RI (2004-present). Provide classroom instruction in English and American Literature as well as in grammar and composition to eleventh and twelfth grade students. Serve as coach for the volleyball team.
- Prepare lesson plans and other course materials as well as assigning essays, reports, and other writing assignments.

MUSIC and **PHYSICAL FITNESS & COORDINATION INSTRUCTOR.** Self-employed (1996-2003). In addition to marketing my skills as a private piano and language arts instructor, also developed, successfully marketed, and was contracted to implement an athletic skills development program at child development centers as well as through the Providence Parks & Recreation Department.
- Designed, planned, and implemented the "Jump the Gun" program, an athletic readiness skills program for classes of up to 15 students ages three to seven. Developed and produced informational flyers and other marketing and promotional materials for the program.
- Succeeded in "selling" the program to child development centers and to the Providence Parks & Recreation Department, which implemented it at several Recreation Centers; made "cold calls" to local child care directors and civic officials to present the program.
- Trained and directed the work of two teaching assistants in addition to coordinating the advertising, curriculum development, and class schedules for the program.
- As a Music Instructor, provided instruction to students of all ages and skill levels in music performance, improvisation, music theory, and goal setting; developed individual programs of study geared to the skill level and developmental needs of each student.
- Devised a program using piano and gymnastics to assist children with visual perception problems or dyslexia in overcoming obstacles and understanding "how" to learn.
- Instructed high school students privately in English grammar and composition, with a special emphasis on the elements of effective essay writing.
- Expanded my business to the point that prospective students had to be placed on a waiting list, emphasized advertising in newsletters of home schooling resources.
- While serving as a Gymnastics Instructor for a summer nonprofit program in Providence, taught classes of up to 25 underprivileged students the rudiments of gymnastics; devised curriculum for the course and trained teaching assistants.

Other experience: EDUCATIONAL SERVICES COORDINATOR. Everything Canine, Providence, RI. During college, was recruited to serve as facilitator and coordinator for tours of up to 500 students attending this traveling exhibit of robotic dogs.

PERSONAL
Former member of the Providence College gymnastics team and Instructor for Providence College recreation department. Known for my natural leadership ability and exceptional problem-solving skills. Excellent references are available upon request.

CAREER CHANGE

Date

Exact Name of Person
Title or Position
Name of Company
Address (no., street)
Address (city, state, zip)

**WATER SAFETY
INSTRUCTOR
&
TABLE TENNIS
COACH**

Dear Exact Name of Person: (or Dear Sir or Madam if answering a blind ad.)

I would appreciate an opportunity to talk with you soon about how I could contribute to your organization through my education in psychology as well as my experience in counseling and motivating others.

You will see by my resume that I recently earned my B.S. in Psychology from East Central University. While attending college, I learned to manage my time effectively while teaching and coaching both adults and children. I easily develop rapport with others and am known for my ability to motivate others to excel. During my time with the Ada Boys and Girls Club of America, I coached table tennis and swimming and was successful in building team morale as well as a healthy respect for competition. One of my table tennis students is ranked number four in the nation for her age group.

With my newly minted degree in Psychology, I am eager to utilize my degree for the benefit of others in a human services environment. I am confident that I can quickly become a valuable asset to an organization that values initiative and intelligence. I offer a reputation as a mature young professional with a talent for putting others at ease, listening to what they have to say, and knowing how to reach and motivate them to put forth their own best efforts.

I hope you will welcome my call soon to arrange a brief meeting at your convenience to discuss your current and future needs and how I might serve them. Thank you in advance for your time.

Sincerely yours,

Shane Charles

Alternate last paragraph:
I hope you will call or write me soon to suggest a time convenient for us to meet and discuss your current and future needs and how I might serve them. Thank you in advance for your time.

SHANE CHARLES

1110½ Hay Street, Fayetteville, NC 28305   •   preppub@aol.com   •   (910) 483-6611

OBJECTIVE   To apply my background of success in counseling adults and children to an organization that can benefit from my ability to "bring out the best" in others through my motivational skills.

EDUCATION   Earned a **B.S. in Psychology**, East Central University, Ada, OK, 2004.
- Completed specialized course work including the following:

general psychology	crime and delinquency
research methods	theories of learning
experimental psychology	behavior modification
developmental psychology	principles of sociology
clinical methods	theories of personality
industrial/organization psychology	statistics (sociology)
sociology of deviant behavior	psychology of personal adjustment

- Was named to a 2001 task force which brought in college graduates to present motivational talks at various sites around the campus.

EXPERIENCE   *Contributed my talents as an excellent listener with insight and sound judgment in several capacities with the Boys and Girls Clubs of America, Ada, OK. Completely financed my college education through the following jobs, 2000-present:*
WATER SAFETY INSTRUCTOR and **LIFEGUARD.** Refined my ability to work with people of all ages and skill levels; developed my own teaching methods.

TABLE TENNIS COACH. Provided the leadership and instructional skills which motivated young people to "sharpen" their games and succeed in competition.
- Coached Amy Johnson who is ranked number four in the nation in her age group by the United States Table Tennis Association. Improved the morale and built a sense of team spirit in my players. Polished my organizational skills while making arrangements for out-of-town tournaments and setting up fundraising events.

ASSISTANT SWIMMING COACH. Played an important part in raising the morale of team members while building my teaching skills.
- Helped children learn to enjoy swimming and have fun in competition.

Gained supervisory and practical experience, Ada (OK) Parks and Recreation:
ADMINISTRATIVE ASSISTANT. East Central University, Ada, OK (1998-00). Provided the Dean of Physical Education with office support by filing papers, answering phones, inputting data, and acting as a courier for intercampus correspondence.
- Became skilled in using computers with Microsoft Word software; built my typing speed up to 70 wpm. Designed and prepared test materials for physical education majors.

SUPERVISORY LIFEGUARD & WATER SAFETY INSTRUCTOR. (summers during high school). Oversaw six lifeguards as well as scheduling their work hours/in-service training and advising them of their responsibilities. Learned to supervise others and develop them into a team concerned with ensuring the public a safe place to swim and relax. Taught both children and adults the skills they needed to swim at any depth with confidence in their own abilities.
- Provided classes in CPR and First Aid to students of all ages.

PERSONAL   Am very effective in helping young people maximize their potential and achieve results.

CAREER CHANGE

Date

Exact Name of Person
Title or Position
Name of Company
Address (no., street)
Address (city, state, zip)

**WELLNESS CENTER
DIRECTOR**

Dear Exact Name of Person: (or Dear Sir or Madam if answering a blind ad.)

With the enclosed resume, I would like to make formal application for the job as Director of the Wellness Fitness Center.

As you will see from my resume, my background is tailor-made to your needs. I earned a B.S. degree in Physical Education with a concentration in Exercise Science, which was financed by working in a full-time job as a fitness center assistant manager throughout college. In that capacity, I implemented and managed a corporate wellness program, organized and directed a football league, and developed fitness programs for all fitness levels. Through this education and experience, I have become well acquainted with the nutritional and diet component of fitness/wellness programs.

Even in high school, I demonstrated my strong interest in fitness and athletics. I was named in the "top eight in Wisconsin" for my weight class in wrestling, and I was named "most valuable player" in cross country in both high school and college.

Previously I proudly served my country in the U.S. Air Force and was promoted ahead of my peers at a time of military downsizing. I excelled in training and supervising people, managing multimillion-dollar assets and warehouses, and in organizing and directing special projects which required strong leadership and problem-solving skills. Although I was considered to be "on the fast track" in a successful career in the U.S. Air Force, I left the military in order to establish a career in the fitness/wellness field.

After contacting the enclosed references, I feel certain they will assure you of my natural drive, hard-working nature, and proven leadership ability. I am confident that I could rapidly master your requirements and become a valuable asset to you. Being a proven performer, you would not be taking a chance!

Please consider me for this position. I am confident that I could demonstrate during an interview that I am the person you are looking for and could count on. I hope I will hear from you soon so that we can set up a meeting at your convenience to discuss your current and future needs and how I might serve them. Thank you in advance for your time.

Sincerely yours,

Gregory Connor

GREGORY CONNER

1110½ Hay Street, Fayetteville, NC 28305   •   preppub@aol.com   •   (910) 483-6611

OBJECTIVE

To benefit an organization seeking a motivated professional skilled in developing and managing corporate fitness and wellness programs who possesses sound bottom-line judgement along with excellent communication, management, and problem-solving skills.

EDUCATION

Bachelor of Science, Physical Education with a concentration in Exercise Science, Cardinal Stritch University, Janesville, WI, 2004.
- Financed my education in a full-time job as an assistant manager of a sports club.
- Gained expert knowledge of the diet and nutritional component of fitness and wellness.
- Was named **Most Valuable Player** as a four-year letterman in **cross country** while in college, and was also named **Most Valuable Player** in **cross country** in high school.
- In high school, was ranked in **"top eight in Wisconsin"** for my weight class in wrestling.
- Was 10 credits shy of a minor in Athletic Training.

EXPERIENCE

FITNESS CENTER ASSISTANT MANAGER. McRae Fitness Center, Janesville, WI (2000-present). Learned to manage my time wisely while simultaneously excelling in this full-time job and handling a full load as a college student; manage 10 people and routinely was in charge of this fitness center which offers a wide range of membership services.
- Implemented and manage a corporate wellness program; perform fitness testing and develop individual fitness/wellness programs.
- Organized and directed a football league.
- Earned a reputation as a creative problem solver and polished communicator in the process of resolving employee dissatisfactions and customer complaints.
- In charge of new membership sales, increased the customer base; sold sporting goods.

SUPERVISOR/MUNITIONS SYSTEM SPECIALIST and **TRAINING DIRECTOR**. U.S. Air Force, Eglin AFB, UT (1996-00). Based on leadership skills and intellectual ability, was selected for, and then excelled in, one of the Air Force's most challenging career fields—the operation, repair, and management of munitions systems; at a time when the military was downsizing, was promoted six months ahead of my peers to Senior Airman.
- Trained and supervised up to 12 people while managing multimillion-dollar inventories, operating warehouses, and directing special projects; was commended for the strong personal example and leadership I provided while continuously working with munitions and hazardous materials in environments where there was "no room for error."
- Devised and implemented a method of protecting munitions from inclement weather which saved more than $130,000 during one special project.

WRESTLING COACH. Central Senior High School, Janesville, WI (1992-96). Established training programs which motivated average wrestlers into competitive levels; built pride, dedication, and sportsmanship in each team member while instilling in young athletes the drive to excel.

Other experience:
LIFEGUARD. Applied water safety knowledge, CPR skills, and supervisory abilities.
TEACHER. After graduating from college, taught physical education to kindergarten through sixth grade students at Hampton Elementary.

SPECIAL SKILLS

Offer a wide range of skills and knowledge related to these and other areas:

pool maintenance	planning/setting up fitness programs
CPR and First Aid certified	operating computers/word processing

Date

Exact Name of Person
Title of Profession
Name of Company
Address (no., street)
Address (city, state, zip)

Dear Player Personnel:

With the enclosed resume, I would like to formally make you aware of my interest in the Women's National Basketball Association (WNBA) and my desire to play for any expansion teams as well as the following teams in particular: Chicago Sky Scrapers, Seattle Salmons, Honolulu Surfers, Dallas Lone Stars.

As you will see from my enclosed resume, I earned my B.S. degree on a full four-year scholarship and won numerous college honors while excelling as a season leader in scoring, free throws, rebounds, and block shots. My style can be described as inside post-up player, rebounder, and shot blocker. I received numerous honors including being named team MVP, All CIAA, Outstanding Sportswoman, Nike All-American, and College Sports Information Directors' Association All-American. I was recruited and received an offer to play professionally in Canada but declined the offer.

Single (never married) with no children, I am available for relocation anywhere, and I would welcome the opportunity to talk with you about my desire to discuss my strong qualifications. I am a dynamic, crowd-pleasing ball player known for leadership ability, personal reliability, and exemplary character.

Please look over my resume and give me your best advice about how we should proceed in finding suitable opportunities for my exceptional talents and skills.

Sincerely,

Teresa Mills

TERESA MILLS

1110½ Hay Street, Fayetteville, NC 28305   •   preppub@aol.com   •   (910) 483-6611

OBJECTIVE I would like to contribute to an organization that can use an accomplished basketball player who desires to play professionally on a team which will help me to continue to develop my skills while providing me with an opportunity to make a significant contribution to the reputation and winning record of a respected organization.

EDUCATION Received **B.S. degree in Athletic Administration,** Marquette University, Milwaukee, WI, 1996. Received a full four-year scholarship.

GAME DATA
- Right handed player
- Best shot: Turnaround Jumper
- Style: Inside Post-up Player, Rebounder, Shot Blocker

HONORS AND AWARDS
College:
- All CIAA – 2002-03, 2003-04
- MVP (Team) – 2001-02, 2003-04
- Outstanding Sportswoman, 1998-99
- College Sports Information Director's Association All-American, 1994-95
- Nike All-American, 1993-94
- Was recruited and received offer to continue playing in Canada professionally but declined

High School (River Falls Senior High School, River Falls, WI):
- All Conference
- All City County
- MVP (Team)
- Regional Tournament Team
- Most Outstanding Offense
- All-USA Team
- Milwaukee Post Christmas Tournament MVP
- Coaches East-West All Star Team
- Honorable Mention All State
- Friendliest Senior
- Most Athletic Senior

HIGHLIGHTS OF COLLEGE STATISTICS
- From 2002-03, played in 91 games, scored 1017 points, and averaged 12.86 per game
- Was a season leader in **Scoring**; averaged 19.1 in '03-04 and 18.9 in '02-03.
- Was a season leader in **Free Throws**; in '02-04 averaged .754.
- Was a season leader in **Rebounds**; in '01-02 averaged 12.0 and averaged 10.3 in '02-03.
- Was a season leader in **Block Shots**; averaged 0.7 in '00-01 and 0.3 in '01-02.

WORK EXPERIENCE
ASSISTANT BASKETBALL COACH. River Falls, WI (2003-present). Volunteer my time in training and preparing female athletes at River Falls Middle School.
POLICEWOMAN. River Falls, WI (2001-03). Held Secret security clearance.
RECREATION AIDE/COACH. River Falls, WI (1998-01). Coordinated athletic activities and services and coached youth basketball.

PERSONAL Am a hard worker who leads by example. Mission oriented, coachable, outgoing personality.

Date

Exact Name of Person
Title or Position
Name of Company
Address (no., street)
Address (city, state, zip)

YOUTH ACTIVITIES DIRECTOR

Dear Exact Name of Person: (or Dear Sir or Madam if answering a blind ad.)

I would appreciate an opportunity to talk with you soon about how I could contribute to your organization through my versatile background in the areas of planning, directing, and providing administrative support for recreation and community services programs.

As you will see from my enclosed resume, I offer a wide range of skills which include budget formulation, program development, personnel management, public speaking, and contracting. In my most recent position as a Youth Activities Director and Recreation Program Director in Ft. Bragg, NC, I supervised as many as 65 employees while supporting three teen centers, eight youth centers, and four youth sports programs which served from 100 to 175 people a day.

Through my versatile experience, skills, and knowledge, I could make an impact on the quality of your organization's programs. The recipient of several "on-the-spot" awards for contributions and professionalism, I have consistently found ways to improve the quality of the sports, leisure, and recreational programs at each location. The opportunity to work in overseas locations has given me numerous chances to plan trips in Europe. I have also refined my knowledge of equipment and assets such as sound systems, scoreboards, computers, sports and field equipment, and switchboards.

I have a reputation for being able to deal with people at all levels from community and civic leaders, to parents, to children and youth, to supervisors, to my subordinates. I get along well with others and can be counted on to get the job done.

I hope you will welcome my call soon to arrange a brief meeting at your convenience to discuss your current and future needs and how I might serve them. Thank you in advance for your time.

Sincerely yours,

Karla Yates

Alternate last paragraph:
I hope you will call or write me soon to suggest a time convenient for us to meet and discuss your current and future needs and how I might serve them. Thank you in advance for your time.

KARLA YATES

1110½ Hay Street, Fayetteville, NC 28305   •   preppub@aol.com   •   (910) 483-6611

OBJECTIVE

To offer my experience in planning, directing, and administering recreation and community services programs to an organization that can benefit from my knowledge in formulating and justifying budgets, supervising employees, and organizing youth and adult activities.

EXPERIENCE

YOUTH ACTIVITIES DIRECTOR. U.S. Government, Ft. Bragg, NC (2003-present). Wear a variety of hats as acting director, program manager, and recreation which includes three teen centers, eight youth centers, four youth sports programs, and special events.

- Supervise up to 65 employees in facilities which provide activities for 100 to 175 people on an average daily basis.
- Implemented instructional classes which resulted in a 50% increase in revenue.
- Planned and implemented a summer day camp which was cited as the best in NC.
- Developed a strong volunteer force which enabled the program to enjoy a 25% decrease in operational costs. Develop employment contracts to hire Camp Counselors and provide summer jobs for area youth.
- Handle publicity to ensure awareness of the availability of programs/resources.
- Plan and supervise programs ranging from instructional classes, to gymnastics and tumbling, to karate, to piano, to baton twirling, to modern dance, to cultural events.
- Implemented an after-school peer homework helper program and regular counseling.
- Plan trips for football games, museums, amusement parks, and ski resorts as well as day camps, horseback riding, swimming, bowling, and a variety of other activities.
- Apply organizational and written skills preparing standard operating procedures (SOPs), policy letters, employee performance reports, and a range of other reports.
- Analyze and execute two operating funds totaling more than $1.1 million annually.

RECREATION PROGRAM DIRECTOR. U.S. Government, Italy (2003). Handled a multitude of daily activities including supervising five employees, planning and conducting special events, providing new residents with information and assistance, coordinating with various local agencies and offices, and ordering supplies and equipment.

- Dealt with local vendors: had the authority to approve purchases up to $10,000.
- Coordinated accommodations, car rentals, and other details for tours/recreation activities.
- Represented the recreation center with presentations and slide shows for local groups.

RECREATION ASSISTANT. U.S. Government, Ft. Stewart, GA (2000-02). Assisted in planning and implementing programs for youth from ages six through 19; these programs included social, educational, recreational, cultural, and competitive activities.

- Prepared a minimum of five well-attended and successful programs a month.
- Implemented an outreach recreational program for families in outlying areas.

RECREATION AIDE. U.S. Government, Germany (1997-99). Received several "on-the-spot" cash awards for my contributions in planning and conducting a wide range of youth-oriented recreational, cultural, and social activities including teen clubs, summer camps, classes, talent shows, team sports, and ski trips.

EDUCATION

A.S. in Recreational Management, Cape Fear Technical Institute, Sandhills, NC, 1998.

PERSONAL

Was praised for my organizational and "people" skills as coordinator of a highly successful program involving 200 people which brought 15 Russian adults and 65 youth to Italy for two weeks. Consistently earned laudatory remarks for summer camp programs and was singled out among coordinators throughout Italy for exceptional programs.

ABOUT THE EDITOR

Anne McKinney holds an MBA from the Harvard Business School and a BA in English from the University of North Carolina at Chapel Hill. A noted public speaker, writer, and teacher, she is the senior editor for PREP's business and career imprint, which bears her name. Early titles in the Anne McKinney Career Series (now called the Real-Resumes Series) published by PREP include: *Resumes and Cover Letters That Have Worked, Resumes and Cover Letters That Have Worked for Military Professionals, Government Job Applications and Federal Resumes, Cover Letters That Blow Doors Open,* and *Letters for Special Situations.* Her career titles and how-to resume-and-cover-letter books are based on the expertise she has acquired in 25 years of working with job hunters. Her valuable career insights have appeared in publications of the "Wall Street Journal" and other prominent newspapers and magazines.

PREP Publishing Order Form

You may purchase our titles from your favorite bookseller! Or send a check, money order or your credit card number for the total amount*, plus $4.00 postage and handling, to PREP, 1110 1/2 Hay Street, Fayetteville, NC 28305. You may also order our titles on our website at www.prep-pub.com and feel free to e-mail us at preppub@aol.com or call 910-483-6611 with your questions or concerns.

Name: _____

Address: _____

E-mail address: _____

Payment Type: ☐ Check/Money Order   ☐ Visa   ☐ MasterCard

Credit Card Number: _____ Expiration Date: _____

Put a check beside the items you are ordering:

☐ $16.95—REAL-RESUMES FOR RESTAURANT, FOOD SERVICE & HOTEL JOBS. Anne McKinney, Editor

☐ $16.95—REAL-RESUMES FOR MEDIA, NEWSPAPER, BROADCASTING & PUBLIC AFFAIRS JOBS. Anne McKinney, Editor

☐ $16.95—REAL-RESUMES FOR RETAILING, MODELING, FASHION & BEAUTY JOBS. Anne McKinney, Editor

☐ $16.95—REAL-RESUMES FOR HUMAN RESOURCES & PERSONNEL JOBS. Anne McKinney, Editor

☐ $16.95—REAL-RESUMES FOR MANUFACTURING JOBS. Anne McKinney, Editor

☐ $16.95—REAL-RESUMES FOR AVIATION & TRAVEL JOBS. Anne McKinney, Editor

☐ $16.95—REAL-RESUMES FOR POLICE, LAW ENFORCEMENT & SECURITY JOBS. Anne McKinney, Editor

☐ $16.95—REAL-RESUMES FOR SOCIAL WORK & COUNSELING JOBS. Anne McKinney, Editor

☐ $16.95—REAL-RESUMES FOR CONSTRUCTION JOBS. Anne McKinney, Editor

☐ $16.95—REAL-RESUMES FOR FINANCIAL JOBS. Anne McKinney, Editor

☐ $16.95—REAL-RESUMES FOR COMPUTER JOBS. Anne McKinney, Editor

☐ $16.95—REAL-RESUMES FOR MEDICAL JOBS. Anne McKinney, Editor

☐ $16.95—REAL-RESUMES FOR TEACHERS. Anne McKinney, Editor

☐ $16.95—REAL-RESUMES FOR CAREER CHANGERS. Anne McKinney, Editor

☐ $16.95—REAL-RESUMES FOR STUDENTS. Anne McKinney, Editor

☐ $16.95—REAL-RESUMES FOR SALES. Anne McKinney, Editor

☐ $16.95—REAL ESSAYS FOR COLLEGE AND GRAD SCHOOL. Anne McKinney, Editor

☐ $25.00—RESUMES AND COVER LETTERS THAT HAVE WORKED. McKinney. Editor

☐ $25.00—RESUMES AND COVER LETTERS THAT HAVE WORKED FOR MILITARY PROFESSIONALS. McKinney, Ed.

☐ $25.00—RESUMES AND COVER LETTERS FOR MANAGERS. McKinney, Editor

☐ $25.00—GOVERNMENT JOB APPLICATIONS AND FEDERAL RESUMES: Federal Resumes, KSAs, Forms 171 and 612, and Postal Applications. McKinney, Editor

☐ $25.00—COVER LETTERS THAT BLOW DOORS OPEN. McKinney, Editor

☐ $25.00—LETTERS FOR SPECIAL SITUATIONS. McKinney, Editor

☐ $16.95—REAL-RESUMES FOR NURSING JOBS. McKinney, Editor

☐ $16.95—REAL-RESUMES FOR AUTO INDUSTRY JOBS. McKinney, Editor

☐ $24.95—REAL KSAS--KNOWLEDGE, SKILLS & ABILITIES--FOR GOVERNMENT JOBS. McKinney, Editor

☐ $24.95—REAL RESUMIX AND OTHER RESUMES FOR FEDERAL GOVERNMENT JOBS. McKinney, Editor

☐ $24.95—REAL BUSINESS PLANS AND MARKETING TOOLS ... Samples to use in your business. McKinney, Ed.

☐ $16.95—REAL-RESUMES FOR ADMINISTRATIVE SUPPORT, OFFICE & SECRETARIAL JOBS. Anne McKinney, Editor

☐ $16.95—REAL-RESUMES FOR FIREFIGHTING JOBS. Anne McKinney, Editor

☐ $16.95—REAL-RESUMES FOR JOBS IN NONPROFIT ORGANIZATIONS. Anne McKinney, Editor

☐ $16.95—REAL-RESUMES FOR SPORTS INDUSTRY JOBS. Anne McKinney, Editor

☐ $16.95—REAL-RESUMES FOR LEGAL & PARALEGAL JOBS. Anne McKinney, Editor

_____ **TOTAL ORDERED**

_____ **(add $4.00 for shipping and handling)**

_____ **TOTAL INCLUDING SHIPPING *PREP** *offers volume discounts on large orders. Call us at (910) 483-6611 for more information.*

THE MISSION OF PREP PUBLISHING IS TO PUBLISH
BOOKS AND OTHER PRODUCTS WHICH ENRICH
PEOPLE'S LIVES AND HELP THEM OPTIMIZE THE
HUMAN EXPERIENCE. OUR STRONGEST LINES ARE
OUR JUDEO-CHRISTIAN ETHICS SERIES AND OUR
REAL-RESUMES SERIES.

Would you like to explore the possibility of having PREP's writing
team create a resume for you similar to the ones in this book?

For a brief free consultation, call 910-483-6611
or send $4.00 to receive our Job Change Packet to
PREP, 1110 1/2 Hay Street, Fayetteville, NC 28305. Visit our
website to find valuable career resources: www.prep-pub.com!

QUESTIONS OR COMMENTS? E-MAIL US AT PREPPUB@AOL.COM